Time for Awakening

"Constance Casey is a genuine and accomplished spiritual adept who shows us what is possible in opening to freedom. Propelled by remarkable dedication and compelling honesty, this Midwest mother and carpenter takes us on a profound meditative journey into the depths of insight and awakening."

—JACK KORNFIELD,
co-founding teacher of Spirit Rock Meditation Center;
author of *A Path with Heart*

"Part memoir, part guide to self-knowing, *Time for Awakening* is a spiritual coming-of-age story that serves to inspire and accompany those drawn to the path of liberation. Through curiosity and vulnerability, Constance shares her transformative experiences and embodied wisdom, inviting us into a deeper understanding of the human journey."

—SHARON SALZBERG,
co-founding teacher of Insight Meditation Society;
author of *Real Life* and *Real Happiness*

"*Time for Awakening* takes the reader on quite a spiritual journey from Twelve Step meetings to a strict Buddhist monastery in Malaysia and back home to Minnesota. Constance Casey, a Midwest mother of modest means, is willing to undergo extreme hardship and challenges in pursuit of deep spiritual awakening and, gratefully, finds what she is looking for.

The Buddha exhorted his fol   ...l-~ come and see for yourself.' Constance Cas   and dedication to discovering li¹   hows us

D1534100

that deep transformation is possible. We not only follow her process but are inspired to undergo our own journey of awakening."

—JAMES BARAZ,
co-founding teacher of Spirit Rock Meditation Center;
co-author of *Awakening Joy: 10 Steps to Happiness*

"A captivating and intimate exploration of how authentic awakening unfolds...this book is chock-full of spiritual wisdom."

—TARA BRACH,
founding teacher, Insight Meditation Community of Washington;
author of *Radical Acceptance* and *Trusting the Gold*

"An interesting, inspirational story of a midwestern woman who begins to search for a deeper meaning and added strength in her life... Casey's step by step process in her success story could be a perfect tool for another to follow and reach their goals as well.

Pleasure and pain, elation and despair and other triumphs and struggles are authentically documented. Constance Casey learned to live the mantra, "Trust the process," and her book is a well-written, meditative account of how and why she did it... Her story was so transparent that I felt I was experiencing her life through her words and thoughts. I commiserated with the remodeling challenges and embraced her spiritual awakening... Truly an inspiration and enjoyable read."

—NONFICTION BOOK AWARDS,
2023 SILVER AWARD WINNER

"Over the course of this memoir, Constance Casey successfully presents a spiritual quest narrative that has the potential to inspire readers who find themselves similarly dissatisfied with modern life... An earnest and personal tale of searching for oneself."

—KIRKUS REVIEWS

"Constance Casey's *Time For Awakening* is unlike any other memoir I've ever read! Steeped in Twelve-Step programs, Anne Wilson Schaef's Living in Process, and decades of intensive Buddhist meditation practice, this courageous woman has forged a unique understanding of the strengths and limitations of each approach to spiritual growth. The unusual synthesis of these healing paths opens Constance Casey to deep wisdom and high levels of consciousness. She remains grounded, however, in caring for her family, renovating their Minnesota house from basement to attic, running her tech business, and later serving as a hospital chaplain.

Anyone interested in meditation and how a young mother followed the big questions in life to move beyond thinking, beyond self, beyond suffering, and into enlightenment will love Constance Casey's extraordinary odyssey."

—NANCY MANAHAN,
author of *Living Consciously, Dying Gracefully:
A Journey with Cancer and Beyond*

"Constance Casey offers readers a shimmering gift. This is not a memoir of a spontaneous and disembodied mystical awakening, but of knowledge of Stillness arrived at through an intense and extended quest. Her openness and detail in regard to the material and financial aspects of her homelife in conjunction with her life of meditation, learning, traveling, and healing are refreshing in a spiritual memoir.

Ultimately the overall impression of the book is one of fullness, fullness of the vibration of life, and its infinite universality. This book reminds us, with kindness and camaraderie, to be humble and persistent as we seek skillfulness in our inner and outer pilgrimages to practice embodying the gifts of compassion, love, and peace."

—SUN YUNG SHIN,
author of *The Wet Hex* and *Where We Come From*

"In *Time for Awakening*, the unique, distinct voice of one woman's realization story weaves seamlessly with the unmistakable voice of Awakened Mind. In the words and between the words, through the story and through the silence under the telling, Constance Casey transmits a knowing that offers encouragement to the reader's human experience and recognition for what's always, already awake in us all. This book is a catalyst and companion for anyone on any stage of the awakening journey."

—BROOKE TEISUI MCNAMARA,
Zen teacher at Dragon Lake Zen and
author of *Bury the Seed* and *Feed Your Vow*

"*Time for Awakening* is a classic story of struggle and transformation. Rooted in the Buddhist model of enlightenment with an underlying thread of 12 Step recovery, it tells a timeless tale with modern resonance."

—KEVIN GRIFFIN,
author of *One Breath at a Time* and *Living Kindness*

"Constance Casey provides us with a remarkable spiritual travelog of her travels along the path to deeper and deeper understanding. Her dedication to moving towards awakening shines as an inspiration for all of us in her spiritual memoir."

—LEIGH BRASINGTON,
author of *Right Concentration* and
Dependent Origination & Emptiness

Time for Awakening

A Memoir

Constance Casey

Time for Awakening: A Memoir
by Constance Casey

Published by
Constant Expressions LLC.
Minneapolis, MN, USA

This is a work of creative non-fiction. Certain names and details have been changed, whether or not so noted in the text.

Notice
This memoir is solely for inspiration and encouragement. It should not be treated as a complete guide for awakening nor should it be used in place of medical advice, therapy, or counseling. Consult with the appropriate healthcare professional if facing physical or mental distress. Readers are responsible for their actions and decisions based on the information in this work. Any outcomes are not the fault of the author or publisher. Mention of specific companies, organizations, or authorities in this book does not imply endorsement by the publisher, nor does mention of specific companies, organizations, or authorities in the book imply that they endorse the book. The Internet links provided in the book were accurate at the time of publication. The publisher and author disclaim any responsibility for the content on any third-party websites referenced in this work.

Cover design by Preston Casey Palmer & Cathey Flickinger
Cover photo by Preston Casey Palmer
Book design by Preston Casey Palmer & Forrest Casey
Set in Georgia, size 10/14.695

The Library of Congress Cataloging-in-Publication Data will be updated here as it becomes available.

ISBN-13: 979-8-9891535-0-3 (paperback)
ISBN-13: 979-8-9891535-1-0 (ebook)
Ebook will be available in 2024.
Check www.constancecasey.com for announcements.

For Preston and Forrest,
with all my love.
May you practice well.

Table of Contents

To the Reader

TIME FOR AWAKENING is a work of creative nonfiction. This book is my recollection of events, processes, and training that impacted my spiritual practice during an intensely transformative time in 2007 and 2008. In the early chapters, I provide you with the atmosphere of my home life, encompassing both the construction of my home and my long-time participation in recovery. My focus when writing was less on my childhood history and tilted more toward sharing my recovery and awakening story. This background naturally formed the basis for the spiritual call that ignited within me in 2007, weaving together my lifestyle with contemplative practice and supports along the way.

This book is meant for those interested in living a gentle, peaceful life and awakening to ultimate spiritual Reality. Friends and family who have heard me share some of this journey encouraged me to write this story. None of us know how long we have to live, or what may come along in our path, so writing this now is important while I have the capacity, and to leave behind a record encouraging my two sons to practice well.

Entering the first stage of deep, abiding enlightenment, which is typically called "stream-entry" in Theravāda Buddhism, was a process that deeply facilitated knowing my humanity through and through. It was a falling away of a separate sense of self, a dying before death, or knowing an enlightened view in a profound way that changed me permanently. You too can listen and learn with that subtle, energetic Presence that is right here, right now, even as you read these words.

Each one of us is being invited to train our minds and create conditions for this shift in consciousness in our everyday life. It is only considered extraordinary because, for the most part, this sacred passage is not discussed in the open. It may seem impossible to strive for realization when it is already available right here and now. This is true, and it is not the whole truth. We as human beings are capable of conscious reflection, and in that reflection, we are given a gift of Knowledge. It is a deep aspect of our humanity that transcends intellectual understanding.

I respect the perennialist view that regardless of differences in culture, biology, conditioning, or background, anyone can awaken to a universal profound Truth. In light of these distinctions, I also realize that each person will have a different journey toward and experience of this Truth. There are some consistent pointers in numerous bodies of religious and scientific work; classical maps that detail transformational processes along this path to awakening. I also respect religious pluralism, and I bow deeply to the histories and nuances of each religious tradition's teachings that are rooted in the basic tenets of honesty, love, and peace for all.

Writing this story gave me an opportunity to learn from the process of writing; to reflect on these experiences which I initially wrote down in 2009-2010. Since then, I needed to gather support and watch it spring forward with readiness. Going away on retreat allowed me to let go of the many roles in my life. I needed that space to look inwardly, heal, and practice the art of meditation.

I'm editing this in the midst of our worldwide pandemic and ongoing climate crisis where retreat centers are often closed due to community standards for health care. Most importantly, whenever we come together to sit, or meditate, and share this inward gaze, I feel encouraged, and perhaps you will too. Of course, if you want to awaken, then all of life is meditation, not just time spent on the cushion.

The people, places, events, and adventures that I share are all real. While memories are elusive and selective, I drew upon pictures, videos, journals, notes, emails, and conversations to maintain accuracy in recalling the details. For narrative reasons, I've taken the liberty to compress some chronology of my travel arrangements after being at the Malaysian Buddhist Meditation Center. For brevity, I tried to convey the overall spirit of what I needed to share from the experience. Some names and identifying details were changed to maintain anonymity and protect the privacy of the individuals involved.

This book only provides a small sliver of the vast compendiums of Buddhist knowledge and teachings. As a result, I've kept the focus more on my experience and not so much on terminology or psychological jargon, even though many references were helpful along the path. Yogi, for example, refers to a Buddhist meditation practitioner. For convenience, footnotes are provided to refer to some helpful terms that you can peruse for deeper study. Some of them refer to wisdom teachings that I studied after the time-span of this memoir. It is helpful to use the glossary, especially in the second half of the book. I've also noticed that the mind and body operate closely together, so sometimes I prefer to say "mind/body" and not separate them.

Buddhism has been passed down over the millennia through the ancient Indo-Aryan languages of Pāli and Sanskrit. In Theravāda Buddhism, Pāli is the sacred language that was used to preserve the oldest written texts or suttas after a period of oral recitation, whereas Sanskrit is primarily used in Zen, and other Buddhist traditions. Both have many similarities; for example, the teachings of the Buddha are called Dharma in Sanskrit and Dhamma in Pāli. You will see Pāli terms used more after I transitioned from Sōtō Zen practice to Theravāda practice. While Pāli terms are often first italicized, I have chosen to artistically deviate from that convention in this work and utilize italicization to signify deep thoughts or to convey emphasis.

Throughout this book, I refer to our transcendent dimension in many different ways. I use words like God, Awareness, Divine, Higher Power, Universe, Spirit, Mother Earth, Her, Heart of all Hearts, Love, Mystery, Being, Truth, Reality, Life, Faith, Grace, Knowledge, Stillness, Brightness, Suchness, and Presence. The essence of the numinous cannot be put into text, but I am using these variations to communicate this story to you. I capitalize and interchange these terms to illustrate how many ways this difficult-to-describe knowing can appear.

We each have different preferences and backgrounds; please substitute the label that resonates with you.

While my story may be entertaining, entertainment is not my intention. I desire to activate the most subtle aspect of your consciousness which wants to awaken fully. This story may agitate the hindrance of doubt and pull at you. Good.

The limitation of this story is that language can only do so much. It doesn't let you just be; it wants a subject, focal points, and discussions. Sometimes, this stirring of the mind with Being and practice is just what we need on our varied paths for integration. Hopefully, this story will encourage you to go for it, and explore your own unique process in Stillness with your own wonderful expression.

May you be well. May you awaken and know.

CHAPTER ONE

Beyond Ideas

THE LATE SUMMER WINDS tossed around a few dying yellow oak leaves on the windshield as I drove down a familiar Minneapolis road to the grocery store. I'd been this way a thousand times with one or both of my sons while we went over the shopping list. It was late August 2007, and this time I was alone in the evening rush hour traffic, which had lined up over a block long. I had been reflecting on my long-term Twelve Step recovery work, asking myself from the bottom of my heart: What step or tool had I not given my absolute full-tilt-pedal-to-the-floor attention?

As I sat there on Xerxes Avenue, waiting for the light to change, my eyes caught a glimpse of a sign on the corner, "Dharma Field Zen Center one block right." Over the decades, I'd meditated in hermitages practicing contemplative prayer, but I knew I needed more guidance. I sucked in a deep breath as I gawked at this sign against the blue sky until a beep from behind broke my trance.

While putting apples in the shopping cart at the store, my heart raced about the center. I wanted to go home to look it up online and find out more. This was before we had cell phones with Internet. I had recently acquired a flip phone, which only worked for phone calls. I wondered, how would a Zen center fit into my life? My days were full of parenting, and rebuilding the house that we had totally gutted a few years earlier. I had temporarily set aside my healing facilitation practice for women in recovery and shifted my focus to my home web design business due to its more reliable income at the time. This all stirred an intense urge to reassess my priorities while looking more deeply within.

Later that evening, I made time to sit down at our computer and learned that Dharma Field is in the Sōtō Zen tradition continuing from the Minnesota Zen Center founded by Katagiri Roshi, who studied with Shunryu Suzuki. I had sat there in earlier years of my life, but didn't feel a great commitment at that time; nevertheless, the book by Suzuki Roshi, *Zen Mind, Beginner's Mind*, had been helpful. I often reviewed passages in daily life reminding me to begin again, just as I was doing.

What drew me toward Buddhism is that they called it a *practice*. Each of the many different schools of Buddhism offers an ethical and insightful practice to consider rather than a set of doctrines to adopt and uphold. If questions arose, you were encouraged to sit with those questions.

As I considered this Sōtō Zen tradition along with other Buddhist traditions or lineages, like Theravāda, or Vajrayana, what came up for me was that I needed help *now*. I didn't have time to shop around. Dharma Field was the closest place to home, and therefore, the most convenient. My days were filled with appointments with contractors and clients, the children, their schools and homework projects, and growing technical needs—I needed simplicity. I felt a pressure to go and sit, to see if any guidance could complement my ongoing practice in Twelve Step recovery. Given that the sign on the street had seemed to shout out at me, I went to the next introductory session.

The one-story stucco house with a basement sat on the corner of a residential neighborhood surrounded by a wildflower garden. When I walked up the steps in front, I noticed that there was no entrance ramp attached to the building for those who needed it. The steps made it impossible for someone using a wheelchair to enter on their own.[1] I inquired immediately to the volunteer greeter inside the door. She didn't have an answer. I stood stock still as I thought about my friends with different abilities. I almost left. Then, I happened to look up and

---

1   I was told later that the building is registered as "historic," and the entrance to the building cannot be modified.

read the hand-painted Rumi quote above the door: "Out beyond ideas of wrongdoing and rightdoing there is a field. I'll meet you there."[2] Pausing for a moment in light of this quote, I dropped these ideas and placed my sandals side by side on a shelf.

As I stepped barefoot through the tall maple doors into the spacious creamy yellow zendo, the sun shone brightly through large western windows, casting a golden glow on the old maple floor, warming my toes. One of the head priests, Norm Randolph, greeted about a dozen of us newcomers with his kind bass voice. He was a tall, white, older fellow with thick-rimmed glasses, robust at the waist, wearing a black hippari shirt and black pants. He began the session by explaining how one enters and leaves the zendo in a way that creates an environment with little confusion. If everyone does everything in the same manner by entering and exiting the same way, one can focus inwardly, and there is a peaceful rhythm and flow within the space.

Norm discussed how the body was to be held erect and natural. We each sat on soft, round black cushions called "zafus," positioned atop flat black futon squares called "zabutons". While Norm spoke to us about posture, I glanced around to see that there were no women or people of color, and I considered my feelings of apprehension and unease at this lack of diversity.

It seemed luxurious to be invited to *just sit*, and be aware of the breath. After he stretched slightly to each side, he instructed us to "sit like a mountain" and spoke of different postures: the Burmese (with legs to the side), the lotus, or half lotus were all acceptable. We all sat facing the center of the room for about twenty minutes, with Norm positioned toward us. Normally, we each face the wall in forty-five-minute sessions, but it helps to have five minutes to get settled before the session; you are probably in a session for fifty minutes. Then there is walking meditation, or kinhin, walking in single file, all together in a circle; and another forty-five-minute sit begins again. If you have to leave, you can bow out during kinhin, near the doorway, go to the bathroom, and return before the next session. The doors are closed at

---

2   Rūmī Jalāl ad-Dīn, "A Great Wagon" in The *Essential Rumi: New Expanded Edition*, translated by Coleman Barks.

the beginning of the sit. There is to be no interruption. If you are even one second late, you sit outside the hall.

When there was a chance to speak with Norm, I asked about the other Buddhist communities in town. Both the head teachers, Norm and Steve Hagen, had both been at the Minnesota Zen Center before, so I inquired about what they were trying to do at Dharma Field that might be different. He said it was true, they had practiced at the Minnesota Zen Center with their teacher, Katagiri Roshi, for several years, but since he had been at Dharma Field for so long, almost ten years, he didn't have anything to offer about the differences. His answer seemed evasive at first, yet there was something modest about his lack of interest in figuring it out.

Still, I asked him, "What is this center all about?" He shrugged slightly and leaned ever so gently toward me and said, "That is up to you to find out." He seemed pleased to just be there—in the moment— and that was all that really mattered. I nodded, feeling more curious about how he held himself, and appreciated that there was no push to know anything.

There were no paintings or objects on any of the tall walls in the zendo. I expected to see a sitting Buddha statue, but instead, there was a roughly hewn large gray rock, about three to four feet tall, resting on a wood platform in front of the room. A small candle, a vase of flowers, and a little stick of burning incense were set atop wood blocks on either side of the rock.

The arrangement resonated with my spiritual view—grounded in the elements of earth, wind, water, fire, and space. In Buddhism, flowers often represent a symbol for sīla, or ethical conduct; the lotus flower is often seen as purity. The candle represents a balance of emotion, seeing that wisdom is like light. The incense is a symbol of clarity into impermanence: all that arises, passes away. I also thought about how Buddhism came from Asia, and without a sitting Buddha figure it seemed quite unusual. Just the same, even though it took a little while to get used to the rock, I understood that they were trying to lessen the idea of worship to an outer authority.

Norm showed us how we must bow when we cross the threshold to enter or exit the zendo. We bow to each other and to our cushions before we sit, and we bow when we stand up. There seemed to be a lot of bowing. I wondered if I'd be able to remember it all.

I would never be able to bow down before any personality. When I did bow, it was to a vital Mystery. I had bowed plenty of times at the feet of my children, surrendering to the energy I sensed within me and in them, often in total exhaustion. Like other children, they wanted to extend playtime, so I had to find opportunities for relaxation and renewal throughout each day. If they would not agree, I sometimes found myself bent on the ground at their feet, not pleading for them to cooperate so much as asking for *that* in me and *that* in them to find a peaceful meeting ground. Being little boys and reflecting innocently, they often bowed back to me, our heads touching in the tiny hallway, and then rising quietly to walk into our separate rooms to rest.

What was *that* which we touched in those moments? The willingness to attend to the process living within me, one breath at a time, felt intensely sacred. For the time being, this place of bowing with sitting and walking, this zendo, seemed to be a good enough place to settle and focus inwardly with others.

CHAPTER TWO

Reconstruction

AFTER PUSHING MYSELF UP at 5 a.m. to carefully check measurements for doors and shelving, I went to the used materials warehouse to look at what they had in their haphazard arrangement spread out all over the place. When I got home, I took a breath and reviewed my calendar. I saw that I had to call the plumbing store to order a faucet for the bathroom and check the Internet for the right type. The building inspector was going to stop by at any time, and I had to get our plumber here for a pressure test. *Ok, work with it.* I had an expense spreadsheet to fill out for a couple of options for cabinets, but I saw the warehouse was having an auction that I could attend in the coming weekend that might help with our budget. I had an appointment to set up with the electrical contractor to double-check our wiring. A meal needed to be prepared for supper. Then, I saw empty tissue boxes to put into the recycling bin, and flipped on the shop vac to gather sawdust. One thing led to the next. Oh well.

There was still much work to be done. My calendar was pretty much how I held things together—an attempt at structure for my daily tasks amidst the unpredictable house-building and parenting adventures. Swirls of energy somehow found their way into my process; I saw them as gifts. Sometimes, I just wanted to sit. My back ached, my knees creaked, my fingers tingled, yet my feet still tread onward. When nighttime came, I let it all go, recalled the feeling of ease at the Zen center, and considered: *One breath at a time, oh, just be.* Sleep came.

~~~

Our house in Minneapolis was built in 1906 as a summer lake home, equipped with an open front porch to soak in the cool breezes from the nearby lakes and be close to the exciting events at the local pavilion for summertime concerts and swimming. It was a quiet area of the city, mostly inhabited by white, lower- to middle-income schoolteachers and trade workers, apart from the higher-income households who live on the lake parkway.

For a brief period in the early 1900s, our neighborhood was actually home to a diverse community, until a racist campaign to push out African-American households through racial housing covenants succeeded. Over time, the land has been subdivided into smaller lots, and houses now sit tightly packed together. With the increased attraction of the nearby lakes, our neighborhood gradually became gentrified. We've watched beautiful old houses get torn down by developers and replaced by larger and more expensive ones. Familiar neighbors left and new commercial enterprises moved in, which has created something alien to us.

My husband, Stewart, and I became established in the neighborhood in the late 1980s by sharing a job as caretakers of a rental building for five years while we saved up for a down payment on a mortgage. When we bought the house in 1992, it had been a severely neglected rental house, which is why we got it at a lower price.

One evening in 1997, as we stood in the kitchen, water started dripping on our heads. In order to find the leak, we tore out the ceiling, exposing a host of other major problems from the original 1906 construction that we hadn't expected. Since every penny we had was invested in the house, we had no choice but to completely gut it and rebuild it one step at a time.

In 2003, after we refinanced the house, with the help of two hired men I framed walls, screwed down subfloor, ran electrical wire, and supervised the installation of plumbing. I still had my hands full with parenting my two beautiful growing young men, Preston, age fourteen, and Forrest, age eleven. Stewart worked long hours to support us all.

His work was project-based, working out of town for months. With him gone and without any local family support—no grandparents, uncles, or aunts to help out—I felt like a single parent. There were times when both Stewart and I struggled to find work, and our building project slowed. Regardless, the reconstruction rested firmly on my shoulders as the general contractor and carpenter.

When excavating our yard, we discovered peat mixed with a cornucopia of old bottles, plates, tins, and cans, indicating that the land had been used as a city garbage dump. This set us back quite a bit, as peat retains water and is considered a very poor soil type for a foundation. This required significantly more effort and time as I strategized with an engineer. Subcontractors were often unavailable or uninterested due to the complex nature of our narrow site, which required supplemental inspections for an engineered foundation using helical piers.

Our old two-and-a-half-story balloon-framed house had a tiny kitchen, dining room, and family room on the main floor and three bedrooms on the second floor. Our reconstruction included an addition, opening the back end of the house to the yard, and finishing the attic as a studio office space that we could eventually use.

In 2007, the house still required a great deal of insulation and structural work, which meant that the garage, which we built in 2000, became our primary abode during this process. We set up an office and resting area in the little upstairs garage attic, where you try to remember not to hit your head.

Doing carpentry in the house enhanced my enjoyment of working creatively with wood. Carving and whittling had been one of my fun pastimes. Out of a dying oak tree on our property, in the late '90s, I worked with a master carver, Kevin Showell, to create a seven-foot sculpture of a Dakota mother. I had seen her in a vision, collecting firewood for her family, and catching sight of a beautiful deer in the forest. It was as though I gazed out through her eyes of wonder in seeing the beautiful deer, and often called me to pause more and take in the beauty of tranquility whenever an opportunity arose. This profound respect for Mother Earth felt inscribed on my bones, supportive and nurturing, providing everything for human survival. With her presence in our backyard during our reconstruction, I was compassionately reminded every day of the heritage of our ancestral land and the values that we shared.

Resourcefulness was carved into each step of this process. In the rough framing stage of construction, I found many pieces of wood for backers, supports, and shimming in dumpsters. Contractors would rip out sections of a house and throw the entire thing in the dumpster, (we would always check with them to make sure there were no hazardous materials). We'd spend Sundays, all day long, on the driveway teaching our boys to use a crowbar to pull nails out of old boards and stack them neatly for later use. Using reclaimed materials made puzzles out of projects, but it reduced our expenses by thousands.

On occasion, out of curiosity, and because I could always learn something new, I'd stop by a job site; sometimes I was given full sheets of plywood or microlam beams they were not going to use. They said it would have been a bother to return them. I kept a set of screwdrivers in our van to remove beautiful antique engraved iron pin door hinges, doorknobs, drawers, and faucets for later use in our home.

It was amazing to me the treasures people throw away! We gleaned plenty of needed wood scraps for backers and framing, good pieces of pipe, doors, knobs, hinges, drawers, shelving, trim, tiles, toilets, sinks, extra utility buckets, angle iron, etc., to keep things going. I scrounged through old junk warehouses with a flashlight looking for the right pieces. In one warehouse, up on the fourth floor in the dark, I found a tiny old porcelain sink that was perfect for our half bath. At my insistence, Stewart painstakingly compressed every piece of scrap aluminum siding and bundled all copper or steel from our demolition for me to take to a recycling facility. We reused some of the original studs from 1906 and refit them into the new framing. Later, I made mirror and picture frames out of old stair treads. We filled boxes with plaster and lathe and hand-dumped our debris at the local city dump ourselves more than ten times, using every free permit we had available to us.

It was hard to see things go to waste. One day when we were at the dump, I saw a pedestal sink just sitting up there, so we took it back home to use. Reusing good materials fits with my core value to not dump onto Mother Earth what can be used because it comes from her to begin with.

Somehow, with diligence and cooperation, we slowly rebuilt the house together. I could ask my sons for a one-and-five-eighths-inch screw, distinguishing between a fine or coarse thread. My older son, Preston, spent the summer on the ladder with me, screwing in aluminum plates for the installation of the radiant heat among many other chores. My younger son, Forrest, gave a presentation in school on radiant heat installation for his "how-to" booklet assignment in sixth grade. He described how he supervised the handling of the tube uncoiler and shouted out the numbers on the spool, so he wouldn't uncoil too much tubing as the three of us stood on ladders threading it into the predrilled holes in the joists, hooking it into the clips (or plates) like lacing a shoe. Teachers perched near the classroom doorway, watching his presentation and asking him questions afterward so they might learn the same thing for their house.

We felt a connection with the renters across the street and a few distant neighbors, some of whom were also building their own homes or additions. We were close to Marge, in her eighties, who had lived next door for fifty years and raised her children in that house. Her son Jeff, in his sixties, had moved back home to live with her. Jeff made Adirondack chairs and vintage-style tables for special order in their garage after moving in with her. He often stopped to talk about life. Watching him tread the well-worn path to the garage and back three or more times every day was a regular pattern for us to see. They both welcomed a knock and a visit in their living room on any old afternoon for a chat.

Marge loved having us close by; she said it made her feel safe. She loved the motion sensor light I installed on our side door because it cast a light for her when she parked her car at night next to her house. If our trash can was full, she'd repeat, "Use mine!" In learning how frequent our trips to the library had become, she'd ask us to pick up and drop off books for her too. Forrest and Preston helped her with yardwork and shoveling, and she graciously allowed us to use her yard for playing with our dog, Ruby.

One neighbor showed me a tiny classified ad in the back of the newspaper where a local contractor wanted to unload a truckload of hard foam insulation at a very low price. I called the city's housing inspection office and came up with an innovative plan for insulating our vented roof to an R54 rating, well above the code requirement. Then, I quickly arranged for the truckload of insulation to be dropped off at our house. Since most of a house's heat is lost through the roof, this would eventually lead to substantial cost savings! The roof insulation, done by hand in the way I designed it, took over six months to complete. It was a relief to have the roof and siding finished. Our makeshift basement kitchen-laundry-workshop room provided for our basic needs.

Weeks turned into months, and then years, as we slowly collected materials and rebuilt structurally sound spaces. Our van doubled as a truck, which I needed every day for picking up lumber, supplies, and groceries. Having a bus stop nearby was helpful, as it allowed Stewart and the boys to get around town when the car was in use. I learned to break everything down into smaller components within the project and to do what I could each day.

One time, when the boys and I were moving a sheet of foam insulation to the attic, I stopped and realized that I had to be even more patient with this rebuilding process. It was a bigger project than we ever expected it to be. Everyone always asked us: "Are you done yet?" I reflected on that question because I heard it so often. It made me contemplate life, work, and craft. Aren't we always involved in the art of living in some way or another until death? *Are we ever really done?*

I was constantly reframing our messy circumstances into positive and empowering experiences for us all. We had to shut off the water while we installed valves and pipes, so it was a great time for the kids to be involved in swimming lessons at the YMCA where we could all get showers and come home fresh and clean. Sometimes we made mistakes and had to keep the water shut off until we figured out the problem and using the laundromat helped us connect with more people in our community.

Minnesota winters are harsh, and the pipes could easily freeze. Because we were installing our own radiant heating system during that time, we had to wait until the warmer season and the insulation was completed before we filled the pipes with water so they would not burst. Shut-off valves helped somewhat, but we had to make sure we were integrating it all together in the right way.

This took more than a decade to work through. It was a complex process that involved shifting strategies for installing tubing and plumbing, systematically insulating, and designing electrical avenues little by little throughout the house on a tight budget.

In the summer of 2007, with the help of my dear old friend Dave, we tiled a bathroom and installed a few of my own painted tiles. One read, "Breathe in peace, breathe out love," a good daily reminder during each step of the process. Once we had that bathroom, we were able to let go of the portable toilet on the boulevard and enjoy some of the newly functioning aspects of our house.

Fortunately, the city did not require a deadline for the entire project; they only expected to see progress every six months, and albeit slowly, progress was being made. Going slowly helped eliminate mistakes that would have been costly, and gave me the patience to learn as we reconstructed our home.

As I write, I keep finding better ways to express myself. These words will be published, this book completed, but it is rather like a leaf floating down a stream that bumped into you and you are now holding. Now, twenty years later, our caulking needs replenishing, our boiler needs replacing, our front steps—crumbled.

Everything changes.

CHAPTER THREE

Study

H AVING FOUND A PLACE to meditate away from our messy home project, the practical nature of my mind wanted to explore some supportive literature on meditation. How would I find the time to read more and add formal sitting practice to my already full schedule? To make sure my reading was going to be most effective, I visited our neighborhood library to look up some books. Initially, I did a broad search under the subject "meditation," and found thousands of entries! It reassured me that there was much to study, but it terrified me more. How would I sort through it all?

The library catalog had too many options. I took a deep breath and exhaled as I organized the authors from A to Z. Since anything I read would reflect the style and practice of the author, I made sure to carefully go through each of the first twenty listings and familiarize myself with each of their works. One of the first listings was by an author named Adyashanti for a book called *Emptiness Dancing*. Although his book had to be sent from another library, I ordered it anyway because it sounded fun.

The next day, during one of my frequent visits to my neighborhood library, my fingers landed upon a book that had an edifying effect on my mind: *The Life of Ramakrishna* by Romain Rolland. While my study of spiritual literature had begun long before discovering the Zen center, somehow reading the beautiful portrayal of Ramakrishna Paramahamsa's spiritual journey opened a web of inward pathways.

When I spoke about it with a trusted friend, Wes, he said, "If you continue to read along those lines, by and about enlightened teachers, you will put yourself into an arc of energy that will bring you into communion and open a wider path in life." I sensed this had happened in him and saw it in his sparkling eyes, and in the way he moved with such intention. He wasn't caught up in busyness, but a sense of Stillness permeated his presence.

That fall in 2007, I also asked around at my Twelve Step meeting if anyone had read helpful literature on meditation. A friend mentioned *The Miracle of Mindfulness* by Thich Nhat Hanh. He had found the book on tape at the library, and listened to it in his car, so I ordered it. Being mindful sure seemed like a miracle. Any time I remembered to be present was a gift! I felt inspired by his background in activism; continually advocating for peace and reconciliation even amidst the brutal campaigns of violence happening during the Vietnam War leading to his thirty-nine-year exile. He pointed to a supranormal form of presence with spiritual awareness dependent on one's own effort.

The library responded quickly to my request with a notice that Adyashanti's book had arrived. Even though I had several errands to run, I drove to the library before it closed that night. As soon as my chores were completed and my sons were settled down, I started reading *Emptiness Dancing*; every word danced on the page. The book resonated within me like a soft feather tickling my heart.

I looked up Adyashanti. His name sounded like some guru from India, but I saw that he is a white guy who teaches in California, around the Palo Alto area, and is a little younger than me. He seemed pretty down to earth, though I had no idea what the culture would be like around him. Given that he had done Zen practice for about fourteen years and was open about sharing his experience, I really wanted to learn more about him.

There was an invitation to sign up for a retreat in April of 2008, at Asilomar in Pacific Grove, through his Open Gate Sangha website. *Could it really be possible for me to go?!* There was no scholarship. The cost of the retreat was a little high, about $275 for the five days; the airfare and lodging were above our budget. Still, my index finger clicked forward, even with some concern—the next thing I knew, I had entered my name in a lottery to attend his spring retreat in California! I needed to move forward. I wouldn't know whether I'd get in for a month or more. If I didn't get in, there was nothing to lose.

Many of us have a natural curiosity that grows as we reflect on our interests, feelings, and experiences. But at this point in time, clarity about what it is to be human was my primary goal. And clarity comes through direct experience. At a certain point, I had to stop the curiosity that took me into the Wikipedia footnotes, opening tab after tab, reading until dawn—preventing essential meditative practice.

In front of me was an overflowing list of unfinished projects, but it was like time had stopped. A ferocious desire to *truly know* myself kept arising. I felt a fundamental dissatisfaction with my understanding of what it is to be born here, to be born human. Whenever I paused to mindfully breathe in and out, my body said, more than anything else:

Stop. Sit. Be.

CHAPTER FOUR

Recovery

D URING THE EARLY 1980s, whenever I found a free evening, I'd
light a candle and do some contemplative journaling. Those
candlelit nights with my thoughts and feelings were the beginning of
my healing. I needed to heal because my dysfunctional family background had been so difficult that I required a complete rebuild.

In 1983, when I was single, before I had kids, I was attending a
women's support group run by the county's social services department.
Some of the women talked about how the Twelve Step program was
helping them recover from harmful relationships and work with their
own codependence. I could see the improvements they were making
in their lives so I inquired about joining one of these recovery groups.

I was immediately struck by the way the program talks about
addiction to "people, places, and things,"[3] pointing to how all aspects
of the human experience can become addictive. The First Step in the
program talks about being powerless over alcohol and that our lives
are unmanageable. I understood the word "alcoholic" to mean anyone
struggling with intoxication, which can include any avoidance of our
humanity. This was reinforced by the literature the group provided,
"...admission can apply to many other difficulties we feel we should
be able to control, but are not. I do have a power...If I exercise that

---

3   Al-Anon Family Groups, *How Al-Anon Works for Families & Friends of
     Alcoholics*

power wisely, the problems outside of me will work out without my interference."[4] What this meant to me was to admit that we sink into ignorance and acknowledge that the unhealthy patterns we learned are not beneficial. In ignorance, we are not able to see our choices and appropriately manage our lives. By being honest about not knowing, we open to a larger field of wisdom. Therefore, I gravitated toward the Twelve Steps, and appreciated that the message was to be carried to anyone interested in moving beyond stressful addictive patterns.

Nearly everyone I knew seemed to be addicted to one thing or another. Some faced substance addictions like drugs and alcohol, while others were strongly pulled to sugary, salty, or fattening foods. Since food has been so connected with my survival and well-being, I've struggled from time to time with overeating and using it as a source of celebration. Beyond these were also process addictions to exercise, work, busyness, gambling, and sex; each appeared to be conditioned habits to avoid being in harmony with Reality. The Buddha, Jesus, many of the saints I studied, and the founders of the Twelve Step Program were like good addiction counselors, directing us toward a fundamental understanding needed to break free from these entanglements.

My primary personal struggle revolved around codependency because I needed healthier boundaries and more-functional relationships. I worked hard for love and connection. As a child, I learned to mask my feelings from my unsafe family of origin and deny personal needs. With a more sensitive nervous system to the emotions of those around me, building skills for emotional maturity was especially critical on my path. Relating with other women gave me the faith and community of support I needed for learning new ways to handle the breadth of life's challenges.

At my first regular meeting, a basket of seven index cards, each with a tool written on them, was passed around. Seven members were invited to take one of the cards and share how they had benefited from using that tool in the prior week. I set about using these seven tools right away:

---

4   Al-Anon Family Groups, *One Day at a Time in Al-Anon*

- Attend meetings and work the steps
- Connect with others; use the phone list outside of the meetings
- Engage daily in meditation and/or prayer
- Read informative and wise literature
- Write or journal about your questions and concerns
- Get a sponsor and meet with that person regularly
- Be generous and provide support to the group with service

Using all of the tools helped me learn to embody the values of the program, make progress in living an authentic life, and connect with my community. I was finding serenity and making progress, but struggled with finding wise support. After a meeting one day, I connected with the openness of a member during our small group discussion, and asked her to be my sponsor. She agreed, and we talked over the phone once a week.

During our brief chats, I remember reaching out with ideas to try new things. The first thing I wanted to talk about with her was taking a day off work from my minimum wage job for my mental health. What I remember most about this sponsor is that she often replied with "Why not?!" I could take time for myself and it was not harmful. As we continued to connect, I'd hear her voice in my head at times while considering choices. *Why not?* Living with very little income made me choose carefully. I learned to value solo bike rides, solo camping, attending protest events, community potlucks, volunteer ushering at theaters, and picnics with other friends in the program.

I remember her thoughtful dating advice. She suggested that when I went out on a date, I could fold a $20 bill and a quarter in a cloth and safety pin it inside my bra. If I needed to get in touch, I'd use the quarter and phone her on my date as needed, and if I needed a sober lift home, I'd use the $20 bill for a cab. At times when my date drank too much and/or became aggressive, both ended up coming in handy for getting home safely. There were times I had to take away the car keys and firmly set my boundaries.

The donation-based program offers an egalitarian atmosphere of honesty and intimacy, with different members sharing each week. Where else can you go and hear people speaking openly about painful problems in their lives with an intention to learn and grow? I had hung out with a few friends and had visited many different places of worship, but had never heard people sharing as openly at meetings like this before. To find others who accept themselves, start over, take a breath in the middle of a conflict, and try again, is a rare gift in our busy and disposable relationship society. Only through listening and feeling supported did I eventually step up several years later to share my story with others.

The program reached into my gut for intuitive wisdom, constantly asking me: What is really important right now? This inner work helped me realize that there were many options besides my two-sided thinking. Multivariant thinking is to see an open system that includes many options and paradoxes. I came to see that I am not outside of any problem or solution—I am, and we each are active participants in this life.

Our group held a regular group conscience review that invited accountability and learning. If there was an indiscretion, it was part of the program's ethics to discuss issues that arise within a group. For example, a few old-timers might gather after the meeting to discuss it and bring it to the attention of the whole at the next meeting with a gentle reminder of the traditions. After all, we are still human and have our shadow side, so attending a group for a while can be wise to see if it is beneficial.

A basic idea in the program is to choose your own concept of God as everyone had their own way of interpreting their spirituality. Even though the steps are strongly worded in Christian monotheistic terms, folks of other traditions are welcome. Many people I met were spiritual but not religious. I became accustomed to sharing using first-person language, which encouraged owning my experience. When I listened to someone share their story of struggle to find peace or love amidst the chaos of their family life, I knew I was not alone.

Over the years, I noticed that in some Twelve Step groups members identify themselves by referring to their addiction, such as "I'm an alcoholic..." Labels can serve a purpose, but they can also be dropped so that recovery, which is like discovery, can take place. In my home group, we just say, "My name is..." This felt friendlier, less focused on the pathology of addiction and more on recovery.

What I also noticed about my group was a focus on honesty, accepting the way things are, nurturing a healthy relationship with a spiritual presence, and learning to lovingly detach and respond appropriately around people who are in various degrees of harmful behavior to themselves. It was a clear premise to me that any harm to oneself is also harmful to others. It didn't take long to learn that the primary aim was learning to accept myself and develop my own sense of a Higher Power through working the steps, traditions, and using the tools. The community helped me learn a gentler view toward my feelings and my growing pains, and offered a safe place to review my mistakes.

Before I became a parent, I went to at least four meetings a week at different locations. Sitting in all those church basements with those who were trying to function in a healthier way enlivened me! I was blown over by this incredible community of support, truly an under-ground revolution of intimate change in cities and towns all around the world. I saw that those who worked the steps with patience and used all of the tools were finding ease with functioning. I learned to name my feelings by listening to those who were admitting them and to reflect on my choices, whether it be constructively refraining from action or cultivating new, healthy habits. Eventually, as I began to sponsor others, I listened from a deep place of understanding that we each have our own path in life and just need someone to listen.

Sometimes, I'd ask for help after the meeting to role-play a scenario for trying new ways of communicating. I began studying nonviolent communication. My curiosity grew as I worked the program. Studying the causes of addiction at the library inspired me to go back to school in 1987. By 1990, I was a certified addiction counselor. Following my work in various treatment centers, I established my own private practice. In my counseling work, the cycle of abuse was always clear to see. It worked its way round and round, and the only way to change it was to interrupt the process with a new set of skills and the support necessary to cultivate a deeper openness to change. What I saw working most effectively was a sense of openness to a Higher Power—a deeper Love that underlies all.

In May of 1990, I brought my first newborn infant, Preston, home from the hospital after a very traumatic birthing process where I almost died. Because I had no family support or experience with an infant, I reached out to a new sponsor, Joan, who had a wealth of experience from having raised five children. She firmly instructed me to rest whenever possible and to call her the next morning. Knowing I had that call got me through the night.

When I called her the next morning, she asked me to reflect on a series of questions: What was happening right now? What was the feeling at the moment? Can I sense a power greater than myself also at work? Can I generate positive feelings for learning to be a new parent? We spoke for about fifteen minutes. Our calls were always brief, with no extensive story. This went on daily for over a month. I really learned about living one day at a time from our simple daily contact.

Every call ended with her saying, "Call me in the morning," and I only had to think of that day! Whatever happened the night before, even if I was up all night with a crying infant, wasn't as important as what was happening right now. The night had passed; could I be gentle and go mindfully into the next moments of the day and let that go?

Months later, when I felt more agility in handling my baby and had ventured out successfully, we talked once or twice a week. She said if things got tough, she'd be there for another call, but if not, use the phone list. Her support and the support of the recovery community gave me a sense of something larger than myself.

I found a new home group where childcare was provided. Having this additional support helped me to let go by exploring my feelings and options with caring attention. Each day I'd open the daily readings from *One Day at a Time*, or *Courage to Change*, for wisdom and reflection. The readings fed into my journaling practice to reflect on what I was struggling with and what my thoughts and feelings were each day.

Politics are not discussed at Twelve Step meetings, but cultural and political contexts fed directly into some of the causes of my codependency, or people-pleasing behavior. Over the years, I watched the illusion of "trickle-down" economics, the lessening of support for the homeless, the failure to ratify the Equal Rights Amendment, and the persistence of unequal pay for women. I was constantly reminded by the media that I was not pretty enough, not thin enough, and not rich enough. In workplace after workplace, I saw men, and sometimes women, in power get away with outrageous behavior. Many assistants often made excuses for the inappropriate conduct of the managers. I could see how far we had not come in the preceding decades. The combination of this cultural schism and being born sensitive has made it challenging for me to learn how to navigate this life.

This made me want to find a lifestyle that worked. To train my sons to become caring and responsible young men in our Midwestern American culture, and with their father unavailable as a co-parent, I needed flexible work options. My private practice and home business helped me be present for our children and gave me joy in seeing others grow in wisdom and develop a healthier way of life.

Parents are constantly asked to sacrifice the self. It is written in their bones the minute they accept the role. Without a supportive home during my own childhood, I felt it would be foolish for me to add any further dysfunction to the chain, so the moment I became pregnant I wanted to do everything in my power to be the best parent I could be and provide a safe home. This was an enormous responsibility since Stewart was often away for work. Children have many immediate needs. Parenting was my primary concern and a heavy karmic responsibility. Honoring my vulnerability in my recovery work helped me learn to take better care of myself and the children.

Even though there was often childcare at the meetings, it was sometimes difficult to get out the door in time with both kids in tow. In 1994, when my older son, Preston, was three, and my younger son was three months old, Preston suddenly developed Lennox Gastaut Syndrome (LGS), a rare, degenerative form of epilepsy that was complicated to treat. His body began having thousands of different types of seizures a day. My heart's wish to comprehend the karmic connection surrounding Preston's condition led to many powerful dreams and mystical experiences, such as my vision of the Dakota mother. Because his care involved around-the-clock mindfulness, I was praying and meditating intensely, the Eleventh Step in recovery. With faith and practice from the program, I found new coping skills I didn't know I was capable of—patience, trust, and love for simply being with my children along with intelligent discernment with medical professionals.

By 1997, Preston had made a full recovery, and with several more years of education and training, he regained full use of his faculties. Given the severity of Preston's illness for many years, I believed that my body was just as vulnerable and open to illness and death at any time. While still on this earth, I could not take my own life for granted, and worked hard to transmit some crucial life skills and understanding to the children.

Our children carried their own desires, hatreds, and delusions, and were searching in their own ways, just like me, for some deep understanding of this human life. As they grew, they became familiar with and attended their own Twelve Step meetings and potlucks. We blossomed with the principles of the program, which I also saw overlapping in other spiritual traditions: honesty, hope, surrender, courage, integrity, willingness, humility, love, responsibility, discipline, awareness, and service. I'd sometimes ask the kids to shout out some principles when out driving, and they'd do it! One of my sons set up a "sober room" for his senior prom, which became the most popular room during the dance for kids to feel safe to enjoy the party and not drink alcohol. We also supported the community with our web design skills and created a website for regional use.

Some of my favorite slogans that I heard at meetings were and are: "This too shall pass," "First things first," "Easy does it," "Take what you like, and leave the rest," "Keep it simple," "One day at a time," "Keep an open mind," "Live and let live," and "THINK: Is it True, Helpful, Inspiring, Necessary, Kind?" For example, the children often requested a movie, a treat, or a number of other things. But I'd stop and reflect on a slogan such as "First things first," and see what came from that. Often, I'd say, "That depends on each of you, and us together," which meant, "It depends on whether you will cooperate, fulfill your own duties, and we move together peacefully to evaluate what needs to be done—then what needs to be will be. Are you getting ready for bed? Do you have homework? Do you need something before the end of the day?" We need to be true to first things first. We worked together to honor and respect each other's needs for harmony. And, sometimes, our need for play brought up an "Easy does it" form of spontaneity and we changed direction to discover something new.

Book-ending is another powerful tool that I used with clients as well as myself. If there is a new situation coming up that might be stressful, I'd call someone on the phone list or my sponsor and talk about my concerns before the event. Then, I'd check in afterward to review my experience so I could learn from it with support. Often, whatever I was experiencing was exactly what the other person also needed to discuss at that time!

While working from home in my private practice and later as a website designer, I noticed the subtle changes season after season. I felt shivers in my body, sweat dripping on hot days with no air conditioning, and listened to the creaks when I tiptoed across a cold floor. It seemed like I was melting into a wisp amidst the chaotic construction. It wasn't easy for the children to listen to the flapping tarp overhead as a temporary roof for months in one of the worst Minnesota winters in forty years, and watch exterior walls being removed as they headed to school. It was hard to keep their hamsters safe, and not have a cozy place to bring friends home to play.

Even though I was in the role of guardian—*Life* was the boss. I didn't know what God was, or what a "Higher Power" might be, I just knew it wasn't me alone, so I often turned to that deeper subtle presence throughout the day, asking, *What is this*?

In daily life, I gave attention to the children in the simplest way possible by shifting between parenting and self-care. I'd check on them, listen to my body, look around the house, and rotate again. There was a tender and loving balance in making mindful transitions. We played together and quietly rested in moments between chores and errands. If fingernails needed clipping, there was clipping; when we needed to eat, there was just stirring the bean stew—tasting, smelling, hearing the kids play, and watching; listening to the house, listening within, and fixing what needed fixing with quiet appreciation. Often, I'd wait to work on my web business until after the kids were settled down. Or, since it was paid work, I'd stop and take care of client needs, putting off other chores, to make some desperately needed income.

After many years, I noticed this sense of *me* drifting away, so one day in 2006 I called my prior long-time sponsor, Joan, who had moved out of state. I shared with her that when this feeling arose, and the kids were in school, I'd sit peacefully for hours while thoughts just flowed through. She said, in a really worried tone, that I must have really let myself go. She proceeded to coach me into acquiring a goal of ambition. She also suggested I see a therapist and/or get on an antidepressant.

Had I become drowned out by the children and the house? I had been taking good care of my body, my weight seemed average, and I was in good health. I did not want medication. Nor did I want to use drugs or alcohol.

Sure enough, I had changed in many ways. I'd stopped wearing uncomfortable shoes decades ago. I rarely wore makeup as I let go of worry about outside perceptions. I preferred hiking clothes, because they were double-stitched, and made of durable fabric with deeper pockets. I found a tool bag to use as a purse. I stopped participating in the conditioning from media and women's magazines to look pretty in the way women packaged themselves for men. Although, I still sometimes like to adorn the body, and play with my hairstyle for fun.

When I asked Joan about her grown children, she boasted that they were busily rising up in their careers, getting their kids into better schools, and buying vacation homes. I was glad that her kids were thriving and doing so well. I just didn't feel I could handle any more than I had already been doing. I had often considered her feedback helpful in the past, but it didn't help me evaluate what was happening. I was keeping a clean and functional home plus building it while raising two sons. That was a lot already! Still, I wondered if there was something wrong with me.

As I reflected on this, I found a book that outlined a model of different stages of growth. On one axis, the horizontal axis, are psychological personal growth, skillfulness in self-care, and career growth. On the other axis, the vertical axis, are transpersonal or mystical stages of growth, representing a different path altogether.[5] The horizontal and vertical interact all the time. The horizontal axis is typically

---

5   Wilber, Ken. *The Integral Vision.*

outlined in society and what we need to attend to for survival, like building our resume and climbing that career ladder. But, none of this can be taken along at death.

The vertical axis was calling me, opening me to the Truth with an inward focus. It is about relinquishing any sense of self without causing harm. It's not about getting or having anything. Spiritual development is supported by doing less and keeping things simpler as I had been doing for many years. This process is the living breath of life, our Spirit.

It was always reassuring when I remembered to feel the breath energies, and try to welcome feelings as they came and went. *What is happening now? What is needed right now? What are the options?* Okay. Accept. Keep it simple. One step at a time.

Still, I wondered if I needed to be doing more after listening to Joan. It isn't easy going against the stream. We were low-income and struggling. I thought I might earn more as an attorney and work on causes that align with my values. The year before, in 2006, I had taken a logic class and sat an LSAT test. I sat three of them. During each test, the silence in the room felt perfect amidst the concentrated fervor of the students. I sat there in Stillness, knowing that with each ticking second, I would miss more questions if I didn't focus and stop listening to the quietude. Again, those thoughts just flowed without concern. In the middle of my last LSAT, where I was moving along just fine with all of the questions, suddenly, I heard a deep orotund voice rumble within: *This isn't it.* A resounding resonance in my gut told me that my very existence, my entire being, was here to learn something much more fundamental. The desire to study law vanished.

But, I found myself torn to some extent. I had a full-time job for a while, but it often required overtime, and the cost of daycare was more than what I earned. I had been approaching writing as a career where I could develop my work at home. During Preston's illness, I had worked with a local writing teacher, Carol Bly, who encouraged me to write. She sent me boxes of books from her own shelves, and said that I must read, read, read, as much as I can. We were engaged in finishing my memoir, a story of our family experience with Preston's epilepsy, together in 2007 when she got ovarian cancer and died a few months later, which felt devastating.

Somehow, with having worked a program of awareness in every area of my life for so long, it seemed like the program began working *me*. I was being acted upon; chased by something bigger that I kept turning to look at. Ideas about myself, like what it is to be a woman, wife, and mother were melting away. My focus turned intensely inward to that seemingly something that sees or knows. *What knows everything in creative unison and provides the basis for all that we need? What was it? God?* I didn't know. The more I sat with difficult feelings and worked the steps, the more the pull strengthened within to follow that vertical transcendent process.

For several years, my only trips out of the home had included visiting state parks, taking cheap vacations close by, driving the usual well-worn road to the warehouse for building materials, and going to the grocery store. I could hardly remember the last time I had left Minnesota, other than a drive to Chicago to visit my paternal cousins and my stepmother for an occasional Thanksgiving. I liked being home. It was hard to travel. And to use our few resources for a trip just for myself seemed quite extravagant.

Over the years, I had a series of different sponsors, and I stayed in touch with a few of them occasionally even after they moved away. In 2006, I needed a new regular weekly sponsor and asked Guy for help. Guy was open to me and the boys, and invited us to his apartment for social gatherings. He was retired, and therefore available for weekly in-person meetings. Our time was usually spent contemplating a step of the program alongside a current dilemma in my life. His calm listening helped me notice when I was worrying and drew me back into an undercurrent of faith.

In the fall of 2007, after practicing at the Zen center, Guy and I had our weekly meeting, and as usual, he inquired about the kids. I launched into a story about the growing police presence in their public schools, the new iron bars on the windows, and how I had to park farther away. Due to recent horrifying school shootings, it took much longer to enter the school as new security measures were being implemented at the entrances.

We paused to take several breaths for a minute.

"Well, times are tough now. Enough about them. What about you?"

"I *was* talking about me. I'm a parent and had to see their teachers about their work, and inform them of choices. I don't know what the best options are."

He nodded. "That's true."

My life and my sons' lives overlap. But I could see what he was getting at, so I blurted out, "I just made plans to go to California on a personal retreat!"

"Huh?" His jaw slackened.

"Yeah, I have a good feeling about it. I want to go away to practice meditation for a whole week, but it's not until April."

"Okay. Do you know anyone there?"

"No."

I could see his surprise so I added, "I won't know for at least a month whether I get in."

"Oh?"

"Yes, there is a lottery, and it might be full."

He gave me a quizzical look.

"I've been going to a local hermitage for decades and feeling somewhat stuck," I explained.

He nodded. "Why do you want to go to this place?"

"I need a broader perspective with intensive meditation and time to meditate continuously." After a pause, I said, "I'm so tired of my doubt."

"Mhm," he murmured.

"Do you know much about meditation?"

"No, not really."

We turned our eyes out the front window.

A stillness settled in as we sat with the quiet of the room.

~~~

Thousands of families and communities have been driven apart and isolated in these troubled times. Taking inspiration from Lois W., the co-founder of Al-Anon, I made it an annual tradition for several years to invite members of my home group over to my house to watch

"When Love is Not Enough: The Lois Wilson Story."[6] Whenever I attend a meeting, I often imagine Lois, as she's depicted by Winona Ryder, knocking on the car windows of all the other wives who are sitting alone and waiting for their husbands to come out after their AA meeting. She invited them to her kitchen table to talk about their lives and how they were also needing support. How she holds the practice of the Twelfth Step, carrying the message to others, is the same that I intend in this writing, so that others can learn about the support available.

Given that Twelve Step programs are offered freely and based on a tradition of attraction rather than promotion, anonymity is an important value, which also protects its members against the stigma surrounding addictions in our culture. Although, Lois writes in her memoir that "the degree of anonymity we practice is a personal matter... If AA and Al-Anon groups do not let the public know of our presence... we block ourselves off from those in need."[7] I see Lois as a role model for how to carry the message to others. Our society has greatly benefited from those who have testified publicly before the U.S. Congress and Senate to advance legislation supporting insurance coverage for treatment. A shining example is Betty Ford, who courageously acknowledged her struggles with alcoholism and founded the Betty Ford Center in 1982. It is through such open sharing of personal stories that treatment centers have been established, leading to global support for families in need.

Stories like these helped me find the willingness to transform resentment into acceptance and love. I really feel that today we need to remember Lois's example and find ways to gather in our own backyards, front stoops, kitchens, and on the Internet to share and support one another.

---

6   Harrison, John Kent. *When Love Is Not Enough: The Lois Wilson Story*, DVD (United States: Hallmark Hall of Fame, 2010).

7   W. Lois, *Lois Remembers: Memoirs of the Cofounder of Al-Anon and Wife of the Cofounder of Alcoholics Anonymous*

CHAPTER FIVE

Deeper Recovery

G OING FROM a women's support group to Twelve Step recovery groups while doing therapy did not meet all of my needs for recovery from the trauma I had experienced as a child. In early 1987, while I was studying addiction counseling, I happened across a flyer on a bulletin board at school for a talk being given by a feminist author, Anne Wilson Schaef, who had written a book called *When Society Becomes an Addict.*

Seeing addiction everywhere affected me tremendously. I noticed the materialism around Christmas, avoidance of intimacy in my relationships, and workaholism among my family members. I didn't know anyone who wasn't caught up in busyness or rushing around to do things or get things. Who knew how to live in balance?

I immediately bought a ticket to go hear Anne speak. With each question from the audience, Anne would pause, and invite the questioner to feel into her own question right away, right there! She was interested in the welfare of this woman and her inquiry process. She noticed if a question was dualistic, how the dualism restricts the mind and options. I appreciated the way she rephrased questions to allow for something new.

There was a woman who asked if she should stay in her marriage or leave. She asked how to know if it was her or her partner that was the problem. Anne encouraged her to consider ways in which she may have already left, perhaps emotionally, or how the differences between them could be honored and truth could be explored more openly without feeling threatened. She talked about there being many facets within each of us.

Anne asked her where in her body the question might be coming from, because prior trauma and a history of built-up tensions and desires can be held in the body and triggered in conflictual situations. This prior trauma could be preventing her from feeling like she could be herself in the relationship. She asked her if she was more concerned about how the relationship was perceived by others or about what she was seeing for herself. To what degree was she trying to manage or control the relationship instead of engaging in an intimate relationship where honesty and truth are all right? Was she willing to learn new skills for healthy relationships? She invited the woman to look into whether she was really taking time to listen and hear her partner. Anne admitted she had been married twice and learned the hard way. Without healthier inquiry, the decisions are often in a stuck place.

By the end of that day, layers of tension and stress in my body opened up to new ways of perceiving. I signed up immediately to attend one of the intensives being offered that month by two local therapists who had worked with her. By welcoming in bodily wisdom, she was going beyond the therapeutic paradigm being taught, offering an abundance of reflections to enrich my Twelve Step practice.

After reading *When Society Becomes an Addict*, which describes many characteristics of addiction, I decided to use four that Anne highlighted as a daily tool for reflection. I created my own acronym for them, called D.I.E.D., which helped me recall this four-part checklist during the day: denial, illusion of control, external referencing, and dualistic thinking. Or, sometimes, I thought of it as dualistic thinking, illusion of control, external referencing, and denial.

Denial: To deny the truth is a form of dishonesty with others and with ourselves. This also includes subtler forms of dishonesty like passivity, not speaking when necessary, and defensiveness. There are various kinds of denial, such as denying the negative outcomes of my own actions, and also denying the negative impact of another person's actions on myself. Denial thrives when we are not really present to take into account our own needs and/or what is needed in our current circumstances in life. One lies to oneself first and then carries it out-ard, so I worked to be more intimate and honest with my basic needs, desires, and transgressions of basic boundaries. Regular check-ins, journaling, and choosing nonviolent communication increase clarity and reduce denial.

Illusion of control: Believing we can control what we cannot control is engaging in delusion—unacknowledged pain is usually hiding there. Surely, we are responsible for our own behavior, but we also need to see the ways in which our actions have limits, learn, and let that in. We want what we want when we want it. And we also don't want certain things. That noticing is important. The serenity prayer helped me to reflect on this:

> ...*grant me the serenity to accept the things I cannot change,*
> *the courage to change the things I can,*
> *and the wisdom to know the difference.*[8]

For serenity, I had to stop more often, pause, feel, and notice my options to move in a positive direction. The "things" in the prayer invited me to notice and name various patterns, situations, and places where my skills were challenged. My unskillful behaviors had been learned and reinforced in our workaholic culture of busyness. Contemplating this illusion of control also brought forth a question: If I can't control a process, where does *my* responsibility begin and end?

External referencing: Thinking primarily in terms of how we are perceived by others, without sensing our own inner wisdom, is another form of dishonesty. Praising or blaming a single event or person

---

8   I left out the word "God" at the beginning of the prayer because each person has to find their own meaning for that word. It was often taught to me as a punishing form, so I held that word with caution because I intuitively felt that God could not be punishing. I also knew I had to put in effort with intention to make progress in recovery. I couldn't just rely on some deity outside of myself.

is also a way of participating in external referencing because there are many causes that go into events. We need to look at our participation in our own lives. I'm inspired by many people, but take care to see that others support them too. Nurturing my own creative offerings to the world involved developing a trust and love with my unique way of being.

Worrying about what other people think and spending more effort on the perceptions of others obscured my ability to recognize my own needs for growth and support. I thought something or someone could provide happiness or relief and did not turn inward to see what is going on within. The feedback I receive from other people can be tremendously helpful, and yet I need to carefully look at how it feels in the body and whether it truly resonates. How someone else does something is not necessarily how I need to proceed in a particular moment. It was important for me to discuss my choices with my sponsor and friends as a way to rekindle an internal focus and illuminate my options.

Dualistic thinking: There is a tendency in our culture to communicate and solve problems in an either-or mentality. It's important to know one way or another about things. Are the dishes done or not done? Does the car start or not start? And, we are humans, not electrical switches. By stopping to notice if I was engaged in dualistic thinking, I could bring a paradoxical view and a new framework toward the situation. When it comes to our intentions, thoughts, and feelings, they are more complex and subtler than this polarized response to life. In my own house, if a person needs transportation, we can explore using our shared vehicle, the bus, a bicycle, or a combination of options.

Dualistic thinking limits options; thinking an outcome has to be my way or your way, and not seeing that there may be a compromise, or something new altogether. Words like "always," "never," "everyone," "no one," "everything," and "nothing" can dramatize a situation in the thinking mind, making it more of a solid story. Scarcity is built into it. It is a learned pattern based on immediate gratification. We need to dig deeper to bring up new questions. With a blended discernment of opposing views, constructive options for reflection are offered up, gradually loosening stiffness within the mind into a softer, more workable batter.

Even the breath becomes an opportunity for learning. Often what is being learned or explored has many levels of understanding.

Each of these characteristics also feeds into one another. External referencing can be a form of denial and the illusion of control can often be driven by dualistic thinking; my way or the highway. With these concepts in my toolbelt, I became skilled at identifying how addictive systems were operating in my life and the world around me.

The combination of working a Twelve Step program and reflecting with D.I.E.D. was a profoundly changing experience. I humbly learned from mistakes with my kids, teachers, and institutions. I was sometimes blunt and pointed out the either-or thinking and the few options for discussion. The way I approached D.I.E.D. was to notice and feel if one or more of the characteristics were arising. If one was there, I could see how subtly the others were there too. I would go find somewhere to rest and reflect, or ask my process to wait until I could get to a safe place to sit with my pain, sorrow, despair, overwhelm, doubt, anger, confusion, etc. I might find a bathroom toilet, or a bench, or sit in my car. Stop. Be. Listen. And so, when I experienced stress, I may have laughed, cried, trembled, or rested...but at the end of my respite, I frequently thanked my process and moved forward with a more relaxed view.

In the news, I saw endless headlines framing the world in dualistic terms: "Is it time for war or peace?" How about the commonly used phrase in the deteriorating media ecosystem about the "War on Terror?" War raises terror. Any war is a process that is happening to all of us. How we use language can limit our intelligence and our ability to negotiate new ways of being in the world or solutions to problems.

Often when there is talk of "war" on viruses or cancer or whatever the new crisis is circulated by mass media, few healthy solutions are offered for more peaceful cooperation among human beings. We can develop a variety of solutions for problems. Nothing is going to be perfect; we are all in this process of learning, but language that includes interdisciplinary, intelligent, compassionate approaches informs us with more options.

I invited my children to notice dualisms when they were in kindergarten. One day, the teacher showed a picture of a sky with a cloud in it and asked them: Is the sky clear or cloudy? To the consternation of his teacher, it was obvious to my son that there was a sky with one cloud in it; therefore, it could be called partly cloudy or partly clear. When Forrest was just five years old, he stopped me in the store. We did not have enough money to buy the transformer toy he wanted, so he tugged on my sleeve and asked if he could pay me back out of his piggy bank at home, or if we could come back soon and then he could purchase it himself.

By the second grade, they were recognizing dualistic language around them and questioning things. In elementary school, Preston often did not want to comply with some of the lessons and would get up from his chair and quietly check on the turtles or other animals in the back of the room. He was being pressured to conform amidst his efforts to recover from LGS.

Unfortunately, this added awareness put them in a different place of maturity among their peers. They were often bullied and silently ostracized. To question that system of language and belief can be an affront to others' identity. Communication skills could be taught in schools to facilitate more creative discussions and paradoxical thinking among students, even young children.

Sometimes I brought up these topics with other parents and the school principal. I was told that unless my suggestions were accepted within the core curriculum and teacher training, it was what it was. Teachers all across the country have been struggling to keep up with growing classroom sizes, lack of resources, and unrealistic standards. There was a sense that everyone was already overwhelmed and busy. I didn't have a role as superintendent or principal. I could only work with my children to the best of my ability.

The boys had a few kindhearted teachers through the years. One teacher allowed me to keep my sons at home for a day or two when they needed to finish difficult projects or needed a break. She worked with me and not against me. It was definitely against the rules. While I should have had a doctor's slip for keeping them home, she trusted me, and I trusted her, which was rare.

I really didn't know how to best affect the system when there were so many rules and regulations in place. Every night, Forrest and Preston were expected to complete a sheet with seven columns detailing their reading history. The sheet took quite a bit of time to fill out and stirred up the mind, especially when going through a whole array of books. They were to hand in the form weekly. This process required writing down the titles, the author, the number of pages read, the publisher, as well as the starting and ending page numbers if the book was not finished.

I decided we wouldn't fill out these sheets, and I sent them back with a note saying, "We are not going to do this." The teacher called me at home, astounded. They had this idea that if the form was filled out then they could be satisfied that the kids were reading at home; this was a long-time practice.

I talked with other parents and they said they just filled it out, that it's really for the parents to take care of. This made me feel alone in the process. They agreed it was a huge waste of time and energy and upset the bedtime routine. One parent said she just grabs a stack of books and fills it out each week; it makes the system happy. That seemed dishonest. For us, it created a busyness scenario with work after we'd had a fun and relaxing story time. I wanted our bedtime routine to be about *enjoying* reading, which also included cuddling, looking at the pictures, considering the themes and plots, the morals in the story, and even learning about the authors before transitioning into sleep.

So, I refused to fill out this sheet and told the children they did not have to fill it out either if they did not want to do it. They soon told me they were the only ones not handing in the sheet and felt different from the other kids at school. Still, they also chose to not do the form. From first through fourth grade, this came up as a type of rule-breaking for us at every teacher meeting. I also had to speak with the principal about it where she explained the good intentions of the form, but I said that it could be voluntary with more discussion about enjoyment of reading instead of reporting how many books or pages one has read. I often felt misunderstood and alone because I didn't agree with many of the rules of control. Rules are typically formed with good intentions, but stringent adherence without consideration or flexibility is dangerous to me.

The classroom often did not provide a peaceful learning environment. When Forrest was seven, a kid in his class constantly yanked at his rat tail. The school wouldn't do anything about this bullying unless they caught it in the act. One day, the teacher and I were standing in the doorway looking at Forrest just as the other kid passed behind him and pulled his hair. Boy, was I lucky to be standing there with her watching it happen! He had also been poking Forrest with his pencil and leaving marks on his back. Forrest was a gentle boy and did not want to fight. All the teacher could do was move my son farther away from him so that the other kid had no reason to pass Forrest on his way to sharpen his pencil.

She did not confront the boy hurting my son. The fear of conflict among the teachers created a system of avoidance—not a learning environment for compassion and honesty. Forrest appreciated the intervention and began talking more about problems at school. These issues felt really complicated and difficult for me to stand in my own shoes and work with the system.

With the help of the Twelve Step program, I developed my own system of picking up, starting over, and trying new options. Seeing the addictive characteristics arise and how I had acclimated to recovery around them pulled my attention inward more and more. I saw that parts of me were dying, and a deeper perspective was unfolding. I kept getting drawn toward a paradox between my spiritual mystical knowledge and skillfulness for loving and respectful human relationships. There are skills to learn and—*What is it that is always here within it all?*

On the one hand, I recognized innocence in myself and others, while on the other, I'm surrounded by this messiness of conflicts, desires, and aversions. Courage allowed me to discover new options for circumstances in my life. Using D.I.E.D. on a regular basis reduced the feeling of self-importance. I could die at any time and needed to pay attention to my participation in this very life.

CHAPTER SIX

Trusting the Process

A NEW LEVEL OF OPENNESS that I hadn't encountered before came through Anne Wilson Schaef's teaching. While it was a hardship for both my husband and me to take part in her Living in Process retreats, we worked out a six-year payment plan with Anne, and for my second year, she offered me a full scholarship. These retreats took place at various locations around the country, most within driving distance of the Midwest area, and every retreat was held at a place that was physically accessible for folks with different needs.

At a typical hour-long Twelve Step meeting, you might get five minutes to check in, which is fine, because the time limit encourages you to become more succinct and a better listener. Generally, you do not receive feedback unless you specifically request it after the meeting. However, at Anne's intensive retreats, people had as much time as they needed to tell their stories, share their feelings, and receive responses from others. I was often amazed by the level of honesty and the willingness to gently approach emotional pain, be it grief, anger, or fear, while also learning to let in joy and gratitude. I never knew that such a thing was possible!

The group was usually facilitated pretty well. Sure, problems and conflicts came up, but, more often, folks used that as a chance to look into their own conflicted feelings and discover what was hidden from their initial perspective. Then, they would come back to the group to share their new understanding. In this way, we were invited to see how we were active participants in life and challenged our adherence to certain belief systems.

Most everyone did their energy work, or healing process work, often called "deep process work", in the same large room where we met as a group. A number of mats in the back were available for people to stretch out and move in connection with their feelings, and ask for facilitation. The available mats and openness took the shame out of the process of having feelings. It normalized them. People could be seen doing energy work in a wide variety of ways: standing, lying down, sitting, keening, or quietly resting, etc. You could go back to your room if it felt more comfortable, but often folks did their work out in the open with kind support.

A deep process explores the felt sensations of being in this painful. human life. In Anne's book *Beyond Therapy, Beyond Science*, she explains, "all of us have unfinished deep processes rumbling around inside of us," and this is not just a "catharsis or the expression of feelings."[9] She emphasizes that they encompass something greater, offering a level of healing that transcends intellectual understanding. It's about intimacy with oneself, which takes a variety of gentle healing forms; it can include tears, a quiet walk in the woods, a shared meal in the community, or sitting with oneself in peacefulness.

Not hiding this process had a tremendously freeing effect. It removed the self-consciousness of grief and the shame—even the shame for having shame! The key was assessing my intention, to honor the wisdom in my body and learn: *Was there any indulging, retraumatizing, or running away from my deep process?*

During my upbringing, I had learned to repress my feelings and lie about them in order to take care of others in my dysfunctional family of origin. I would hide in my room or outside in the cold with my feelings. I was taught to never make a public display of emotion.

This group helped me feel safe in my vulnerability and see that I am not alone; that we all experience grief, loss, or any number of feelings and can explore them in a safe and comforting environment. I remember Anne saying, "I have never seen anyone get hurt from sitting

---

9   Anne Wilson Schaef. *Beyond Therapy, Beyond Science*

or stretching out on a mat, seeing what comes up for them, and staying with it along with some gentle, nonintrusive support."

Anne's wisdom and facilitation were powerful and lasting. It was not only her writing but the way she led intensives that impressed me. First of all, she insisted that if someone didn't wish to be in the group, it would be respectful and caring for them to consider other options, like a walk or time to sit in nature. This allowed me to look more closely at why I was there, and what I needed in the moment.

The idea of rigidity around attendance had been instilled in me, so I experimented with this at first and slept through a group meeting one time and received some valuable rest. I realized that my absence didn't cause any issues for anyone else. I also noticed there were natural consequences because if something important had been shared in the group, and was being discussed later, I wasn't as well informed as others about the context. Sometimes, I went to the meetings and talked about my ambivalence about being there and received support for being honest. I learned to find my own rhythm and connect with my body in a nonjudgmental way.

Anne also hosted many wonderful women-only intensive retreats. She set them up in remote locations so we could dance, swim, play, grieve, let our sounds out, and be ourselves. Anne noticed when someone was talking out of their head and appeared to be wandering in their check-in; so sometimes she'd share her feelings of boredom or concern, and invite the person sharing to draw upon the depth of their feelings more. How many times had I sat and listened to someone complain at length without saying anything to them?

One beautiful summer, Anne led a ten-day women's retreat on an island near Ely, Minnesota. At the outset, we set our schedule as a group. One day, she was delayed taking care of herself and lost track of time. When she arrived about thirty minutes late, she was surprised that we had been waiting for her. She asked us to look at what was going on within as we sat there. She asked us to share our assumptions. She asked us to reflect on what we did with our minds, our feelings, and our actions during that time. Her gentle invitations had such intimate care in them. If we were concerned about her, why did no one go and see what she was doing? Due to the island's rugged terrain, she could have tripped or fallen. We could have taken the initiative by sending someone to check on her and still gotten the group started. Did some people space out? Did some get impatient? Did some feel relaxed and open to just being? Did some look for another facilitator to step up?

There were a variety of responses. I didn't think we could start without her, so I also waited. Anne invited us to look at how each experience is an opportunity to see how we are participating. Bringing awareness to our conditioned reliance on her as an authority encouraged us to tune more into our own inner wisdom. She said she was uncomfortable with having that much power in the group. She didn't want to feel that we needed her that much; we had to turn within. Her thoughtful and patient manner seemed to really permeate into each of us. I considered my dependence on authority. No leader I ever knew had asked me to reflect on that!

She also stretched out and did her own grief work. I sat with her during some of her deep processes. We stood in line together for food, and sat on the dock in Northern Minnesota, the land of the Dakota and Anishinaabe peoples, discussing her Cherokee heritage and the importance of Mother Earth. As the sun set over the lake, we peeled apples for juicy pies; she cooed at my infant son and hand-stitched a baby blanket for him while leading the group. I felt her loving warmth and connection with the community around her during this era when she was leading intensives.

Even Anne's mistakes were teachings for me. She sometimes alienated people with her impulsivity and irritations. Some group members left, taking their wisdom with them. I didn't need her to be perfect. No group leader can meet everyone's needs. We all sometimes fail at communication, and we are all mirrors for one another. Seeing how we all have our flaws and are inherently human, I learned to accept what's real and work on opening up to different points of view. Realizing this helped me accept things as they were, including Anne, in all her brilliance and all her struggles.

Anne often said that she did not want to be a therapist, and that she was offering an alternative to therapy. Drawing from her experience as a trained counselor, she discussed the disempowering effects of overusing certain therapeutic techniques, which she observed in

certain group situations. In working with her around this, I learned that
a technique is an experiment, test it carefully, and be open to abandoning it. She wanted people to just relate with one another, be truthful,
and notice any avoidance of intimacy. It didn't require any special
skill to sit with someone who was in a deep process. I often sat with
folks who spoke another language I did not know, offering that simple
presence of compassionate being as they worked with their process.

She encouraged the facilitator to not interfere; simply allow, and
provide safety and support. Or if a facilitator felt a need to interfere, she
encouraged them to look at what was going on within—instead of sitting
with that person, they could stretch out and see what was coming up.
Her approach was: to "wait with" and be honest about your choices.
When facilitating: be present, provide a glass of water for one, a box
of tissues for another; let there be space between you both. Above all,
be careful not to make a solid interpretation of what another person is
experiencing. Check things out. In doing that for another, each person
can allow what needs to be revealed to come.

Her main message was to trust your inner process. I had never
before in my life come across a teacher who so embodied this understanding. Seeing folks do their own work and come back refreshed
taught me to trust in the dignity of each one of us to understand
ourselves. This also reinforced my commitment to let go of my pattern
of caretaking others that I had learned growing up. Much of that
conditioning dropped away. Opening up to emotions was not necessarily a breakdown. It can be simple, gentle, and at one's own pace.

There were usually two three-hour facilitated meetings a day
where folks could check in, share their life stories, or experiences.
People would call out a need for a certain type of Twelve Step meeting,
and folks would come together in the evening as arranged. The
spontaneity, intimacy, and freedom that these groups expressed were
beyond anything I had ever seen or imagined.

At one intensive in Montana, I remember a woman sharing her
story in detail of how, through her denial, she had slowly killed
her beautiful stallion by the way she participated in the horse-racing
industry. Halfway through her story, people started to weep. As she
continued to share, more began connecting with an immense sorrow

within themselves for her and her horse. By the end of the story, she and all of about sixty people in the room were brought to their knees in various stages of pain, anguish, sorrow, or other feelings I did not know. I remember nursing my baby and looking around the room, knowing I was involved in something powerful and compassionate.

One time, I changed my ten-week-old son's diaper and went to sit near an older woman who was weeping and rocking while holding herself. There was a place for me to rest against the wall and hold my baby. I asked her if I could sit with her. She nodded.

I laid out tissues for her while feeling touched by her pain and the beauty of her being. She had strong feelings coming up from listening to another story and being offered the space. I didn't know until she told me afterward that she carried an additional depth of sorrow over the death of her son.

She told me it felt challenging for her to see me holding my son because, ten years earlier, her only child had died from cancer. My presence and my baby appeared to serve as a living mirror for her, allowing her to grieve while also granting her body space to heal and move after all of those frozen years. What struck me was her willingness to trust her feelings and stay with her process. I often felt that when I had someone sit with me in a nurturing and patient way, their presence allowed me to access a unified field of compassion. I value this mysterious dance between any two people that allows for intimacy and learning.

One of the main skills I took away from the groups was to turn toward the center of the emotional pain whenever it arose. If I was feeling angry or irritated, wanting something to be different, I turned toward that anger. Underneath the anger may have been fear, and underneath that was some tension or pain, and so I felt the sensation of the pain. The more I did this, the more intimate I felt with my body. I also began to notice how many emotions blended together—even gratitude for knowing the feelings and turning toward them. Drawing attention to the pain directly and feeling it is a sign of both strength and vulnerability.

The body has a memory and needs to be honored. After an intensive, I might have just put this training in the past, but I could not.

Something profound had shifted in me. I set up a little process area in our basement where, if I felt triggered by something, or if I had a break from caring for the children, I would go and stretch out or sit. I had a foam mat and some big pillows, a few blankets, a box of tissues, and a glass of water. I was often tired and would nap.

In moments of raw vulnerability, intense fear intertwined with pain, coursing through every fiber of my being. The grief of losing my beloved father, the absence of a functional mother, the homelessness in between foster care, the void of a stable and nurturing home during my childhood, and the trauma from sexual assault in those years would bring on some trembling and shaking under the weight of it all. These intense feelings pulled me inward to see hidden beliefs attached to ideas of aloneness, of feeling separate and unloved. I struggled at times to release these identities that were connected with these core ideas, but turning to a tender inquiry revealed my unconscious participation in them. Without facing my pain, my mind would go back to inhabiting old ideas of inadequacy.

Regularly taking time slowly and gently to explore these deep processes brought relief, spontaneity, and playfulness. It reduced chances of conflict with others by helping me mature as a sentient being. I felt this suffering and wanted to heal and be a loving mother for my children. I found bodily wisdom for my family to live in my heart and discovered capacities to be with things as they were. In addition, nightmares that had happened over and over again, stopped. Newer dimensions began to blossom.

Sometimes, worry for Preston's life brought up tears. Preston's seizures involved more and more invasive, painful tests and proce-dures. My heart split open with the challenges. I had to continually accept what was happening with his decline, and make medical deci-sions for his care. He lost his ability to speak and walk while enduring thousands of different types of seizures a day. After a certain point, I vowed that I would do anything to help him as I surrendered every last particle of my being. The only way I knew how to get through that was by remembering my work with Anne, who invited me to feel and know my experience. Thoughts that fed into overwhelm were revealed to me. Often, a simple pause to feel, recognize a heartfelt intuition, and listen to my thoughts from a more relaxed perspective helped me make decisions spontaneously for the children and for all of us.

Later, when Preston had improved, around age eight, we drove a few hours south for a weekend family biking trip. I arranged for us to sleep in a garage someone had turned into a tiny living space that I found on the Internet because camping seemed too complicated for that trip. It was another one of my very inexpensive weekend adventures. After one fun day of bicycling, Preston developed an eye infection, which rapidly worsened. I knew he needed a certain medication for his eyes, but it was back at home. We had four bikes, our equipment, and everything ready to enjoy another day of biking the trails. We all needed this space and time away. That night, during a loud thunderstorm, I sat and prayed for guidance.

The next day, I knew I simply had to get help for him, so we packed up the van to go back home. On our way out of town, I stopped to fill up the gas tank, and the cashier asked how I was doing. I opened up to him and said I felt sad that we had to leave due to my child having an eye infection. Then I spontaneously asked, "You wouldn't happen to know of any mothers in town with small kids?" He said that the local pastor had two sets of twins and lived just around the corner. He called him up right away on the gas station phone. After speaking with the pastor, he kindly wrote down the address and said to go over to their house right away.

When I arrived, the pastor's wife said her kids had dealt with the same thing, and she brought out two bottles. I verified that it was the correct medicine and that it had not expired. I asked for a few drops, and she said, "Why don't you just keep the bottle? I have two of them." This was more than I could have hoped for.

I wanted to thank the mother and the attendant, so we returned to the gas station, and the attendant was so happy to have helped us. Then I bought a pack of diapers and put it on the mother's doorstep before we went back to the garage to unpack. I put some drops in Preston's eyes, and he healed quickly the next day. He was fine. We ended up having a great weekend trip! How does that happen? I do not know, because there are many streams that come together all the time in mysterious ways. I enjoy being open to possibilities.

Medications have their uses, and we each need to find our own path with them. I didn't feel I needed to take pharmaceutical medication to deal with my stress; instead, I stayed with my process. Some people need to take medication, and it is important for them to participate carefully in their own healthcare plan and do what is right for them. In the early '70s, I experimented with LSD, psilocybin, and marijuana, but these experiences were exhausting and transient, and held no appeal for me. My understanding is that certain psychedelics can give a temporary reprieve or insight, but I wanted to find a peaceful way through and *know*. My gut told me that facing pain one day at a time, one breath at a time, would work better for me because my feelings often shifted with kindness.

When I approached the sorrow arising, I aimed to honor it and let it come. I learned over the years to not push the process, to take breaks, pace myself, and go slowly. Birthing came with wave after wave of contractions. Most people decide they are finished after letting out one teardrop. They wipe their faces and move on. Many get all tense when someone cries and hug them to stop the process, afraid of feelings. At that time, in a therapy session, there was limited time and no cushions or space to stretch out on, move, do qigong, or let your sounds out. I asked a therapist once, "Can you just sit there, be a comforting presence, and put out tissues for me, so I can see what this is about?" She said, "No, that is not what we do here; we are looking at your story to figure things out." However, I had grown tired of my story. Many settings do not allow time and space for one to explore on a *feeling* level. Gradually, I learned that healing included bringing a gentle inner willingness toward peace and not knowing. I am humbly learning this again and again each day.

When lying or sitting on my soft daybed on the basement floor, I'd rest and let the mind dream and drift for a while. Waves of various feelings would arrive, sometimes deeper in the gut, lower, and more intense. Paying attention to my own unique process and honoring it enlivened me. Relaxing the body and moving with the flow of wave after wave sometimes brought forth a mystical experience where I felt connected with all beings. At other times, I'd know: *I am thirsty.* Then I would simply get up and pour a drink of water.

Forrest and Preston grew accustomed to my deep process work because, for them, I returned gentler, less brittle, with color in my cheeks, ready to play, go outside, and do what was needed next. They often came home from school exclaiming how they were told, "Boys don't cry," and they felt oppressed by that. Many are not taught to trust their bodies and emotions. For those who aren't, it can lead them to lash out and pass judgment onto those who do. I made sure my sons knew they could stretch out and cry if they needed to, and I would not try to stop it. I would just sit with them. They did their own healing work and trusted it.

Sometimes an idea for what to do or say to a specialist for my son would come up. I might jot it down. Following that, I might shift back into exploring other feelings. I did not try to figure them out. I just stayed with my bodily flow of feelings and thoughts. Understanding arose on its own. Sometimes I'd weep for five minutes and experience a visceral release.

Many mystical unions and insights followed. I often encountered this sense of being lifted by another force, both beyond and within, which bewildered me, yet offered up so much relief that there was only a sweet wonderment afterward. Feeling whole for the moment, I was able to move onward with my tasks and cultivate patience. Tuning in was a form of worship; each tear, each wail upon the cushion—a prayer, a grateful seeking and finding at the same time.

As I was healing, the intelligence of these insights radiated out-ward from somewhere deep within—nothing was untouched as other planes of existence were known. I sensed as though prior generations in my family had been affected through my work. Could that be? And, it appeared the cellular levels of those genetic imprints were healing and releasing.

I started to notice sensations similar to swiftly descending on a Ferris wheel, and I called them my "Ferris wheel feelings." These subtle, lilting sensations made me pause, reflect, and consider ideas of "me." Sometimes, if someone sat with me, I could access this quiet place in the center of the pain that had an incredible openness. Over and over again, I abandoned ideas, and simply wondered, curious and relieved to know that no matter what, life was my teacher.

When shifting through a cycle of pain to openness, freedom, and joy, I'd feel this little niggling sense that *I am so close.* Close to what?

I wondered about death, the great doorway we will all pass through. When I was six, a school friend died from a congenital heart problem. I asked the nuns about death when I stayed after school to wash the chalkboard. They said, "You go to heaven." But, I asked, "Where is heaven?" They shook their heads and just gave me more erasers to clap outside, and taught me the prayer: "Now I lay me down to sleep, I pray the Lord my soul to keep; if I should die before I wake, I pray the Lord my soul to take." I'd lie in bed at night terrified that I would die during the night. *Where will I go when I die? How far can it be? Why be afraid of God taking me if we're supposed to have faith in God?* I sensed that it couldn't be far because I felt a kinship with my friend who had died, and a subtle connection with her.

Our children had similar questions as they grew up. Not knowing what to say, I often told them, "That is a good question for the Great Mystery. Let's let that question work within us." Were there any answers beyond that? I didn't know.

All I ever wanted was peaceful living, to love and feel loved. I often felt peace deep within, but then that peaceful feeling would recede. If even peace comes and goes, what was there to trust? Feelings of love also came and went. And, there are many different kinds of love. Eventually, my feelings and any identity with them had to be examined more closely. What was I clinging to around ideas or feelings? What ideas of peace was I holding in the body? Was I being too idealistic? These inquiries pulled me toward practicing Sōtō Zen Buddhism.

One day, while bowing to my practice in the zendo, I remembered an intensive with Anne in 1993 or 1994, where she stopped and asked me about my deep process. I told her I had a hard time finding any words for it; it was like being pulled into a Great Mystery, experiencing a sense of being less than a particle, yet incredibly vast, boundless. She mentioned something called "kundalini awakening," but she did not know more about it. She said it appeared I needed *a different kind of support; that I was going deep.* The word "kundalini" sounded interesting and yet foreign to me, connected to gurus and cultures of which I had no idea how to access. And, as a parent of very young children during those years, I was committed to staying with them.

By the time I reached out to the Zen center, my awareness of mind/body in recovery had been well-established for nearly twenty-five years. My sons had become teenagers. I could let go more.

I had also spent considerable time watching and listening to people. I heard dualistic thinking in the news, in conversations, in meetings, and in how people related to one another. I often saw people avoiding and isolating themselves. I saw a lot of denial on television, in community processes, and at workplaces. I encouraged my children to recover from dysfunctional teaching environments after coming home—to remember their own feelings again and again, and to understand with compassion that many people are under a huge amount of stress of all kinds. A friend told me, "They just have to go through it." It is so hard to let this truth in. Somehow or another, the boys jumped through all of their academic hoops to receive good grades, which amazed me considering all of the time they spent facing the computer screen and absorbing the effects of consumerism and unhealthy self-images. I worried that as their brains were developing, they were taking in too much information and wouldn't know how to process it.

In the midst of all the work on the house, I sensed what Anne was referring to, and her words haunted me. I needed help with my meditation practice. I knew I could only see for today what I am doing in the present, take a breath, and move onward. I worked on trusting the process; parenting with my own level of wisdom and awareness. I noticed that relationships are happening moment by moment, and there are many new negotiations all the time. The Ferris wheel of life appeared with more subtle sensitivity and variety in the breath energy, offering a light curiosity into experience.

As my desire for inner peace grew stronger each day, I wondered: Perhaps if I sat with others in a Zen setting, more clarity would come? Kundalini awakening is an awakening of the Divine energies in the body, so looking back, I see that it was just as Anne had suspected.

Open me to see,
    all of us participating
        in our own suffering.
We are afraid.
We are ashamed.
We hold onto ideas.
    As I turn my attention
    onto Thee,
        allow me to see our reflection.
        Help me find a willingness
            to sit in the cool, clear Stillness
        and see.
Not above.
Not below.
Not in front.
Not behind.
        Make me a vessel for Thee.
            Make me into a jar to carry Thee.
                Move me into the stream.
At home, always moving.
    All liquid flowing.
        Return my attention to Thee.
Insipid is the dying breeze.
Inspired is the weeping tree.
Luscious languid dancing souls,
    together and apart.
Not inside,
    nor outside.

~ Poem from my 2007 journal entry ~

Anne Wilson Schaef & me, 2018

CHAPTER SEVEN

The Noble Path

IN MY ESTIMATION, the Buddha was the best addiction counselor in history. The Four Noble Truths point to a process that begins with knowing one is experiencing stress, then investigating the causes of stress, which leads to release. The ways in which Buddhist texts addressed stress by paying attention to the body further accentuated and validated the somatic process work I'd been doing for decades. It unfurled the possibility of a new level of intimacy awaiting this mind and body. The basic tenets of Buddhism offered the promise of peace and happiness *right now* in *this very life.*

Once the kids were in bed and the basic housework was done, I started some more serious research into Buddhism. In the simplest terms, the Buddha taught about stress and release from stress. This comes from the Buddha's very first sermon on the Four Noble Truths that attend to life in a practical way.

1. The Truth that life includes stress (dukkha).[10]

The first of these Truths is self-evident. No one can go through life without experiencing pain, disappointment, sickness, grief, old age, disease, and death. Everything in life is inconstant, unstable, fraught with suffering, and without selfhood. The Buddha spoke of dukkha,

---

10 From the Pāli word, dukkha, which I use interchangeably as "stress" or "suffering" in this book.

which is commonly translated as suffering, but I prefer to use the term stress since it is more commonly used now. The term dukkha originates from the analogy of a wheel being out of kilter. When the axle hole of a wheel is not centered, it leads to a bumpy ride. Anyone who has sat for one hour in meditation knows stress.

This felt a lot like the First Step of the Twelve Step program, where we acknowledge our powerlessness and the unmanageability of a life spent constantly repeating the same mistakes and failures. My work in the program, attending meetings, dialoguing with sponsors, honoring my deep processes, all of it had helped me develop skills for approaching life with clarity and focus, but there was more to be done.

2. The origination of stress happens in the mind.

This was also validating. There are many difficulties in life, but not all of them necessarily make us suffer. It is the mind's tendency to cling to concepts, ideas, perceptions, and judgments that creates seemingly separate senses of self, "me," "mine," or "I" around them, leading to stress (dukkha).

Through my Fourth Step work, I had taken many moral inventories as the program prescribes, and explored some of these originations. As much as I had engaged in prayer and meditation through the steps, I still encountered sticky states of thought; old patterns that yearned for release. So, I did not see this Noble Truth as blaming, but instead as liberating. It meant the world around me, with all its challenges, did not have to become perfect in order for me to find peace.

3. There is cessation of stress, or an uprooting of the causes of stress.

This was the gold I had been looking for, a promise of attainable salvation in this life that was offered to all beings. It is like going to a well-trained doctor, who sees that you are suffering and has diagnosed your illness. Knowing that the illness is all of your clinging allows both of you to identify the cure that will truly end your suffering. True happiness and contentment are possible. The prescription is to follow the Noble Eightfold Path. Intention and attention must be combined in an all-encompassing path of practice for letting go of the weight of cravings and aversions. My sincere and true desire for this cessation is what carried me through the journey I describe in this book. It anchored me in faith to go deeper into the practice than ever before.

4. The path to the cessation of stress is the Noble Eightfold Path: Right Understanding, Right Thought, Right Speech, Right Action, Right Livelihood, Right Effort, Right Mindfulness, and Right Concentration.

The Buddha's Fourth Noble Truth consists of developing wisdom and balance with everything: understanding, thought, speech, all action, livelihood, effort, mindfulness, and concentration. Each aspect of the path begins with the word "right." This translation's use of the word "right" might create a subtle tension in the mind, triggering ideas that come from Christianity as though the teachings on "rightness" are commandments passed down by the Buddha. Instead, the concept of right and wrong is framed in relation to the Third Noble Truth. We can know for ourselves that certain actions lead to more stress and that these actions, in pursuit of the cessation of stress, are not right actions. Looking at what is most appropriate or skillful in the moment is what the Buddha was pointing to when he encouraged the Eightfold Path of practice.

There are different levels of relative truth around what is appropriate as awareness deepens; more nuanced clarity and agility become available for the current context. For example, someone might assume they are aversive in the midst of hearing too much information, but with practice, they can open the field of mind to letting data flow and discern what parts of the process are helpful or unhelpful in a given exchange.

The Buddha also traced three unwholesome roots for stress: greed, aversion, and delusion. Greed is clinging to a desire. Aversion is pulling back, avoiding, or running from something. Delusion is about being confused, having a dull affect, complacency, apathy, and not choosing to investigate. Each of these unwholesome roots has opposing wholesome roots: greed can be attenuated by generosity, aversion by loving kindness, and delusion by wisdom. All living beings carry thoughts and actions that come from past tendencies, supported by craving that comes from contact between the senses and the objects of the external world. By following the precepts and looking into the bare awareness within these unwholesome roots, one can find release from stress.

In Buddhist practice, grieving is often considered to be a process happening on the gross, or heavier level. It is recommended to notice sensations on the subtler level through intensive meditation or samādhi. That seemed difficult for me at first, given that I have an emotional center, yet I leaned toward this subtler form of investigation, and had been teasing out the thoughts within the feelings for some time. Some people have an intellectual center where thoughts dominate their responses to life, or a kinetic center where taking action comes up first before they feel or think. Having an emotional center means that I am deeply attuned to the world, feeling every footstep, bow, air across my face, drumming in my ears from rain on the roof, or the pulse in my eye from the glinting sun—all evoke a myriad of subtle bodily sensations.

Over the decades, it was my experience that many organizations prioritized intellectual discourse over compassionate communal support. While I am drawn to logic and reasoning, I feel that a lack of balance between our hearts and minds creates a rift, a divisive framework that promotes rigid independence at the expense of unity and emotional maturity. My experience in doing my deep work with others at the Living in Process retreats with Anne was that it opened my heart, allowing for compassion, understanding, and patience amid extremely difficult and trying times.

In monastic settings, feelings of grief are often seen as indulgent and counter to the practice. Many monks do not admit to taking time to open their hearts through occasional weeping (if it arises), or process trauma from their past, perhaps due to the, often, stoic military style of many monasteries and the emotionally dismissive forms that men and boys are enculturated into, even before entering monasteries.

But honoring my emotions is fundamental to my entire way of learning to live as a whole human being. Within me lies a deeply felt memory of generational trauma, fueling a cardinal aspiration to break free from the patterns of abuse, neglect, and shunning handed down by my biological family. In our patriarchal society, the female energetic system often remains overlooked, amplifying my feelings of alienation in the shadow of male dominance. These patterns are carried in my body and inherited in my genes, shaping the intricate web of my nervous system and cellular structures.

For me to move forward and practice intensively within a Buddhist hierarchical and patriarchal system, I had to directly confront my reservations. Attenuating the three unwholesome roots by cultivating their wholesome alternatives of generosity, loving kindness, and wisdom fostered clarity in trusting the process. Each day, an inner distress signal grew louder and louder, its resonance deepening into a profound willingness to walk this Noble Path through every breath, every bow, every step.

CHAPTER EIGHT

Posture

IN THE EARLY FALL of 2007, I sat many times a week in the zendo where there was always quite a bit of emphasis on posture and how we sat. It was in the atmosphere to remain still and firm. The teachers would sometimes reiterate, "Sit like a mountain."

Generally, it was expected for one to sit on a mat, but at this point, I hadn't found a comfortable way to do so that worked with my body. Fortunately, in each corner of the room, a chair facing the wall was available for those who needed it. Upon sitting down, I tried stabilizing my legs, but it was an orchestra chair that slanted downward in front. This put pressure on a bad knee I'd been dealing with for many years.

The posture provides feedback as to one's state or energy. I tried a variety of ways to sit in the zendo over several weeks, but sensations in my body shifted all over like an ant colony discovering a picnic basket. At home, I'd been sitting comfortably in an old armchair for up to an hour or more with a pillow for my lower back. Or, sometimes I used a lawn chair in the garage. I also hadn't been facing the corner wall like in the zendo, which brought up some sad memories from grade school. Usually, I looked out a window or towards the center of a room to have more open and spacious awareness.

It was hard to accept that the zendo required sitting in a different way than I was used to. The kneeling Burmese posture, with calves to the side, seemed comfortable enough, but then, it pulled painfully at my knee again. I often waited for the forty-five-minute meditation to end so I could find relief. I had to find a posture that fit for me, like a mountain, so I could learn to be as still as the other practitioners.

I thought that if I could just speak with someone about how they coped with this problem, that might help. But after meditation, people generally left as quickly and quietly as possible, vanishing into their cars and driving away before I had zipped up my jacket.

I signed up for a dokusan, or meeting, with one of the teachers to discuss posture and get acquainted. Since Norm had provided the introduction to meditation, I decided to visit with him. It was awkward for me at first, not knowing their customs for a dokusan, or rules for what to discuss in their meetings.

The first thing I asked Norm was more about himself. He leaned back, surprised, but then he accommodated my request, and we exchanged a few details about ourselves. I told him about my sons, Preston and Forrest, and how I had brought them to the center so they knew where I would be on many evenings, plus I wanted them to know about this resource for themselves as well. They were so sweet and open-minded about the center and wanted to learn about meditation too. Forrest even came and sat for a forty-five-minute sit in the zendo. Norm asked me a little more about my family, and then I brought up my main dilemma: How to hold the posture and sit still? He suggested I add another zafu and sit higher.

Later, I tried sitting higher, but one leg or the other fell asleep as I sat. When the bell rang, my foot was so soundly asleep that I had to be very careful getting up. As I stood up, I rotated one foot in circles, while pins and needles shot through my leg down into the foot coming back to life. Someone at the center actually tore a tendon in her ankle when standing too quickly on a foot that was asleep. In those early meditation sessions, my focus was often on watching my foot fall asleep and trying to cope with that, rather than anything else. This was a problem. If I couldn't get settled into a posture, then how was I going to be able to meditate properly?

A long time ago, I was hit from behind in a car crash, and ever since then, I've had to work with the pain that resulted from a permanent fracture in my vertebrae just between my shoulder blades. If I don't rest my back on the floor throughout the day, it will spasm.

Occasionally, lying on the floor with a rolled-up towel under my back helped ease the pain. Hot baths or a sauna at the YMCA would also relax it. As the weeks wore on at the Zen center, my back pain was increasing and lengthening all along the spine.

It was unusual for anyone to move more than an inch in the zendo once the bell had signaled the beginning of meditation and everyone had settled into a posture. One evening, I adjusted the cushion underneath myself and glanced around the room. I saw the teachers sitting and facing the center of the room and the remaining dozen or so men sitting straight upright and facing the wall, all perfectly still. I wanted to leave, and as I turned to stand up, the head priest, Steve Hagen, opened his eyes wide and leaned toward me with one eyebrow raised to reprimand me for moving. I felt my stomach twist with a sense of shame. I stared back at him for a moment, acquiesced with an exhale, and turned back to the wall for the next excruciating twenty-five minutes, waiting for the bell to ring.

The stress during meditation—the squirming, the pain, the itchiness—couldn't have provided a clearer understanding of the first of the Buddha's Four Noble Truths: Life includes stress; we must meet it.

~~~

From 2003 to 2006, I visited the same bench in the Lyndale Park Rose Garden every day for at least half an hour while my sons were in school. I'd walk the mile-and-a-half distance, or drive there on busier days through the changing seasons. I felt steeped with delight to just breathe in the open air and feel my feet touch our earth as everything emptied out. There was a felt call to rest in this place of pilgrimage, a feeling of safety and shelter and connection with nature amidst the construction on the house.

I loved to sit without time constraining me and watch the sunlight change on the lake and in the sky. Sometimes, in the pouring rain, I leaned into the trunk of an old horse chestnut tree for shelter. I grieved through difficult states, reviewed how little I could control, meditated with the falling leaves, watched the ice forming on the lake, the melting snow, the spring mulch removal, the first buds of the roses, and the blooming flowers with bees all around as the gardeners waved them off. Then the cycle would repeat. Why could I not find that inner calm at the Zen center? I wondered if perhaps it was not the place for me to practice as I sat on my old bench near the crab apple trees and loafed around the lakefront. *Isn't our whole life a practice?*

~~~

After that suffocating meditation experience, I knew I had to find a way to sit in the zendo. I looked around the center after a session and introduced myself to a man cleaning the toilets. I'd seen him sit there before, so I asked him if he'd take a few minutes to talk with me about posture. He agreed, and we went to the basement classroom.

His attention felt personable and kind. I asked him to show me how he sits and to describe how he finds stability. We ended up having an interesting discussion about posture as we tried different ideas. He suggested I use an additional small cushion in the mid-thigh to lift the knee and produce more circulation in the legs. He also suggested alternating between the modified lotus and the kneeling Burmese posture after walking meditation because of my knee pain.

After picking up a used zabuton and zafu, I continued to sit at home twice daily and experiment with different postures. The only finished room I had was my closet. I began to notice a subtle need to have my left leg closer to my body. I sat several times just noticing my relationship with that particular tension in my leg. It felt familiar, possibly going all the way back to when I was in utero. And, I was trying to protect that knee since it had some moderate pain radiating from it. I felt gently curious about the tension and clinging. I had never noticed it in such detail before!

Things began to feel more stable. I noticed how my posture or mudra informed me of various mind states. Leaning forward indicated grasping in the mind. Leaning back indicated avoidance and pulling away from something in the mind. The body moved with these mind moments in subtle ways. As energy waned, my head drooped and I'd gently tilt my chin up. Sometimes my head would slowly twist to the left and I'd intentionally bring it back to center.

Centering my pelvic bones with just the right curve in my back reduced some of my back pain. Holding my hands closer to my belly lowered my shoulders, allowing my chest to lift. When I sat cross-legged, with my legs touching the floor, I decided to switch the legs around by putting the left leg in front of the right leg. I didn't want to do it at first, but it provided more stability to the upright posture. I had become lopsided after my injuries and needed to reset my whole body. I practiced this way for several sits at home, using a few thin cushions under a thigh to alleviate the numbness in my feet. Finally, I found a posture that worked for the time being. I sat, learning to be a mountain with all of its changing seasons.

CHAPTER NINE

The Five Powers

A S I CONTINUED MY EXPLORATION of Buddhist teachings, I encountered the five spiritual faculties: Mindfulness, Energy, Concentration, Faith, and Wisdom. By nurturing and cultivating these inner qualities, they become stronger in our awareness and grow into powers. The Buddha taught that when balanced accordingly, these powers are conducive to enlightenment.

I embraced the practice of being mindful of these faculties on a daily basis by envisioning them as parts of a car. Mindfulness takes the role of the driver, while energy and concentration serve as the front wheels, and faith and wisdom as the back wheels. When I felt like I had gotten stuck in a ditch, faith and wisdom gave me the power to dig myself out. Energy and concentration kept me pointing into the present moment. By remaining mindful of these four wheels, I started rolling along as a vehicle for awakening.

To engage with these five powers, I'd consider a broad or macro perspective, looking at the context of the current situation, akin to observing a landscape, while combining or toggling with a microscopic view, such as bodily sensations. Additionally, a crucial aspect of nurturing these powers involves recognizing difficult states and being attuned to methods for soothing the nervous system.

Excited about this discovery, I'd regularly check in with myself throughout the day to assess how centered I felt with each of these five strengths. It brings me immense joy to share a few reflections, as these powers are truly golden and continue to be a source of ongoing learning.

Mindfulness is directing thought and evaluation to whatever is happening in the present moment. From a close-up perspective, it is feeling the qualities of the breath as it is happening and noticing the changing sensations within the body through the six sense doors: hearing, seeing, smelling, tasting, touching, and thinking. By applying thought and evaluation to what is happening right here, right now, with bodily awareness, I can assess and make adjustments to whether the sensation is pleasant, unpleasant, or neutral. Can I notice it changing as it is happening, its location, and movement?

Taking a broad perspective can mean noticing the overall pan-oramic qualities that make up an unfolding experience. This can be knowing the need to make a meal based on sensations of hunger, or prioritizing what is most important in the current context for myself and our family as a whole. Much of my careful planning and organizing around the house is my way of practicing mindfulness on this broader scale to address essential daily needs.

Energy relates to my mental capacity, joyful attitude, and commit-ment to practice at any given time. I find myself moving along a spectrum of energy, ranging from heightened alertness to the embrace of sleep.

During meditation, an inability to synchronize repeatedly with the object of attention often signals a state of lethargy or low energy. At times I might feel tired or bored, emphasizing how important it is to invite curiosity into these moments of apparent monotony. An intro-spection is needed: What intricate sensations make up the state of boredom?

There are different ways energy is affected by the in-breath or the out-breath. The in-breath raises energy, while the out-breath relaxes energy. Yawning can sometimes actually open up the mind and raise energy. Hmm, I'd inquire: Is yawning uplifting or draining in this moment?

Exploring my internal circadian rhythms improves my function and well-being. Energy levels ebb and flow during the day, with mornings offering increased mental clarity. Although I don't lean towards coffee, I enjoy morning tea but can also skip it. In the evening, I wind down an hour before bedtime, preparing for a restful sleep by dimming the lights, turning off my phone, and setting things aside for the next day.

When tiredness weighs me down, rather than succumbing to guilt or battling weariness, I find it realistic to head directly to bed, set a cooking timer for fifteen or thirty minutes and take a nap. These short siestas rarely hinder my return to focused practice.

On intensive concentrated retreats, taking a nap does not usually end up with dropping into a state of oblivion. Instead, I often remain aware of thoughts, feelings, and perceptions and just lightly rest, which is still helpful.

Too much energy can be unsettling, suggesting the need for an extended walk or mindful movement to allow the stirring energy to dissipate and/or harmonize. Walking after eating also aids digestion. The energy-intensive process of digesting food can hinder concentration. As a result, it is common practice, especially during retreats, to opt for a light snack, a fruit beverage, or even abstain from eating in the evening to improve concentration and focus.

When mindfulness is applied, wisdom assesses whatever is occurring for the sake of energy and concentration. Hydration, proper nutrition, rest, and exercise all need consideration.

Concentration, the eighth step on the Noble Eightfold Path, involves focusing and sustaining attention rather than being driven by conceptual thoughts and outer decision-making. It revolves around keeping the breath in mind and staying attuned to the sensations of breath energy, while also noticing any lapses in attention, and making adjustments as needed.

As a helpful reminder before meditation sessions, I often recall the sensation of cutting a board on my table saw, where maintaining focus from start to finish is crucial. Similarly, I need to be fully present, observing and feeling the breath throughout its entire cycle. It is essential to maintain a gentle guardianship of the mind, remaining present with the experiences of touching, seeing, hearing, smelling, tasting, and thinking as they unfold in real time.

The level of concentration achieved varies depending on the duration of the meditation session. Longer sits, lasting around forty-five to fifty minutes, tend to cultivate stronger concentration by the end. Shorter meditation sessions bring some calmness to the system but often lack the concentration needed for insight.

When distractions arise, I immediately embrace them as objects of attention within the body. For instance, if I feel annoyance towards a barking dog, I swiftly take the vibrating sound itself as the object of concentration, honing in on the sensations it produces in the inner ear and throughout my body. Attentively delving into these sensations transforms the sound of barking into a phenomenon of interest. By mindfully exploring the body's feelings and recognizing sensations as pleasant, unpleasant, or neutral, nonattachment towards the phenomenon naturally occurs. This practice requires perseverance, staying with the object of concentration and stilling the mind, to cultivate inner tranquility and heightened focus, ultimately leading to highly refined states of being.

Faith, in the context of the five powers, is a verb, something I do to examine my relationship with doubt. The simple act of sitting down to meditate is an act of faith, because it requires trusting that I will be rewarded with the natural gladness that comes from that wholesome activity. When my faith is strong, I find myself deeply engaged in the present moment and fully invested in the task at hand. There is a sense of wonder, appreciation, and tranquility that encompasses the moment. This process can involve a broad assessment of the overall state or a focused examination of the sensations of doubt in the body and the sensations of compassion in the heart for the truth.

Doubt comes and goes, often influenced by factors like low energy or taking on too much responsibility. To navigate this, it is crucial for me to be mindful of when faith is high or low, and to trust the process. If my faith is low, then I am not ready for a retreat. Having too much skeptical doubt about the practice can impede progress. Faith needs to be strong to maintain mindful awareness in the ruthless silence of continuous practice.

Feelings of worry, engaging in the illusion of control, and thinking I am the sole controller of my life are all signs of diminishing faith. During these moments, I can restore faith by returning to my reliable methods—coming back to the breath and staying with it.

When I remember with a sense of acceptance that everything arises due to countless causes and conditions at any moment, the burdening thoughts of "me, mine, or I" feel lighter. Whether it be discursive thoughts or slacking off of mindfulness, I try to feel into the body, and rekindle my sense of devotion to the truth.

To return to where I am now is to practice faith because it means letting go of the past and the future. Remarkably, Faith does for me what I cannot do for myself.

Wisdom is the capacity within to discern between wholesome and unwholesome actions. This can take a variety of forms, such as pursuing the need to talk with a friend or ask for help. Sometimes, wisdom lies in closing the window to minimize the distraction of a barking dog or adjusting my posture to avoid aggravating my hurting knee. Honoring the call for action with a wholesome discernment of choices is an experimental learning process.

Honesty and wisdom are also closely intertwined. Taking a breath, I truly ask myself, "Am I fully present in this moment?" These honest reflections feel freeing. Without taking the time to reflect on my actions, the mind can run willy-nilly. Even if I am able to roll along with concentration, energy, and faith, doubts sometimes arise, making me feel humbled by the whole meditative learning process.

Funny as it might seem, feeling into the sensations of doubt is helpful and serves my practice. *I can notice whatever is happening in any moment*, even if I am slipping into a ditch. I can gently look with kindness into the bodily sensations. This involves a willingness to stop, pause, and listen, rather than blocking out what is happening, judging it, or holding onto ideas. Wisdom smooths out the edges of my aura, calming my nervous system. Faith fosters patience and gentleness, nourishing creative growth. As I recognize the impermanence of experiences and honestly acknowledge them happening in the present, wisdom flourishes.

My approach to strengthening these powers was pragmatic, incorporating them as valuable tools into my meditation practice on and off the cushion. Often, I found that my hardest-to-recall strength was also my weakest one at that moment. There are no distinct boundaries between them; they overlap and slosh into one another. The act of reviewing this list empowered me. Even though the profound wisdom that I was seeking was beyond words, I couldn't help but notice that these powers had curious capacities all on their own.

CHAPTER TEN

Simplicity & Efficiency

T HE NEXT TIME I was at Dharma Field, I saw on the bulletin board that they offered practice groups. Cool! Perhaps I could ask some practice questions, like the challenges with my posture that had come up. Knowing that one week had already passed, I asked the assistant there if joining late was all right. She encouraged me to ask. With that in mind, I asked Steve if he could make an exception and admit me. He immediately replied, "No," and walked on. My heart sank. I wanted to get to know others there as well as practice.

The following Sunday, I spoke with someone at the center who said he used the peer group as a way to force himself to keep a strict meditation schedule. That is when I realized, I didn't need that kind of pressure. I was already practicing several hours a day in intervals using gentle awareness, toggling between different levels of attention while standing, sitting, waiting in line at the store, waiting for my kids to come out to the car, standing at the table saw before cutting wood, etc. I learned that I couldn't approach every activity in the same way; different tasks required different forms of attention. Formal meditative practice is very different from driving a car or operating machinery. I needed to be present, but also practical.

More and more, I was allowing things to be as they were. I attended sessions at the center when I knew I could really be there without any internal conflicts. At home, I rarely knew exactly when someone would show up. The building inspector, plumber, and electrician were totally unpredictable as to when their trucks would appear. Finding my own "improvised life schedule" allowed me to keep things simple at home, and meditate more often and for longer periods of time than what was asked by the teacher for the practice groups. In Zen, they emphasize practice a lot. Also, the lack of travel time to and from the center allowed me to practice breath awareness in little moments while cooking supper, folding laundry, helping the children with school work, sitting on the toilet, or raking leaves.

The atmosphere in Zen seemed so tough that I doubted my own ability at times. The zendo itself started to feel like a pressure cooker, but how could I find the Truth without being with everyone, doing the same things they did? Even though I was not in the practice group, I attended the Buddhist classes that met once a week in the evening where there were usually more questions from students than the teacher would allow. The meditation I was doing around this time was just *being and knowing*. Receiving the breath, expelling the breath. I made a decision to *be*, wherever I was. No matter what was happening, there arose an interpenetrating desire to *be present*.

As a mother, I often felt I had to be making supper or doing laundry or helping the children right away, but first I decided to focus inwardly on my intention to be present in whatever task I was engaged in, and to include the children in more household chores. With that focus of intention, I became more deliberate about my choices. There weren't ideas of anything in particular, just *noticing and being here and now.*

Thinking carefully about my job as a parent and surveying all of my duties and activities in my life in general, I realized that joining the practice group would have put an additional strain on my availability at home. Not being in the group allowed for more flexibility in my life and more of a private inner sanctum in terms of finding my own practice.

No one in my life was taking time for formal meditation as regularly as I was, except for the people at the center. And, I did not know any of them personally. As I bowed over the threshold, the sight of five or six others sitting in silence evoked a magnificent sense of connection. This connection felt truly magickal, not in the sense of stage illusions, but in the wondrous synchronicity of life unfolding.

While my energy and faith ebbed and flowed somewhat, there was a general upward trend toward meditating more often and reading less. Sometimes a short passage I happened across in my little daily Twelve Step recovery book had an effect on me—like it was the perfect thing for the moment. More often, and sometimes surprisingly, meditating turned into a delightful experience.

To create more space for this process to unfold, I decided to dial down on my news and media consumption. I stopped watching television, reading newspapers, tuning into the car radio, and listening to music on CDs. Most media news was terrible, and often did not focus on solutions. I even canceled my home repair magazine subscriptions after learning they were available at the library. I'd glance through my local neighborhood paper when I could, finding that if there was something I needed to know, someone would tell me soon enough, or the children would bring it up.

I listened to my sons talk about their social anxieties at school and shared some of the benefits I had been receiving with breath awareness. Out of curiosity, my boys came to the Dharma talks on most Sundays. I laughed when Forrest got in the car wearing the shirt he'd slept in. It was a white t-shirt from the Red Cross with GOT BLOOD? blazoned in huge red letters across his chest. That seemed like a great shirt to me. We all have blood. What are we doing here in this human life with this aliveness in each one of us?

I never wanted to indoctrinate the boys into any religion. I exposed them to a variety of places as I explored, and their curiosity grew. I felt they had been baptized in my womb, and we were already in the church of life. Basic human decency informed me that more unites us than divides us. Still, I wanted them to choose what resonated with them. They relaxed knowing that in Buddhism, you are invited to look and see for yourself—to work with your own mind. They knew how dogma binds us to more dualistic thinking. They often asked questions and stayed afterward with me for tea to get a feel for the center. It was natural for them to try out meditation from time to time.

And, I felt compelled to simplify my schedule, do less, and look closer at how I approached problems. I also stopped going to my book club. I simply could not force myself to read anything I wasn't interested in reading, and my interests gravitated toward stories of those who had been through the metamorphosis of awakening. Honoring my true interests felt weirdly refreshing.

The Matrix, which we all saw as a family, was very interesting, with Neo waking up after being deluded his entire life. I wondered the same thing. *Are we all asleep, in a sense? Unaware of a higher plane inherent to our terrestrial system?*

My body trembled around drama; I was not interested in creating crises, but focusing on preventative measures toward peaceful living. I organized the worksite within our house and set up a reasonable work schedule, rising early every morning to examine my current project. I prioritized my errands to only one a day and extended goals for projects even further.

One day at a time, I skimmed down and reduced tasks. I simply could not run five errands in a day anymore. I'd take a week or more to do those five errands, even if it used extra gas to go back to that area. Each errand to pick up supplies and groceries or get something fixed, like a stop at the shoe repair or the computer store, was very intentional.

I encouraged the children to narrow down their outside activities. Forrest wanted to keep up with tennis. Preston wanted to continue choir practice and his community service work. The children responded well to a simplified schedule. We had more time in the evenings to talk and prepare for the next day's demands. We met once a week to review who was responsible for what and when it would be completed. I typed it up and sent an email to each one of us, so we each had a list to refer to. This prevented many potentially confusing conversations throughout the week due to forgetfulness, and provided accountability.

We focused on a more plant-based diet, eating more beans, rice, and vegetables. The adzuki bean is gentle to the body, and we continue to enjoy it. We came up with a delicious vegetarian tostada recipe with adzuki beans and brown rice that the kids ate up in huge servings.[11] I went through our cupboards and threw out anything old or unhealthy. Stewart never drank alcohol, and I only drank a little bit on special

---

11   The recipe can be found at constancecasey.com/recipe

occasions. I changed us over to eating more brown rice and tofu dishes with plenty of green vegetables. We had always preferred to drink a lot of water every day, and Forrest became an expert at making healthy smoothies.

Whatever I could do to find ways to increase gentle respect and enjoyment of our home life, I laid as a foundation for my practice. I had been paying such close attention to each and every small change that, as I look back now, these changes made a significant difference in my lifestyle. It took a while for me to even realize what I was doing, but when I did, I felt quite pleased about it all!

There was only so much time in the day. My practice included more seclusion than I was used to. Worried I'd spend even less time with my friends, I went to the center to speak with Norm. I asked him what I could say, and he suggested I simply tell them, "I don't have the time right now." Sounded easy, but I felt a little conflicted about reducing my social life and expressing my need for more solitude.

I wanted to be with my friends, but I had to be more selective with my use of time in order to create space for my mind/body training in silence. I often felt like a turtle on the side of the road, watching the traffic, as I pulled into my shell and observed the multitude of wild aspects of life swirling around me. Discussions with friends sometimes created a stressful charge because most of my friends were feeling various levels of anxiety when we met. Conversations would often devolve into worries about troubling details that had a digressive, push-pull quality to them.

In a relationship, someone needs to initiate contact to keep it going. I often found myself as the one initiating visits with others who had little time or interest in planning time together. I cared about my friends and received many kindnesses from them, but building and nurturing relationships requires effort on both sides, and without sharing experiences together, they tend to fade. When it came to my family of origin, I frequently took the lead in reaching out and didn't feel a mutual interest. What few familial connections there were in my life, I chose to let them be, respect our differences, and stay with my practice.

Occasionally, I wished for a friend to share a pot of tea with, just *be*, relating on a soft, honest, and intimate level about what was going on, even if it was troubling. I often thought about wearing a t-shirt that said: "We are each experiencing many various challenges in Life. Let's just listen." Or, I often felt like offering a preamble to a conversation in order to facilitate more of a connection: "What I'm about to share isn't a problem, per se; it's just something happening in the field of 'my' life, and there is no need to fix or worry—let's just connect. Some ideas might emerge and that's all good too." People in active recovery appeared more open in this way and easier to hang out with.

Doubts arose when I wondered: How could my practice be generous when I needed so much time by myself? I had associated generosity with my community involvement, but this inner work could only be done alone. It seemed like the Universe was showing me a path, and I just needed to walk it. It was unclear what the path had in store for me. Life includes stress and uncertainty, that's real. By withdrawing from many interactions and living more simply, I was intentionally offering myself to my highest priorities while moving straight into the Heart of all Hearts.

Dear Mother Earth
Please allow only those who are sincere
To spend time with me and me with them.
Allow me to help and support those around me in a true way.
Allow me to serve You in Your way.

~ 2007 Journal Entry ~

CHAPTER ELEVEN

Surrender

Without drywall on our interior walls, pounding sounds echoed throughout the house like an empty cavern. Nevertheless, I was determined to get things done so we could move out of the garage. After talking with another neighbor, I understood that all of the wiring and plumbing had to go through the kitchen walls, so it'd be best to start upstairs and work our way from the top down. It would be difficult to leave the kitchen for last, but it was time to accept that the project would take many years longer than I had anticipated.[12]

One time, I felt so irritated with Stewart about having to re-explain the priorities of the building project that I stated a need for a time-out, hopped on my old bike, rode to the Zen center, and meditated for a couple of hours. Being the CEO of the family, the primary contractor and carpenter for the house project, and the often-lone parent felt overwhelming!

While sitting at the Zen center, I paid direct attention to the sizzling anger. Then, I noticed a shaking, trembling fear lurking beneath it. As I breathed in and out, calming the nervous system, I saw two selves, one who was afraid and one who was angry. The fearful self was worried about the angry self. The angry self appeared to be feeding the fearful

---

12 After eleven years of hard work, we completed the kitchen in 2014. The rest of the house renovation is still underway. Patience.

self. They supported each other. Then, I saw the angry self as just a figment of my imagination—an idea I had taken on. I realized that this angry image came from my upbringing. I had been afraid of this idea of an angry monster inside of me. *We all try to sidestep and blame. Is anger always bad?* It didn't feel so bad anymore.

So many thoughts. Then, just pure fiery anger toggled with freezing cold fear. The more I sat with it, feeling its changing heat and coolness, the more it appeared humorous to me, and something shifted in my perception. Attachments became ever so apparent. Suddenly, I felt delight. I wanted to shout it out loud in the zendo, and stomp around the room, "I am an angry monster. I am an angry monster. Roar! Yeah! I am so bad!" I found it hilarious to finally see it without judgment. I could have leapt into the air. I was seeing these ideas with a sense of spaciousness. And, with a deep sigh, I also understood that Stewart had his own work to do with his anger, that we both needed to continue learning how to discuss conflicts between us, especially since anger was so much about needs and expectations.

When I got home, I called my sponsor, Guy, to share my progress with him and convey my happiness.

He said, "Has the anger been removed?"

"For now." I paused to consider his question. "Maybe it will come back."

He said, "Well then, you haven't done enough."

That irked me. I wanted to feel heard. *Isn't seeing things pass away important?* My effort in meditation had an influence. Anger is not a thing but is made up of some interesting sensations, and contains wisdom about my needs. Still, I was glad to share; to at least have someone to talk with.

He said, "If it hasn't been removed, then God wants you to do something else."

I asked, "What would you suggest?"

He invited me to read about Step Seven from the Twelve Step materials: "Humbly asked God to remove our shortcomings."

Grateful to have some support, I tuned into the wisdom of the Seventh Step prayer, murmuring it over and over again before falling asleep with the *Big Book of AA* on my chest.

I am now willing that you should have all of me,
good and bad.
I pray that you now remove from me
every single defect of character that stands in the way
of my usefulness to you and my fellows.
Grant me strength, as I go out from here,
to do your bidding.
Amen.[13]

~~~

That fall, I took the boys to a Halloween play about life and death that was set outdoors in a nearby cemetery. The acting was remarkably creative, with figures mysteriously emerging behind and around us. As we walked alongside the narrator and the characters, passing tombstones and trees that cast haunting shadows among the dead, the play sparked deep contemplation within me.

It pressed my heart with deep inquiries, challenging my notions of God. I couldn't perceive God as a person, nor could I ever believe any single religious or spiritual group was the only path to the divine. This experience left me pondering: *What is God? What does it mean to be human?*

The next day, I felt refreshed in knowing that something had opened up. I felt lighter, but I also had a curious, tickling doubt sitting beside me. All of these feelings were like dissipating vapors passing through the porous edges of the body. How could my mind and body hold all of this when I was oozing like a honeycomb?

The following week, when I needed to screw down the plywood floorboards for the upstairs flooring, our cordless drill was missing from its charging station, and I searched for it all around the house. When Stewart came home from work, I asked him, "Do you know where the drill is?"

-----

13 Alcoholics Anonymous World Services, Inc. *Alcoholics Anonymous: The Story of How Many Thousands of Men and Women Have Recovered from Alcoholism, 3rd edition.*

"I put it back."

"Back where?"

He stood there in a familiar stance of idle anticipation, quietly awaiting my next move.

"Ugh." I groaned.

Several days later, I eventually found the drill in the joist area overhead where he had been securing an electrical wire during the weekend. I wanted to walk up to him and declare, "I need to be able to find the tools when I need them!" But instead, I went to the daybed and dropped into a bone-deep nap. When I awoke, I heard a deep inner voice clearly say, *It is easy to forget about your chi.*

How true, I thought. Those words stayed with me the rest of the week. How easy it is to get out of balance and forget about how hard we were each working. I felt compassion for Stewart and appreciation for how much energy he put into the project as well.

For many years, much of the wind that blasted through my sails after we were first married had stopped, leaving my sails luffing. I was in the doldrums and needed to wait with the process. Tacking back and forth with his often opposing views pushed me further out to sea. I no longer desired to resist the drifting current storming through my being. I could no longer blame him for anything. Now, I could only turn to a Higher Power to direct my energies.

Since I had signed up for the retreat with Adyashanti, I listened to a couple of his sample talks from his website. He said to allow everything to be as it is, to let go of control, and ask, "What am I? Who am I? Who is meditating?"

Duh. Constance—that's who! What is he talking about!?

Adyashanti said in one of his talks, "Go beyond the meditator; the meditator likes to have something to control." He said that fear is a good indicator, a doorway, and that it means something is beginning to go right. Wow! My sponsor seemed to think something was not being done—that I was not doing enough. That seemed dualistic, until I saw that they both had some wisdom. There is attention to the practice, and there is something that happens on its own within the practice.

Still, it was hard to find clear guidance. I was continually waking up at night with little vague slivers of insight slipping away, and affirmations like "Yeah, yeah, yeah," in the torso with my attention being driven deeper. "Come on now, let me be," I asked from deep within. "Take it all away and let me be. Breathe and be. I just want to know the truth."

Three words kept arising as I sanded windows and finished them with polyurethane:

TRUTH ~ BEAUTY ~ EXPRESSION

What is Truth? Beauty? What is being expressed? I wondered and wondered. These questions smoothed out something inside of me until they faded away.

I kept thinking about the law of diminishing returns as if I were caught in the grip of a pattern of diminishment with less and less "me." My interest in social interactions outside of our family was fading a bit. I was more interested in this internal energy behind everything I saw, felt, and thought, and that took time.

Just. Be. Still.

Different feelings overlapped and sloshed together all the time. Anger told me to stop and consider. Sometimes, behind anger was fear, intersecting with fear—a desire. Other times, behind anger, was a power in knowing the needs of the situation, like a sharp blade cutting through confusion. Boundaries are important both socially and emotionally, but *what else*? Can we go to the root source of it all?

Feelings arose in more subtle ways. The shifting, shaking, pulsating, blinking, labyrinth of sensations was impossible to solidify. My attitude toward an emotion affected how I experienced it. For this stage of my practice, the method of subtraction arose again and again—*no, that was not me*. It felt like venturing into new territory, and with sincerity, I just slipped into it. After all my years of learning to take responsibility for my feelings, I was continually reminded—they are passing phenomena. This too shall pass, feelings change, but to *know change directly* in the sensory moment felt especially liberating.

~~~

It was common among my friends and the culture to provide more leeway to the primary wage earner in the family. Giving the spouse room to decompress after working in what were generally quite exhausting environments with unclear demands, sixty-hour work weeks, and alienating structures was seen as a norm but also a kindness, allowing for the recovery of energy with Spirit. Stewart's working conditions were similarly taxing, and he frequently disappeared for a while after work, so I felt the need to give him some space and time to recuperate. I held onto the hope that, in time, he would recover and meet me where I was, and that we could unite as a couple. I proposed different work arrangements so we could spend more time together. I thought, perhaps we each work part-time, or I take on work when he's not on a job, or we work together in my web business? However, he did not want to consider other options and strongly preferred to stay focused on his own career and the structure it provided for himself and for us. When he could not find work after 9/11, I supported our family with a full-time job. We were both doing the best we could, and we alternated our working lives in the midst of difficult times.

I called an old friend, Carolyn, about some of these challenges, and she said, "Some people do not know how much progress it is to *do less* when one is married to someone like your husband. I know, I'm married to one like him too!" That felt true and helpful. I was prone to overreaching in my relationship with him, trying to find better forms of communication, and I had to let go in the midst of that. Her husband had the same tendency towards individualism as opposed to the communal partnership I had envisioned, so I understood what she meant. Stewart often came and went without any effort to communicate with me. There were other men around me developing more flexibility and openness to their feelings in recovery, trying out different lifestyles and partnerships. The streams come together in mysterious ways, perhaps Stewart and my sons could *know this* too.

When I make a commitment, I do it from a really deep place. I remained loyal in the face of our difficult relationship. I loved him and cared that he was the father of our children, and I did not want to separate. The lack of any family support also influenced my self-reliance. I'd seen others leave and then go right into the same type of marriage. I wanted to learn everything I could to see what my part was and what I could do to transform myself and my relationship with him for the better.

After my call with Carolyn, I continued to wonder: Aren't my marriage problems primarily due to the turmoil of rebuilding the entire house?! How much of my stress is related to my existential crisis? These questions and the particulars of my life played havoc on my mind from time to time. One sponsor said to do less, while another would say I wasn't doing enough. I felt it was best to let it go and just do the next thing in front of me.

If it hadn't been for Ruby, the little Lhasa Apso dog we adopted in the midst of our construction, I don't know how we would have all made it through. Our dear, sweet Ruby had a natural aptitude for letting go and being here now. Ruby's playful and insistent attitude of "Let's relax and play" was the chord we all touched when we saw her. Since I had never owned a dog before, Preston, Forrest, Stewart, and I decided to attend dog obedience classes on Monday evenings. However, it seemed that Stewart had a knack for falling asleep during the classes much of the time. As I was her main caregiver, Ruby and I developed a routine where she'd go and curl up safely in her crate when I started hammering or using saws and drills.

Sawing and hammering every weekend exhausted both Stewart and myself. We needed time to rest, recuperate, and enjoy the kids. A close review of our finances prevented me from hiring additional help or getting supplies. So, I informed Stewart and the kids that we'd have to delay most of our construction and spread it out over several more years.

With this decision, a little creative time opened up for me to sit in a quiet corner and refocus on my artwork. My favorite artistic practice is crafting beadwork sculptures and beaded appliqué pictures with tiny seed beads. In 1983, I learned to line stitch from a member of the Red Lake Nation who owns a craft store at the Minneapolis American Indian Center. Through him, I learned more than just beadwork.

I became interested in the history of the native peoples before and after the land was colonized.[14]

Beadwork is a patient art form. The process of passing the thread through every bead felt reassuring and peaceful. It took me at least a year to design each piece because every element has a sacred meaning. The piece I was working on at the time was aptly named *Surrender*. Each bead felt like a hole in my being that the mysterious thread of energetic light moved through. I breathed through each stitch and lost track of time while beading in silence.

~~~

Being with my children always presented me with something new. Forrest rode his bike to tennis practice after school at a public center. On weekends, I'd watch him play in local tournaments. Competition has often been difficult for me to watch, like a dualistic theater. The losing team limps home, shoulders and heads slumped, while the winning team exchanges high fives and smiles.

One day, Forrest lost to another kid, 3-6, 3-6. I expected him to be upset afterward as I handed him a fresh towel to wipe off, but he exclaimed, "I played better than ever, Mom!" Then he went on to win the next match in the consolation round, 7-6, 7-4, and 6-2. I asked him how that win felt. He watched the other kid put his racket away and said, "I don't know. I like the process of playing more than anything. It's over now; I'm hungry."

What is it that wins? What is it that loses? We can win when we lose. We can lose when we win. Maybe we never win or lose. With the right perspective, we learn to play a little better, no matter what. Watching him play, it occurred to me that our minds are at the mercy of fast-moving, uncontrolled thoughts and feelings.

---

14 Minnesota is the homeland of the Dakota and Anishinaabe people who have stewarded this land throughout the generations. The efforts by these First Nations to protect and recover their land and water rights are an ongoing issue in Minnesota.
Gwen Westerman and Bruce M. White *Mni Sota Makoce: The Land of the Dakota*.

Over supper, he explained that it isn't always easy to accept the loss and move on. He shared that despite having fun, his initial fear led to making more mistakes, and it took a while to build up confidence. I had noticed his stiffness and heaviness toward meeting the ball in his first sets. In the next match, his flexibility and reach became sweeter. We both reflected on how, in tennis, we are at the mercy of the mind states, and how they subsequently affect performance. I learn so much from my kids.

~~~

Once a month, I'd meet with a small group of financially independent, professional, and assertive women where we shared our desires and experiences with our careers and life issues. The next time I was with this group, as my right toe pushed the heel of my left shoe off and onto the entry rug, I prayed silently, *Universe, do with me what you will; take all of me. Cast your net for me to follow. Not my will, but Thy will be done.*

That day, I quietly listened in a more open way. When someone mentioned they didn't feel as connected with me, it surprised me. In fact, I sensed an even stronger connection with them. An electric current seemed to encircle my body, filling me with openness. However, I struggled to articulate these transformative energetic phenomena.

I was the last person to check in. When it was my turn to speak, I didn't know what to say. A career focus or life struggle? My story held little interest for me. Listening to them felt so peaceful and accepting. I asked if there was anything they wanted to know. They said it was strange of me to focus on them, but I didn't feel much of a "me" there. It was as if "I" was not there at all.

They asked what was going on. I noticed my attention kept slipping right behind and to my left, over my shoulder, to some mysterious Presence. I felt *more* present than I remembered being around people in a long time. It was hard to find words to describe this moment, and if I tried, would they even understand? Since I had recently read Eckhart Tolle's book, *The Power of Now*, I asked if any of them had read it to see if we could find common ground. My primary friend in the group shrugged and said, "I read it, but I really don't get what it is about." The rest of them shook their heads.

I suddenly realized from a pulsing in my gut that we were at different levels of truth. I wanted to sit in stillness more and more. I had to say goodbye, and it wasn't easy because I also valued them in my life. I awkwardly shared, "I think I need to end here." They appeared shocked. "Don't you need support for parenting, your marriage, and the stress of the house?" At that time, I had a deep trust that the kids, my husband, and our home were being taken care of in a larger way. Those topics held less sway.

"Yes, sure, I suppose that's true," I said. "I don't know what I am doing, I really don't. I'm taking everything one day at a time and going slowly—more like one breath at a time. I guess I need more time to sit and just be. I really wish you all well. I can't even believe I'm saying this, but there's this pull I feel to not figure things out." It's not like I was ending my relationship with them individually, only my involvement with the group, which to them might have been one and the same. I know I left them in bewilderment. I felt bewildered too.

When I got home, Ruby dropped the ball on my foot and looked up at me as if she were saying, "Just relax and enjoy us. Toss me the ball, will ya?" and a whiffle ball playtime ensued. Oh, how attention moves and shifts. *What was happening to me?*

Sweet Ruby and me, 2007

CHAPTER TWELVE

What Is It?

S TARTING MY DAY by picking up my tools and handling my drill filled me with a satisfying sense of readiness to accomplish. However, mix-ups happened in our shared workspace, and the need to label my tools became apparent to prevent anyone from walking off with them. On my tape measure, I boldly scrawled "MINE" in black marker, a departure from the usual "Casey" label. Strangely, my right hand found comfort in the weight and shape of that hefty tape measure every time I approached a new project, activating my brain into design mode.

Yet, when I glanced down at "MINE," it became a koan: *What is mine?* Rippling shivers cascaded down my spine. I stepped back, letting this thought linger and sink into my bones before carrying on with measuring, fastening, and cutting day after day.

We had another wall to demolish between two bedrooms to extend a closet and change the way the two rooms met, and a stairway to rebuild. I hated this demolition process. It was loud, dirty, and messy. My earmuffs provided little relief. Each wall that came down revealed another lack of proper headers for structural support. It was amazing that the house had held up for as long as it had!

As I fixed one of the hinges for an old door, attending closely to the grain to find the best way to redrill the screws, an energy coursed through my palms, with a question, *What is this door?* Straight away, through an inner vision, I saw a large, tall forest of fir trees and felt a strong connection with them. *I knew the life of this door!*

While moving from one thing to the next, the entire world as I knew it was collapsing. What does death take from us but everything? Death is so close. Every exhale is a death. No one likes to talk about death, but it is a fact of life. We are demolished.

Being called into this reflection had implications that the mind could not fathom. I surmised that what was being done was not just by me, but also beyond the mind. Questions kept questioning, upending every idea or value as I examined the end grain and checked the warp before cutting wood.

This seeking tore *me* down bit by bit. Every now and then, my patience would wear thin, just as flesh hangs from my eyes and ears and mouth.

Meanwhile, I'd notice little red squiggles begin to show around my nose and legs, a close reminder of our mortal, impermanent nature. *We all break down.*

Demolition was in progress whether I liked it or not. There was a fire burning in my chest and raging through my veins as I sat in silence. It had a power over me that I couldn't comprehend. This burning fueled a desire for the Truth, instilling humility through the flames, eating up ideas of "me" or "no me." The Four Noble Truths rang in my ears—the endlessness of suffering, of death, and rebirth. Still, I saw more ideas being added to the fire.

Words floated around while I folded clothes and dried dishes.

Realities. Connection. Coping. Fusion. Spirit.

It seemed to me that the Pāli term, saṃvega, expressed more of what was happening to me than a psychological term like depression. I felt like I had been going around and around in circles forever and that futility had taken a toll on my mind/body. The Buddha had said this whirlwind of shock, dismay, and alienation is a natural reaction to seeing and experiencing the cycles of emotional suffering. I often murmured, What's the point of it all? Why am I here? I saw so much delusion, dishonesty, and violence in the world. An urgent need to know kept kicking my butt, pushing me forward while my heart thumped along to the beat of the continual question: *What is the point of being born human?*

There was another word, saṃsāra; the cycles of life and death, becoming and disintegrating, arising and passing. I allowed my mind to not know, to wonder, to roam endlessly in openness. The children asked endless questions. I thought to myself, *Do I look like Google?* But I simply said, "I don't know."

This inner calling was more important than ever. Even amidst the anger, despair, and agitation, there was pasāda, a serene confidence, a clarity about the way to move forward in the right direction. I tried to find ways to devote even more time to the process. I realized how peaceful it was to sit alone, to slowly drink a full glass of water, to stretch in the morning sun, and to feel the breeze on my face. When touched by these moments of Grace, I had faith to go on.

~~~

The boys and I went on a short vacation in the country. My head and jaw ached at the beginning of the trip. After throwing up on the bathroom floor, and curiously asking, *Whose guts are these?* I left a message with a local acupuncturist in the middle of the night, and he called me back first thing in the morning.

When I visited his office the next day, he said, "This can do the trick sometimes," as he dashed a needle between my eyebrows. My shoulders, arms, and legs went limp. My whole head and body buzzed. The headache vanished. I felt an opening that increased my perception of colors for the remainder of the vacation. The pain lessened, and gratitude swelled as I watched the boys play tag and toss the Frisbee. Sunshine kissed us all as we enjoyed one another.

A few weeks after our trip, a strange urgency pulled me in, like I was being drawn to meet something unknown. It seemed as if an alien squirmed inside me, its growing limbs pressing against my ribs. Like an old radio's dial, an internal mechanism guided me. Attuning to my breath, I sensed a tug in opposing directions. On the left side was fear, swiftly transforming into cold terror. Leaning too far to the right flared a warm rush, a volcanic intensity that demanded clarity. *Turn back to the left, just a little, center in the breath and body. Warm. Calm. Just sitting, aware, no worries, peace.*

How did this happen? I had sensed this once before, yet I could barely remember what I had done. *Did "I" do something?* How did

attention find this peaceful center in the tornado of emotion? I wondered if this experience would be enough preparation for my first
sesshin (period of intense Zen meditation) coming up in February 2008.

After class one night at the Zen center, I wept with gratitude
while telling Norm how deeply I had been touched by the Buddha's
teachings. I told him I wasn't sure what was happening to me. He
listened and said he felt something similar with Katagiri, his teacher. I
nodded and committed to take part in the sesshin.

During the sesshin, Norm talked about how all images or thoughts
are just imagination, or *nothing*, so I tried practicing a form of dis-
missiveness. But then my back started aching. In silence, we moved
as one unit—sitting together, standing together, bowing together,
walking in a circle slowly together. Surely, I didn't imagine my
frozen toes.

The man sitting next to me snored. The coffee didn't seem to
have helped him.

Steve gave a long-winded Dharma talk about the teacher-student
relationship in the afternoon. I hadn't realized there was a "right" way
to do it. I was not looking for a father or therapist, as he seemed to
imply that some others had been doing. It reminded me of a common
saying in the Twelve Step program: We are all at different places on the
path, and we are all the same distance from the ditch. *Weren't these
friendly teachers further along the path and able to help?* That was all
I required. *Aren't we all subject to our conditioning, however skillful
or unskillful? None of us is perfect.* I was puzzled as to why he didn't
just state his concern concisely about the expectations some might be
applying to his role.

On one of his many journeys, the Buddha encountered a group
of people called the Kālāmas, who asked him how they should deter-
mine whether a wise contemplative is speaking truthfully or falsely. In
response, the Buddha validated their uncertainty and doubt as reasonable. He then went on to lay out ten reasons for appropriate skepticism.

Please, Kālāmas, don't go by oral transmission, don't go by
lineage, don't go by testament, don't go by canonical authority,

don't rely on logic, don't rely on inference, don't go by reasoned contemplation, don't go by the acceptance of a view after consideration, don't go by the appearance of competence, and don't think 'The ascetic is our respected teacher.' But when you know for yourselves: 'These things are unskillful, blameworthy, criticized by sensible people, and when you undertake them, they lead to harm and suffering', then you should give them up.[15]

Each of these reasons points to a wisdom that arises in relationships with others in addition to reflection and contemplation. I understood what Steve meant, that I should not blindly accept a teaching just because a teacher says it, but because I can see for myself that certain actions lead to harm and suffering.

There are appropriate boundaries. Over the years, I've come to see that, as humans, we occasionally switch between the roles of parent, child, or peer as we go through various life experiences. Our roles can shift in an instant. When a child offers me a meal they prepared, they are like parents; conversely, when I feel vulnerable and need a hug, I can appear childlike. We can all nurture and support one another in various ways. I didn't want to solidify ideas toward any of my teachers; I regarded them as human beings, imperfect and learning about life just as I was.

I went home late that night and slid into bed quietly, not saying anything to my family. With indefatigable energy, I was back up at 4 a.m., walking carefully over the icy sidewalks back to the Zen sesshin with less sleep than I was accustomed to but didn't seem to need. I asked myself, *Why am I doing this?* Thirty years ago, I might have been afraid this was some kind of crazy cult. But here I was, going in for more back torture to stare at a wall for hours and hours, and paying for it! The legs walked toward the center and up the steps. In Zen, they talked about ending all desires. *What was it, then, that was walking me up the steps?!*

At the end of ōryōki, (a meditative style of eating), we brought our bowls together with the napkin in a special knot, but sometimes I

---

15 Aṅguttara Nikāya, 3:65, "Kesamuttisutta: *With the Kālāmas of Kesamutta,*" translated from the Pāli by Bhikkhu Sujato.

wasn't able to do it quickly enough along with the others. Something in me just *let it go and moved onward.*

Stand. Bow. Turn. Bow. Breathe. Bow. Step. Bow. Sit. Bow.

During the work period, I was assigned to wipe the floor trim in the zendo. I carefully brought a bucket of water up the stairs from the basement sink. Slosh. Slosh. Slosh. Dipping my hands into the soapy water felt warm and calming. Smooth wipe, slide along floor, smooth wipe. No dirt. The room was already quite clean. *Why must I clean what is already clean? I have plenty of dirt at home to clean.* Silly mind. Wipe, swish rag in bucket, squeeze, slide forward, wipe, repeat, and breathe. Simple. Wipe. Be. Breathe. Wipe. Breathe. Bow.

There was only one other woman student there. I wondered if we could connect after the sesshin. I knew everyone would leave right away, so I whispered to her when we were near the basement sink and putting away our rags to ask if she'd like to connect after.

She stepped back, horrified that I had spoken to her. I apologized immediately, bowing deeply. The silence was stricter than I had anticipated. I hadn't meant to cause harm, and made a vow to never do that again.

On the last day of the sesshin, I sat watching the gradations of light changing on the pale-yellow wall in front of me and suddenly heard a deep, resounding voice from within boldly say, *"Who is it that considers the One?"*

A pinch of shock. Wondering. Breathing in and breathing out.

Then, an answer came from a place I didn't know, *"No One."*

A dash of awe. Still sitting.

I had been watching the daylight slowly move across the wall in front of me. I didn't know where this voice came from. Norm often referred to phenomena as imaginations that should be dismissed and not believed.

However, I felt peaceful and at ease with the message. A sensation of uplifting support rose in my belly, like riding a Ferris wheel lifting up. Also, something in me appreciated that voice. It felt strikingly close. I did not imagine it. *What is beyond imagination?* That is the question. In Zen, they say that if it is an experience, it is not the shift into abiding enlightenment. Even so, it was a mysterious event that encouraged me to continue.

The day after the sesshin, I began hearing a hissing sound, like a conch shell or harmonics with varying degrees of intensity. I needed to let hearing be, but my nerves rattled around like loose nails in my tool belt. I made an appointment to ask Norm about it. He paused, staring at me while he checked his hearing. He nodded, "Yes," he heard that too. I decided it must be okay, but it felt pronounced. Is this normal? Is it tinnitus? I had not heard so much before!

Any time I turned my attention to hearing, how loud everything seemed. I called my friend Wes. He said he hears hissing in his ears too, and it comes and goes. We also talked about how my story felt like a feather in my hand, and didn't carry as much weight as before. He gently offered, "Yes Constance, there is something more important to realize, *What are you?*"

CHAPTER THIRTEEN

Be Attitudes

W HEN I LEARNED I had been accepted into the Adyashanti retreat, I thought it wise to hear the gravelly voice of my dear old friend, Helen from New Jersey, before booking my non-refundable plane ticket to California. We had met at an intensive with Anne Wilson Schaef and shared several intensive retreats together over the decades. She is twenty years older than I am, has been an anchor for me, and knows me well.

"Helen, I am about to buy a plane ticket to California for a retreat with some guy named Adyashanti."

"Oh, that's wonderful! You are very lucky to get in. I only got in last year after being on a waitlist. They called me the day before the retreat. I had to run around and get everything ready on very short notice."

"What? You were at one of his retreats? How was it?"

"It was very good. This guy is deep. You have to be prepared, though. They have you doing five meditation sits per day, and you are in total silence."

"I recently did a Zen sesshin, which had about ten sits per day, so I think I'll be okay with that."

"Oh, that's very good."

"And we have the roof on now, so the house can sit too. But what if I start to cry and have a deep process? I've been experiencing some old trauma from my early years."

"You should try to get your own room—see if you can. That way you can just be with your own process and not distract anyone else."

"Good idea."

"I would just go and enjoy it. It is a wonderful opportunity for you."

"We are like two peas in a pod!"

"We sure are!"

Apparently, Adyashanti was not an unknown. Helen recognized the importance that this retreat would hold for me, considering how rarely I found time alone. I had been devoting all my time to the children and house building and community work for many years.

She recommended that I build up more time on the cushion so that I would be prepared for intensive meditation each day. I followed her advice and made sure I sat each morning and evening, occasionally fitting in an afternoon sit as well.

~~~

To be away from home on retreat for one week would be a real test for me, the kids, and my husband. I asked for more initiative and follow-through from them. Forrest struggled with his math homework. When I demonstrated how to solve a math problem, he said that wasn't the way it was being taught, even if we both got the same answer. I didn't understand the new methods, and we couldn't afford a tutor.

I reached out to a neighbor friend, Roger, to get his advice on the math homework. He understood the intricacies of how they were learning it, having gone through the same thing with his kids. Since Roger is a whiz in math and even likes it, he offered to tutor Forrest. He said he'd enjoy helping out. What a gift!

Preston was acting as senior class president. He consulted me almost every night into the wee hours about escalating problems at school, which led to a few missed assignments and some declining grades. After offering ideas, I noticed in my practice a need to stop ruminating and worrying about these problems. I often returned to my mantra to *trust the process and breathe in peace.*

It occurred to me that he needed a second set of ears to sound things out, so I encouraged him to speak with a nonviolent communication practitioner I knew. This would help him address the concerns with the principal and his group of disgruntled students. Eventually, he was able to resolve a dispute over rules between the senior class and the administration, as well as educate everyone involved on useful forms of communication.

As much as I sat watching the story of my life dissolve, I was also in the middle of raising two young men, which involved standing firm and holding them accountable. To go each day from sitting on the cushion in the zendo to meeting them at school with their teachers was like listening to a roaring silence while watching a tragicomedy dance in my head.

~~~

One day after leaving the Zen center at about 7:30 a.m., a fellow practitioner said he had figured out a problem with something at work from his sit. I asked him if he spent his time thinking about his work when he sat, and he said he most certainly did.

I wondered whether that was useful, and being open-minded, I tried it. I certainly had electrical and carpentry problems that had to be coordinated, as well as parenting and other issues. During the next sit early in the morning, I took a mental inventory. But thoughts were impossible to hold onto—they would slip away as soon as I had an idea in place. In the silence, they vanished.

I wanted to solve my problems, but instead, I began developing a horrible headache. It was more common for me to sort through everyday solutions with paper, a pen, and the Internet nearby. The frustration of sitting there without those tools was exhausting. I wondered why my head hurt, and finally remembered I had gotten the idea from a fellow practitioner. Before I knew it, the bell was ringing. It was time to stand up, and my head was splitting. I made a vow to never do that again. I needed to learn to direct my attention to the breath, keep that focus, and evaluate it first and foremost.

The next day, our plumber, Sam, stopped by the house. While we both knelt down to install drain pipe for eventually putting a toilet in place, I told him about my meditation practice. He started to recount the Beatitudes from Jesus's Sermon on the Mount:

Blessed are the [humble] in spirit for theirs is the kingdom of heaven.

Blessed are they who mourn for they shall be comforted.

Blessed are the meek for they shall inherit the earth.

Blessed are they who hunger and thirst for [wholesomeness] for they shall be satisfied.

Blessed are the merciful for they shall obtain mercy.

Blessed are the clean of heart for they shall see God.

Blessed are the peacemakers for they shall be called children of God.

Blessed are they who are persecuted for the sake of [wholesomeness] for theirs is the kingdom of heaven.

Blessed are you when they insult you and persecute you and utter every kind of [ignorance] against you (falsely) because of me.[16]

I remarked at how similar these eight declarations of blessedness were to the eight practices in the Noble Eightfold Path. Both promised liberation from the endless cycle of stress! The one beatitude, "Blessed are the peacemakers for they shall be called children of God," felt connected to the fourth aspect of the Dharma wheel, Right Action, promoting moral and peaceful conduct. In our troubled world, I've often reflected on how I feel like a newcomer learning to live in alignment in this way with others, my family, the house, and for my sons. Right action also meant standing up for the truth when the call was clear. There are many interpretations of the sermon; I appreciated my friend Sam and how we connected on nurturing a spiritual practice and respecting our different forms of devotion.

As we finished up the plumbing project for the day, our discussion extended into a deeper conversation about his regular prayer practice. He asked if I'd be open to sharing a meal, an offer I gladly accepted. In the basement, he opened our old fridge and skillfully whipped up a gourmet omelet using our leftovers, all the while talking with inspiration about his faith in God. Mostly, I listened. I could see an

---

16   Matthew 5:3–10 NIV

attitude of openness and willingness. The willingness to face any irritation provided an ever-increasing openness to seeing solutions. Perseverance arose in the face of any obstacle. What a rare gift to have this conversation with him!

The Buddha said, "For never is hatred settled by hate, it's only settled by love: this is an eternal truth."[17] Coming back to an open mind and heart, admitting how little I knew, asking for help, and persevering with kindness offered a pragmatic and wholesome way forward.

---

17   Khuddaka Nikāya: Dhammapada, 1, "*Yamaka Vagga: Pairs,*" translated from the Pāli by Bhikku Sujato.

CHAPTER FOURTEEN

Not a Thing

BEFORE I LEFT for Adyashanti's retreat in April 2008, the head student at Dharma Field invited me to participate in a precept ceremony. It is a simple and short ritual of standing with some folks to recite the precepts with intention to follow them. The idea of participating in a ritual seemed questionable to me, because I was already applying these principles. Living with them one day at a time was a regular inquiry.

Following the precepts, or sīla, is the moral structure in Buddhism and is a basic foundation for practice because one needs an unbothered mind to sit in meditation. Made perfect sense.

The five basic precepts are the basis for ethical practice in Buddhism:

1. To abstain from taking life or killing.

2. To abstain from taking what is not freely given.

3. To abstain from sexual misconduct.

4. To abstain from false speech.

5. To abstain from intoxication.

Buddhism links moral principles to action through the teaching on Karma.[18] To follow these precepts, one gives attention to one's patterns or behaviors, which allow for less static in the mental forces that one is grappling with in meditation. There is a moral action related to every major intentional impulse. Unwholesome actions create distracting mental imprints that we are bound to encounter when we meditate.

Steve, the head priest, indicated that this was a way of stepping across the line and "admitting" you are a Buddhist. I was never comfortable saying I was a Christian, even though I had done contemplative centering prayer for most of my life and was raised Catholic. I also sat many retreats in hermitages for periods of rest and reflection with the dear Franciscan nuns who guided my contemplative practice over the years. Exploring is part of my nature. Settling on a label didn't appeal to me. But, in keeping an open mind, I wondered if there was something in the process itself that might help.

I met with Norm right away to explore my participation in this ritual with the sangha. I told him, "I am not doing this precept ceremony to become a good Buddhist."

He replied, "What makes you think you have to do it for that reason?"

"Because I see a bunch of other people here doing it for that reason."

He nodded.

We paused, sitting together.

My attention quickly became centered around the sit earlier that morning when I fell into a void, and felt a huge blank openness.

I asked, "What is with this void I see?"

He smiled and said, "That *is* you."

"Oh!" It boggled the mind. "Sometimes I see a bunch of voids."

He spoke calmly. "There can be many voids."

I stopped to consider this affirmation. Then, a memory resurfaced—sitting beside a dear friend on the beach, our hands scooping up sand, only to watch it slip through our fingers as we dipped our hands

---

18   Saṁyutta Nikāya, 35.146, "*Kammanirodhasutta: Kamma*," translated from the Pāli by Bhikkhu Bodhi.

into the water. Our giggles blended with mixed feelings of dread and delight, echoing in the mist.

Norm and I shared a moment in silence.

Then, in the back of my head, as I considered the precept ceremony again, these words came into my mind: "Love the Lord your God with all your heart and with all your soul and with all your mind and with all your strength," "Love your neighbor as yourself," and "There is no commandment greater than this."

I told him, "If I participate, I don't know why I am doing it, and I don't want to harm the process for myself or others."

He said, "Do you have to know why you are doing it?"

"I don't know." I squirmed. "Maybe. Maybe not."

"Well, then," he said in his usual relaxed tone with a nod.

However, I needed a clear intention in my moral development. I was not going to participate in anything like an automaton. As a seven-year-old girl, I underwent a communion ceremony to initiate my participation in Catholicism, though I had little understanding of what it was all about. Again, at age nine, I participated in a Catholic confirmation ceremony. I would often reflect on the teachings of Jesus and find myself deeply moved by the stories, especially when I considered them from the perspective of his mother, Mary. Confessions were also a part of the doctrine, and each chance to be honest about my behavior was something I respected and valued.

Growing up, I experienced more shame than wisdom. In reviewing my mistakes, I learned to transform shame into forgiveness and make amends. Having a sponsor helped me talk about what I had done; how I could learn and let go.

My behavior in practicing the precepts has never been perfect, and I found it unlikely that I'd ever attain any purity of virtue. In the present, many situations are hard to decipher and happen so fast that skillfulness, or the appropriate action for the time and place, is not always obvious to me. Just wanting to not cause harm is not enough to be skillful. Failure is part of the process in life. The precepts allow me to reflect on my participation and *know that I am learning*. Then, I can relax in meditation. I had to keep coming back to beginner's mind, and that this is a *practice*.

Talking with Norm helped me feel supported, and so I concluded that the ceremony facilitated mutual support for all present. My love for the Dharma, Buddha, or Christ, for the sangha, the church, my family, and my community, but mostly my love—above all—for the Truth or the Dharma, called me to participate.

With that clarity, I sighed with relief and decided to recite the precepts and fully devote my practice to the Triple Gem. The Triple Gem consists of the Buddha, the Dharma, and the Sangha. The Buddha is generally referred to as the primary teacher and mentor for students of Buddhism. The Dharma refers to the Buddha's teachings, but it also refers to the unfolding process of Truth that is practiced and eventually understood. The Sangha is a community, church, or any assembly of those supportive of the Buddha and the Dharma. For me, taking part in the ritual represented taking refuge or keeping in step with the Dharma.

In some ways, these three treasures reminded me of the Christian symbol of the Trinity, which is stated as the Father, the Son, and the Holy Spirit. I always thought of the Father as above all, beyond creation; the Son as Christ or universally throughout all; and the Holy Spirit as individually present within creation. The Trinity integrates all experiences of God.

There are also three foundations in the Twelve Step Program: recovery, unity, and service. I'd seen the triangle, or three-sided symbol, on money and on manholes. It was a symbol representing ideas.

All of these diverse perspectives, alive in different forms of three, held many different meanings—aspects of devotion, service, and inquiry, plus much more embodied wisdom that fueled my interest in waking up.

The ceremony helped me integrate the view in Buddhist practice that our actions have consequences. I've definitely wanted to work with being good, but being a Buddhist or a Christian is something I could not be sure about. Those labels hold a great deal of complexity; mean many different things to many different people. And, there are a lot of different kinds of Buddhists or Christians. We are each unique.

Having the foresight to prevent trouble, the wisdom to step back to avoid trouble, and living in peace gladdened my mind and body, extending outward. I often noticed things that needed improvement. My human flaws and awkward ways stood out in my mind, but Life moved *through* my body in all situations and circumstances with profound acceptance. What is *is*. Shunryū Suzuki once said, "Each of you is perfect the way you are… and you can use a little improvement."[19]

Once I clarified my intention, and rested in Being, a sense of inner freedom told me that, at least for now, I didn't have to know what it meant to be a good Buddhist. I could only breathe one breath at a time, take one step at a time, and wonder: *What am I?*

---

19   David Chadwick, *Moments with Shunryū Suzuki: Stories of a Zen Master Told by His Students*

CHAPTER FIFTEEN

Instructions

AT TEA TIME, after the Dharma talk on Sundays, nobody discussed what they did on the cushion. The teachers often spoke in second or third person. People barely socialized. The meditation instructions were continually, "Just sit and keep coming back to the breath," or, "If wandering, just come back." Come back to what? From where? Where is the breath? Is it at the nose, the sinuses, the belly, the chest? Where to focus? Noticing the breath in the belly relaxed me. It was also such a relief to have nothing to do and nowhere to go. Sometimes, thoughts arose that this was self-indulgent, luxurious, and affluent. But I felt compelled to do this.

The April retreat with Adyashanti was fast approaching. *The Shobogenzo*, written by the founder of Sōtō Zen, Eihei Dogen, was a daunting 1,144 pages. I reviewed it for further instructions, but this did not fit with keeping it simple. I had no time for extensive study.

Worried that I wouldn't be prepared for the retreat, I searched the Internet with the words "Practical Meditation Instructions" for advice on meditation. Up came a PDF file called "Practical Vipassana Exercises."[20] (Vipassanā is a Pāli term meaning insight, which allows us to see the mind. However, we first need samatha, a form of meditation that calms the mind.) The author of this work, Venerable Mahāsī

---

20 Venerable Mahāsi Sayādaw, *Practical Vipassana Exercises.*

Sayādaw,[21] appeared to have a brilliant reputation as a highly skilled meditation teacher, and the booklet was only sixty-four pages, simple enough to digest in one sitting with my eager appetite.

The examples provided instructions for noticing the rising and falling of the abdomen as an object of attention, noticing the distinct sensation as it happened, and then watching it come and go in the mind and body. That was incredibly helpful! I had also wanted to know how to notice if, say, the sound of a dog barking came up while I was noticing the breath. The suggestion indicated a noting practice—let the ears hear the sound, note: hearing, hearing, hearing... If a vision arose, note: seeing, seeing, seeing... I found that bringing attention to experiencing what the particular sense door was already paying attention to increased synchronization and relaxation significantly. Doing the labeling felt too conceptual for me. I didn't have to think about the dog barking. I could just feel the barks as vibrations in the body and *know* hearing as it predominated my attention.

I was used to taking the bodily senses into the field of attention through a gentle and open scanning process: feeling the interior of my body, the spaciousness around it, and the environment. Then, after feeling safe in the space, I'd feel the breath at the belly, through the diaphragm, which calmed my nervous system as I let pleasant breathing sensations spread out through the body. I had been doing this in the rose garden, when nursing my children, or while relaxing in the bathtub. As I meditated in hermitages over the years, I'd say a prayer by speaking the words with long pauses between each word, breathing in and out, feeling the breath, and resting in between thoughts. In Zen, I thought I had to do something else; each tradition does have different ways of meditating. Being an improvisational meditation artist worked for me.

Therefore, I didn't feel comfortable with any hard mental noting practice. I preferred to *feel* or *know* the vibrations of hearing, seeing,

---

21 Mahāsī Sayādaw (U Sobhana Mahathera) was a Burmese Theravāda
    Buddhist monk of contemporary Burma and an eminent meditation
    master who lived from 1904 to 1982. He devoted his entire life to the
    practice and teaching of Buddhism in the West and throughout Asia.

smelling, tasting, touching, or thinking, and let those sensations flow along as they happened. It reminded me of my kinesthetic experience from when I did contact improv; you flow with the movements and let movements take you as you interact with others on the floor. Knowing was like a combination of feeling and mental thinking.

After reflecting on these instructions, I wanted some guidance for going on a silent meditation retreat, and up came advice from a man named Dr. Daniel Ingram, MD.[22] He suggested, above all, taking full responsibility for my practice. A good reminder. I sent him an email to see if he had any other tips for me in particular.

Within a few minutes, the phone rang, and it was him! I could hear sounds in the background from an active hospital. He said he was quite busy and only had five minutes. He preferred to be called Daniel. I immediately thought, *We have synchronicity.*

Then he started barking, "Note the arising and passing of all phenomena at all times!"

His insistence and directness surprised me. Again, he kept saying, "Note the arising and passing of all phenomena at all times!" He didn't have much time; he was busy working in an emergency room, but he wanted to get this point across. *Okay. I can do that.* I figured that this had to do with evaluating the breath and seeing it change as it expanded and filled the body. It was certainly better than sitting around watching my mind wander and having some vague idea of the breath. Though I had definitely noticed the slipperiness of thoughts and feelings. So, I interpreted this to mean that I was to experience mental fabrications slip in and out, and notice that entire process continuously as it happens, *feel* it and *know* it, as the Satipaṭṭhāna Sutta[23] described.

He quickly ended, "Have fun!"

Fun! What an ingenious idea, and not something that I'd often encountered at the Zen center, but the more I concentrated and sat, the more fun it became!

---

22 Daniel Ingram, "General Advice on Retreats," Integrated Daniel, 2008, https://www.integrateddaniel.info/retreats.

23 Majjhima Nikāya, 10, "*Satipaṭṭhāna Sutta: The Foundations of Mindfulness*," translated from the Pāli by Nyanasatta Thera.

What I also heard Daniel share was to be diligent and stay focused for the entire duration of the meditation retreat. He said to quickly "note" specific objects of attention as they arise or pass away. And I did; at certain times, it worked as a mental focus. Due to my somatic practice and earthiness, my inclination to perceive sensations was strong. I decided to just be open to learning, see what happened, and trust my own way of being with the practice.

I'd been dismissing "wandering" and not bringing honest attention to "wandering" as soon as it happened. It felt delightful to know that the problem wasn't so much "wandering" as it was failing to notice it as it was occurring in a relaxed way, and attending to the breath at the abdomen again. To notice "thinking" was freeing because a tiny release happened in knowing it; even if there is a thought that is noticing the thinking, it relaxed the attitude toward the wandering mind.

I committed to carefully noticing and feeling "wandering" when the mind wandered and "thinking" when thoughts diverted my attention from the sensations of breathing. It's critical to remember to return to the breath at the beginning of the sit and not wander off for a long time. Sometimes, I'd notice sensations of gratitude for remembering this. Then, I'd return attention gently but firmly to the sensations of breathing, which was a point just above the navel. I found that to be grounding and calming as an object. While I considered his instructions, I also knew that what worked for him might not necessarily work for me.

The founders of the Twelve Step program had been pointing to awakening, as the Twelfth step says, "Having had a spiritual awakening as a result of these Steps..." But to hear that it was doable from someone with total certainty felt incredible! On an online forum, several folks indicated that the teachings of the Buddha, Jesus, and others were attainable for all here and now. This is what the Buddha promised in the Third Noble Truth, the cessation of suffering. How empowering!

In my Twelve Step meetings, folks talked about relative awakenings for developing many skills in how to relate to their families and life circumstances, but I never heard anyone talking about a deep spiritual awakening. If I had, I would have been tapping them on the shoulder and asking if we could have a chat after the meeting so I could learn about what they were doing, as I had often done with those who appeared to have found better functioning in life.

I marveled at the encouragement. Wasn't enlightenment only for monks, nuns, and priests? Or those who live in far-off monasteries, meditate on high ledges in cliff dwellings, or hermits who live in caves? Doesn't it only exist in the past, perhaps among the saints, for the extraordinary sacrifices they performed? Wasn't it only possible for those few who sat at the foot of a guru, offering daily devotions to him (it was usually a him)? Hadn't some astrophysicists, neuroscientists, or those studying quantum mechanics gained some insight into this? Didn't a best-selling novelist try this in India and give up?

I didn't know what to think. I scraped, cleaned, and worked hard, but I wasn't feeding the starving in India every day. I wasn't the mother of Jesus. I didn't fit into any of those categories. I believed I was average. I figured the best I could do was try to draw closer to those who were enlightened by reading and listening to their messages and finding inspiration in them. But this could no longer satisfy.

I reviewed my process, first focusing on settling into the posture and feeling supported from below. Then I felt the refreshing sensations of the breath and kept coming back to the abdomen after noticing anything else, even wandering. Whenever the mind touched the object of focus, there was noticing *that* in the moment as it started, staying with it, and watching it fade away. Each time I did this during meditation, a soothing tingling in my hands and legs intensified, bringing forth a more relaxed and fun sit.

I felt grateful and curious to be going on retreat with others and meeting Adyashanti. I had to hear and see for myself. I wasn't taking any of this at someone else's word. It had to resonate in my gut. Would these additional instructions be helpful? The only way to know was to put them into practice.

I typed up my brief notes from my research, made a few copies, and placed them in separate pockets in my luggage so that I'd have them along with me for review.

I was ready and focused. For what, I had yet to find out.

CHAPTER SIXTEEN

No Way Out

WHEN I ARRIVED AT THE AIRPORT, I was so out of my element that I practically stumbled my way through security, feeling like I had no head. At the gate, a baby's piercing screams drowned out the announcements about my gate and departure time change. Eventually, between screams, I heard my name called and checked to see the gate number had changed. I sprinted as fast as possible and managed to slip onto the plane just as they were preparing to shut the door.

The flight attendant asked, "Didn't you hear us paging you for your flight?"

I just stared at her and said, "Thank you. I'm sorry."

It was my responsibility to double-check all of the details, as details do change. I was relieved to have even made it to the airport after all my pre-trip preparations.

It was delightful to finally sit on the plane to San Francisco and enjoy some ginger ale to help settle my nervous stomach. How amazing to sit in a chair in the vast sky, gazing out at the puffy clouds below!

After landing, in an attempt to save money, I had tried to find a carpool ride, and had no luck, so I thought there must be very few people attending this retreat. At the last minute, I booked a cheap car rental for the week, getting the last available car in the airport area. But, it seemed like such a waste to have a rental car sitting in a parking lot all week long.

When I arrived at the car rental, a couple in front of me were in a heated argument with the clerk because the agency didn't have the infant restraint seat they needed. The clerk threatened not to work with them, suggesting they go someplace else. I stepped in and said to the clerk that it was easy to see how worried and tired they were with their child, and perhaps they could take another look around for something that might work. With a wavering look, the clerk turned to another staff member who looked in the back and brought out an old car seat covered in stinky dried vomit. I told them it could be cleaned up with some soapy water, and even offered to help wash it for them. Another employee then took it out to their garage to wash it down.

Once I signed the contracts for my car and loaded all of my things into it, I grabbed the keys and asked to use the bathroom. They pointed me to one outside around the back. When I entered, the door fell slightly off the hinge and scraped the floor as I closed it shut.

A few minutes later, when I pulled on the handle to leave, the door wouldn't open.

I pulled and pulled, but it was no use. The door stuck. *Really* stuck. Was my pulling making it worse? I tried pushing. I pounded on the door and called out, but there were fifty-mph wind gusts that day, and my voice probably wasn't traveling to the front of the building where the employees were working.

My cell phone and purse were in the car.

The back of the bathroom was connected to the inside of the building, so I began hammering my fists on the connecting wall. I waited, no response. My pounding wasn't loud enough, and my hands couldn't take it. I picked up the plastic waste bin and used it to scrape and hit the wall.

No response.

My skull exploded. Panic gripped me, causing my back to tense up as I scanned the space around me. Of the four light bulbs, only one was barely flickering, and I realized that if I pounded on the wall, it could affect the filament and the light could go out at any point. Perhaps turning it off would reveal a crack showing light from outside where I could insert my key and pull the door toward me. Perhaps pulling or pushing on the door would also squeeze the door into the jamb even further. I took the risk.

No luck. There was no light coming through. I flipped the switch to turn the light back on and, "Tink," it flicked out!

In total darkness, I stood there, feeling my heart thump out of my chest, my skin tingling, breathing in short and out short.

I quickly searched with my hands under the vanity sink for replacement light bulbs. Nothing there. A small plastic toilet bowl brush, nothing more.

Trapped. I leaned on the sink and felt my heart racing with fear. I tuned into the bodily sensations of shock and worry. *These are thoughts.* I knew that the thoughts were causing the sensations. *I can change the thoughts.*

Surely a female employee would need to use the bathroom at some point and would come out to find me there. *Just be patient.* But then I remembered that when I asked to use the bathroom, I saw another one on the inside of the building just for employees. So, there would be no reason for an employee to be back where I was. I realized I might even be there overnight since they would be closing shortly.

Panic.

More fear and worry. How am I going to get out? Do they not see that the car I rented, parked right in front of the building, is still there? They are renting everything in sight.

My shouts for help wore out. *Screaming wears down the vocal cords. How did singers do it? Regulation.* I needed to manage the use of my voice and diaphragm.

Pressing my ear to the doorframe, all I could hear were the mere rustles of sand whistling in the parking lot.

I stood for another five minutes, then I resumed banging on the wall with the bin, yelling, "Help! Help!"

As I yelled, I realized that I had been yelling for help *all of my life*! This whole trip was a call for help.

No response.

It often felt like I went through this same struggle every day.

I searched the garbage can and again under the sink with my hands. Nothing.

I reached inside the wet toilet tank and yanked out the lift lever to use as a pry bar. Using the lever and my car key, I pried the trim around the door frame, scratching my right hand on a nail in the process. Inch by inch, I edged along behind the trim until it finally tore free. Then, I pulled the door handle several times from different angles. No use. Not a single crack of light.

Pitch-black darkness.

I pounded the wall and yelled for help.

Waiting.

No answer.

I removed all of the trim and set it aside in the corner.

The door would not budge.

I tried the panic button on the car key to sound the alarm, but I was out of radio range.

I kicked the door, thinking I could maybe put my foot through it. No use. It was thick solid wood, and my tennis shoes were not the type of shoes for kicking in a door.

The sledge hammer from my garage would make a nice hole with a few swings, I thought.

I ran water over my wrists in the sink to soothe my racing heart, slow down my breathing, and clean the cut on my palm. I prayed for guidance, and then knew it was useless to worry.

I sat down on the grimy floor.

I was safe. I had water. I wasn't hungry. I even had a toilet.

Shaking my head, I had to laugh at how the streams come together in mysterious ways. I saw that no matter what, no matter where I am, *there is no way out.* Wherever we go, we have to face reality. It is a better way to be.

I sighed with a deep breath and asked myself: Why not face it fully and completely in this very moment? Then I remembered the instructions to watch the rising and falling of the abdomen. I noticed how short my breaths were in my upper chest. I slowed down my breathing and took longer breaths, all the while noticing my intention to calm down. Soon, an inner peace arose, similar to what I often felt when I looked with love into my children's eyes after nursing them. A sense of wellness rushed in while time disappeared.

Feeling the need to try again, I stood up, lifted the wastebasket, and thrashed it earnestly against the wall, then rapped hard on the door three times. In my cracked voice, but this time coolheaded, I called out once more, "Help me if you can hear this!"

Like a shot, a man on the other side of the door said, "Are you asking for help?"

Happily, I shouted, "Yes! Please push the door open."

He commanded, "Step back," and with a shove from his shoulder, the door lurched forward, and he stumbled into the bathroom. I peered at him through strained eyes as the brilliance of the afternoon sun poured in, rays of light casting glorious streaks from behind his dark silhouette.

I blinked a few times to adjust from the darkness. "How did you come by here?"

He shrugged and said, "I don't know. I thought I might look around back here for my car rental, but of course, it must be in front."

I grabbed my camera from the car and took a picture of the door trim and toilet, just in case there was going to be a dispute. I was pretty sure I had just earned a discount on my rental. I checked my watch and realized I had been in there for almost two hours. I went into the front office to tell them their bathroom toilet was out of order and that the door was broken, and to please not let anyone use the bathroom until the door was fixed.

The woman at the register asked, "Was that you pounding on the walls?"

I nodded, gave her my name, and couldn't have been more well-behaved. I simply walked to my car to move onward.

Life delivers its own lessons.

CHAPTER SEVENTEEN

Being Called Home

M Y CHECK-IN AT THE RETREAT went smoothly. Soon I was eating supper and getting acquainted with a fellow from Canada named François who had been to other Adyashanti retreats. He was really happy to be there and looking forward to it, which was reassuring.

The retreat was held at Asilomar, a hotel and conference center that had accessibility for people with all levels of physical ability. I had seen signs in the lobby announcing other events and workshops going on concurrently, so the hundreds of people seated in the dining hall made sense to me. But when I entered the meditation hall where we would meet each day, I was amazed to see that, including volunteers and staff, about 350 people were in attendance for this retreat alone! *This many people were interested in meditation?* Incredible! What a treat.

Unlike the Twelve Step gatherings that focused more on the story of one's life and developing inter-relational skills, this was something completely different. It reminded me of the big Gratitude Twelve Step gatherings I'd been to, except this was silent.

There was a chair on a stage in front for Adyashanti to sit on within everyone's view. I felt glad that there was no issue in being able to see him, but I knew he was just a man. All of this attention on one person seemed weird to me, but I was being open-minded and going with the flow. We were both human beings. This was simply a way for us all to hear and see him.

In the Twelve Step meeting culture I was used to, hearing from each person in a circle as an equal was the norm. But I had also gotten used to Zen, where the teacher speaks in front and the rest listen. I knew that each person has inherent wisdom within, and so even though it seemed silly to all be pointed toward one man, it was what it was. I remembered the helpful advice, "Take what you like and leave the rest," and used it here.

The retreat leader firmly shared some simple and relatively flexible rules. We each had name tags that let the staff know we were on silent retreat and that they should not speak to us. The mutual commitment to silence was like a container that supported our individual processes amidst other groups at Asilomar who were not on silent retreat. Here, if you did not want to stay for a sit or a satsang, you did not have to attend. That was cool, and reminded me of Anne. But, if you did attend a sit, you were asked to stay seated for the entire forty-five-minute time period and to mindfully exit at the end. This rule would reduce distractions for the people concentrating and doing longer sits, and it seemed perfectly reasonable.

Meditation can bring old wounds to light at any time. Silent retreat settings do not generally provide the type of facilitation I valued from Anne's intensives, and could feel suffocating for someone working through their trauma. Memories of abuse in my childhood that I had deeply buried would sometimes come up, and I was accustomed to taking good care of myself around my feelings and working with my process. In this way, I valued the retreat's flexibility for folks to join a sit as they felt necessary, which contrasts with a Zen sesshin where everyone is expected to attend every sit together.

The great hall only provided chairs, unlike the floor seating I had adjusted to in Zen. A few folks sat in the far back along the wall on the floor with cushions they had brought with them. There was also an out-door pool and the ocean, both incredibly rare treats for a woman from Minnesota, but I put them out of my mind. They were not as important as attending every sit and paying close attention to the breath and the body.

The next morning I awoke with a smile, ready to launch into meditation. We all shuffled in and bowed to whatever seat came to us.

Many folks urgently headed for the front. Per my usual style, I selected a chair in the back and settled into a new posture. Bowing to the seat is a sweet gesture in Zen where there is an inner agreement to enter into this most intimate space. Everyone in this huge group cooperated without a single hitch. Incredible!

After the ordeal in the car rental bathroom, my commitment was at an all-time high. When they handed us Adya's printed meditation instructions called "True Meditation," I eagerly digested them right away. His instructions encouraged an open attitude throughout the retreat. I decided to combine his instructions with noticing and feeling any breath sensations as they arose, staying attentive and watching them fade as they went. Sometimes I'd notice the in-breath more than the out-breath and tried to even out my focus. This allowed me to quickly feel centered in the body and mind. When I noticed a sound, I turned attention directly to the inner, felt experience of hearing. I allowed consciousness to *know* directly what conscious-ness was doing—feeling down into the ears, letting the rumbling vibrations of sound echo through the canals and structures and reverberate in the entire body.

If there was pain, I noticed it in a soft, loving way and looked at the exact point of the pain. Then, I noticed if there was a point of contact that was also pulling away from or resisting the pain, and as I noticed that, the pain would move and change. Then, I started to recall the advice "at all times," so I kept raising energy to keep going.

Practice became more and more interesting. As my curiosity grew, the awareness of sensations picked up speed. I was noticing at a faster clip, and seeing the pain move off the back and into a shoulder, then under a scapula, and then back to the neck, a little sharp at one point; like small pieces of glass, it would scatter about, then swirl around into the chest. I wasn't even sure it was pain; there was tingling, then tightening, then almost tickling and clenching, then with increased concentration and interest, I would see pain simply vanish and there was no tiredness.

Someone sitting next to me coughed. I felt the wave of sound vibrations coming toward and through the inner ear. At one point, I observed mild irritation at my neighbor's squirming to rearrange their position. I noticed two things. One, a need to adjust my position in relation to theirs for just a second, and two, a feeling of happiness despite what they were doing. I toggled between these interesting phenomena: seeing the clinging to the irritation, feeling the bare sensation, then watching it fade away with gentle breath energies as support. The thinking process, or mental note of pain, was not as important to me as the feeling and knowing of it *as it was happening* and as whatever was being experienced was changing—staying with whatever arose, moment by moment, and feeling saturated with breath energy.

When a sit ended, we took a break. As I returned from the bathroom to get some water, I saw a sign above the water jugs that read, "Resistance is Futile." Perfect! I laughed, remembering the phrase from the fictional alien species called The Borg on *Star Trek*, one of my favorite shows to watch with my family. The intention of The Borg is to assimilate human beings into their collective. It felt comical that Adya and his staff would put up that sign. To fight reality is futile. I also started to see, during the sweet falling away of sensations, that there was no hiding from Awareness.

With an inner smile, I headed back into the next meditation.

~~~

Each sit deepened the silence and concentration. At first, I opened to the spacious awareness that Adya pointed to, then tuned into specific areas of unavoidable pain in my back or legs, and feeling supported by the chair beneath me. Then I felt into the breath energies moving in the torso, which became like little beacons to notice and watch as they flowed and changed. An image or memory might surface, and I would simply see it, not enter into any other thought about it, and notice my eyeballs turning slightly to the left or the right as it departed. An overall pleasantness arose, which increased concentration to the point where I was no longer aware of time passing, nor was I aware of any pain from sitting so perfectly still.

At one point, the effort to hold onto pleasant sensations became exhausting. I had never realized how exhausting it could be. When I returned to my room that night, I was wiped out. I hadn't said a word all day, nor had I processed any decisions other than minor self-care.

I had been meditating constantly. I barely had the desire or energy to take a shower, but I did take a quick one anyway. I fell asleep as soon as my head hit the pillow. When I woke up with my alarm just before the morning bell at 5 a.m., it seemed as though I'd just put my head down the night before.

For the first several days of the retreat, I did not miss any of the satsang talks or sits. However, after lunch one day, I decided to gift myself a brief walk on the beach where I prayerfully wrote a huge "HELP" sign in the sand and watched it vanish in the waves.

Adya had been answering questions for days. During each question and dialogue, I continued to notice sensations with breath energies arising and passing. An enormous gratitude kept welling up because the questions being asked were the same ones that had been bubbling under the surface for a long time.

These kinds of questions felt intensely intimate, and finding someone to talk with on this level is never easy. Yet here I was, and there they were. One by one, people were walking up to a microphone in front of hundreds of people and sharing the deepest questions in their hearts. I felt both shock and joy as each person stood to ask a question. And as I kept my primary focus on the bodily sensations, listening was easy—the words and ideas cascaded through the space of my mind. Life includes stress. We are all subject to stress.

His simple answers and responses resonated with me. He validated difficult experiences. But given the retreat's brief duration, only a small number would have the opportunity to speak with him. It seemed only fair that people—some who traveled as far as Europe—would get the chance to ask questions. Then I remembered to "stay out of other people's stuff." That was a thought, and given that I was meditating, I noticed, "just thinking," and it passed. In the meantime, my mind/body bubbled, swelling like a bean in a pressure cooker at full heat.

After supper that evening, while walking back to my room and pondering if I had the courage to make it to the next sit, I saw François out for a jog. When I opened the door to my building, he threw his hand up with a big smile and waved as he recognized me. I suddenly felt a renewed ability to continue meditating.

Isn't that interesting...how quickly the intention shifted? I thought with a smile as he passed by and my hand rose and waved back. One minute I believed I could not do it, and the next, I could? How changeable the mind could be. It helps to have encouragement from others. How the mind wants and doesn't want and how attention moves along in those directions. *But again, that is just another thought; return to sensations.*

During the final sit that evening, Adya remarked that it is okay if one has strong feelings. He told a story about a monk who, right after receiving news that his mother had died, broke down into sobs in the middle of a restaurant. Then, after finishing his process, he went on his way.

Phew, what a relief that having feelings is okay here. A great deal of fear and tension were shaking my body. This indicated to me that I had a deep process coming up. But, being in an unfamiliar setting, I was also trying to cope.

It felt as though four people were arguing in my head. One was afraid and worried. The second was trying to keep the worried one at bay, telling the fear to wait. Another was the resistance energy of seeing this as separately happening, and being overwhelmed by all the new direct contact. And another was seeing it all as if it were not a problem. Were these all of me? *What am I?* Certainly, they were all clamoring for attention. What was it that was okay with this?

I withdrew to the beach, hoping that the movement and the ocean's mist would help blow it off. Yet as I made my way across the road, rain began to fall, catching me without an umbrella or rain jacket. I didn't want to go back to my room alone. I wanted to be near someone.

After a short time, I realized it was probably best to return to my room. Leaning desperately into the wet wind, I turned back to the brightly lit hall. I considered that perhaps I was just overwrought and tired, but I felt like a shaking live wire. Again, these were just thoughts arising. It was like a beam of attention held fast to every single thing, and I worried my body could not handle it.

When I stepped into my building, I saw an older woman sitting on the floor in the cozy alcove next to a crackling fire in the fireplace. My body immediately slunk down on the floor across from her, bending toward the fire to warm my hands and dry off. Her long gray hair slid over her shoulders as she stared at the fire. I started to sob and blow my nose with tissues from my pocket. She carefully reached for a full box of tissues on an end table and kindly placed it in front of me, then returned her gaze to the fire. I continued to cry tears of relief and sorrow, taking breaths to embrace the gift of being myself, no matter how devastated I felt. The firelight danced in my eyes and hers; she never gave me any indication that she was disturbed by my crying.

I heard an inner voice: *Let it come. Just be here now.*

Once in a while, she added another piece of wood to the fire. I'd stop and watch the wood turn to ash.

Fire. Heat. Warmth. Ash.

Another upwelling of grief came from somewhere I didn't know.

Receive. Just Open.

With that warmth and safety, I surrendered. After a while, I could breathe more deeply again with ease.

I went to bed, slept very soundly, and woke up early and refreshed to sit in silence, walk in silence, and eat in silence among the huge flowing group of human beings. I renewed my commitment by rereading Adya's meditation instructions and my own notes for practice that I had brought along with me. I seemed to be finding my own way, simply happy and fortunate to be there. I didn't know what the crying from the previous night was about, and it didn't matter. Noticing each new sensation continued to bring awareness into the present moment and quickly blew away any lingering thoughts of the past.

The morning flew by like a breeze, and then I felt a lifting sensation when I sat down to meditate. After lunch, my energy level felt depleted, so I went straight to bed, set my kitchen timer for thirty minutes, and woke up with drool all over my pillow. A deep restful sleep. I brushed my teeth while reading both sets of instructions once more. Each set of instructions seemed to feed into the other. I asked myself, "Am I following it all to the letter?" Yes. I knew I was doing the best I could.

In the afternoon, they offered several extra sits with fifteen-minute breaks in between. Some were guided meditations for those who wanted the support. Instead, I thought I would take a walk because the retreat was almost over, and I hadn't had much time to see the ocean beach.

I also noticed that more folks were chatting outside amongst themselves in small groups, and some were going off for a swim. This made a part of me want to head off to play on the beach too, and perhaps get to know some of them.

But, as I reviewed this choice, my legs moved in the direction of the hallway, and I saw my feet cross the threshold. I noticed the changing sensation of my feet touching wood instead of the recent tar walkway, and my mouth changed from a frown into a smile in the direction of the bell ringer, who smiled back as I passed by. Her skirt caught the breeze and flew up, touching my wrist. The decision to find a random spot in the back of the hall flowed automatically as I bowed to the seat, feeling the bones bend and the muscles move.

The bell rang once more, calling me home, reminding me *we are home.*

CHAPTER EIGHTEEN

Removing All Barriers

SILENT MEDITATION is a ruthless way of peering into the labyrinth of consciousness. No garden to stare at, no chores to do, nothing but the simplicity of *quiet beingness*. Staying connected with each sensation, I observed the beauty of the moment—its bare simplicity and gentle softness.

By the fourth day, I'd finally found a comfortable posture. By taking off my shoes and turning them upside down underneath my feet, my knees could then be raised up and not pulled down so much when sitting in the chair.

The experience felt even more pleasant as I relished the added freedom of sitting in a regular chair with a back cushion. This allowed me to attend to my body's needs within the confines of the schedule. I also noticed that it didn't matter where I sat because the sound system was good at any point in the hall. But I started to feel shaky and needed to concentrate more inwardly.

I began to close my eyes to concentrate more and attune to the bells and sounds around me.

Concentration worked efficiently when I focused right away on feeling the breath at the abdomen, and stayed with it, like staying with a beloved child learning to ride a bike. All the way up and all the way down. This synchronization brought up a more open, albeit choppy, type of concentration as more details came into view—as if leaning a little less on the hand holding the bike seat, wobbling along precariously, but balancing with increasing speed. I noticed the pleasant sensations and a vibration gently running up my legs as the pressure and texture of the soles of my upturned shoes kept my posture upright and stable.

As people entered and sat down near me, I became aware of the waves of touch and the movement of the air. A perceptual shift opened to a peripheral knowing as people settled around me. Attention moved through them, passing by as if they were nothing in particular but waves of form. No irritation came from the effort to concentrate. This state seemed very much in line with Adya's instructions to "allow everything to be as it is."

In the deep silence, I was interested in the exact locations of sensations, and I felt the urge to notice more rapidly. I wasn't holding the bike seat for someone anymore—I was the one on the seat at cruising speed and switching through the gears as sensations were pleasant, unpleasant, or neutral without judging them as good or bad, just as they were appearing with mindfulness.

With that knowing, I was suddenly flying very fast, with every bodily sensation jettisoning through space. Faster than warp drive, but seated with the ecstatic sensation of speed and wind. Happiness enveloped me, and I remembered to remain grounded in stillness, taking in each tiny, momentary observation.

A beautifully crafted rug appeared abruptly underneath my knees. As I raced through space, it was impossible to notice the breath because all my attention moved with the acceleration of what I was seeing as just "seeing." I remembered that although this was an important opening, I had to be careful not to attach to it, to just be with and watch what was happening.

The mind moved very fast, and in less than a blink, I became an exploding star.

An inner brightness expanded and cascaded across the universe, causing cataclysmic changes in the cosmos that reverberated into other bursting and pulsating stars. I understood the reason for stars in the first place and their diverse qualities; the chemical elements that went into their existence and nonexistence brought forth more illumination. The natural attraction that each element had to each other, and the different processes of imploding, exploding, and fading away had a perfection that could not be understood in words.

Time was a distant concept. I could only notice people vaguely shifting around me as a new sit began. I didn't need to move, my focus was as intense as ever, so I remained still.

My head transformed into a massive elephant's head, complete with a thick trunk running down the front of my torso. It felt so real, I wanted to reach out and touch it to check. My hands wanted to move into different mudras or positions. I adjusted the tilt of my head slightly, staying focused.

The mind quickly moved onward, and I saw my head being cut off and rolling down some steps. And that was okay. I was okay. I couldn't count how many nightmares I'd had where I woke up sweating with similar visions, so I continued exploring. I felt sweat dripping down the sides of my body as the heat of the euphoria pulled me along.

The bell rang for the end of the sit. I thought about visiting the beach during the next meditation, and the next thing I knew, I was there! I felt the wind and the sand under my feet on the shore and the sun shining high in the sky. I recognized two people from the dining hall walking by. *I am on the beach! But also, not on the beach.* This I realized as an out-of-body experience, yet I was also aware of sitting. I decided to stay seated.

Incredible!

I knew I was experiencing something more powerful than before. I didn't want to move an inch. Adya was giving a gentle guided meditation. I heard him say, "I am encouraging you all…" I had to laugh inside, because I didn't need any further encouragement.

If the mind can be this powerful, it might be a fruitful time to uncover any shadow work that needed to be revealed. I thought that the cause of much of my stress was my beliefs, and since some of those beliefs were hidden, I wanted to uncover them.

With this intention, a vision appeared to me. I was suddenly in a boundless space with a sense of vast darkness. It was so huge that the word *space* itself couldn't begin to approximate the largeness of it. Then a light appeared, illuminating hundreds of tables that extended as far as the eye could see. A series of oak boxes, resembling old library card files, were arranged in rows on each table. I reached down to touch one, and inside I saw it was full of index cards.

As I walked along the great expanse, the space extended out farther like a computer program extending text on an infinite page. I reached for another box. It was also filled with index cards. Some of the boxes looked older, with worn edges, and some were newer. Each card had a belief written on it. Rummaging through every box, I looked and looked. When I finally turned around to take it all in, I understood that every time I needed a belief, one was there.

It would take countless lifetimes to sort through all of the boxes. Some of the beliefs changed as I read them. And I saw that each image or idea was also made up of these changing sensations slipping away. I felt stuck in a repetitive sequence, like looking for my misplaced glasses.

This has been happening forever.

From somewhere within, I sank to my knees, realizing that the only way out of all of this was to stop believing and *know*. I had a faint memory of what Dogen pointed to in the Zen teachings, "Beliefs are foolish." If there is clinging to beliefs then this battle goes on forever and ever. Beliefs are temporary and useful, but they are not the Truth.

This totally shattered ideas of *me*.

There was another sit beginning, and I was barely aware of time or my body, except for the sweat dripping down the sides of my torso every now and then. Astonished, I continued to stare at the illuminated tables.

The next thing I knew, I heard the bell for supper, and felt my energy gradually draining. I'd been still as a statue in the same posture for four hours without stiffness or pain. Some experiences like this had happened before at home, but not with such intense insight and power. At home, they felt more equanimous and relaxed.

I headed straight to the hall for supper. With each step, my feet felt as if they were going through the ground to the other side of the earth. Using mindfulness, just taking the next step forward, intending to pick up the fork, touching the fork, and touching the spoon, helped calm the inner shakiness.

Since I have celiac disease, I reminded the staff by pointing to a sticker on my name tag and the chef put two fresh gluten-free muffins on my plate! One blueberry and one cinnamon apple. Smiles appeared on my face and his as I moved forward, each moment a fresh moment, and with joy I made my way to sit and eat, one bite at a time, swallowing, tasting, and relishing feelings of fullness and gratitude.

I wanted to freshen up in my room after supper, but I sat down cautiously on my bed to reflect. Suddenly the time was spent, and the bell for the evening talk with Adya was already ringing *home*.

When he entered the hall, he said he was not going to do a Dharma talk, but would answer questions from those who were eager to ask. This made sense to me, since many people wanted to talk with him.

Did I have a question? I wasn't sure what I would ask. I kept my attention on the breath, which settled me down a bit. I listened to all the questions with a new understanding of how everything changes.

The top of the head felt scraped away, with tingling sensations under the top of the skull. I put my hand up to touch my head, and it was okay, but it was like my hand was not my hand. It felt as though my belly had been replaced with a wide-open portal into the universe.

As the night wore on, I wanted to talk to Adya, so finally, I raised my hand high, and he called me up. I thought of my children, my husband, my Twelve Step friends, the Christian contemplatives I prayed with, the Zen folks, and all the people I knew who were suffering. *I was asking for all of us.* With each step towards the stage, courage welled up, and a unified fellowship gently guided me.

The microphone was a strange contraption to put between two people discussing something so intimate. I tried to share with him how I had been searching for this kind of support for an eternity and never knew that my questions could be answered.

Adya had a way of tuning into me in the moment and simply hearing my need to know. I asked him about my experience of being on the beach during the sit, and he said it happens all the time. He validated that it was an out-of-body experience. He said, "How can we be confined to just a body?"

This rang true with me, and I laughed inwardly, thinking this kind of meditation experience could affect the travel industry tremendously. Then I had to stop a rush of memories of similar experiences as a child.

In the Twelve Step program, it seemed we were continually in recovery, working the steps. No one was fully awakened, at least as far
as I knew. More than any other question, I needed to know whether he
really felt a sense of being awake and knowing it fully.

What I interpreted him saying was that yes, it was doable. He
appeared satisfied and done with seeking, and that keeping an identity
of "being in recovery" could potentially become another way of holding on. I agreed. I needed to let go of that too.

I was worried about feeling like I had been scalped or that something had happened to my brain. He assured me that energetic shifts
happen and that these are just states of being. We all pass through various states. Since I flew over many states to get to California, that seemed
funny to me. I never heard someone talk about "states of being" before.

I moved on to discuss my question about beliefs with him. I had
been taught that Truth was a matter of belief. But then it would be
unreliable.

He reminded me that Truth can only be known deeply. If the lights
are on, you know it. You don't need to believe it.

I suddenly blurted, "I'm willing, willing to go to any length."

"Well, then, you can't be stopped." He paused and repeated, "You
cannot be stopped."

My head dropped. I realized then, that *there were no barriers.*

This insight magnified the need to reach out for more help to work
with the energies in the body. I asked him where to go for a longer
retreat since, "I was just getting warmed up."

"The real retreat is you," he said. "Being on retreat is nothing but a
state of mind that can be attended to anytime, anywhere."

We dialogued a little further, and I took in what he said with a
couple of sharp breaths, then returned to my seat.

When I exited the hall, François, my acquaintance from Canada,
bopped my hand with his fist and nodded with exuberance while a
sense of wonder arose in me. Truly, being present right now felt right.
And being able to meditate so continuously was supported in many
ways that I could not do at home.

Although, when I sat on the edge of my bed in my room that night,
I felt dissatisfied and disappointed. My intense experiences were only

yet another mystical experience. Life is what it is; each moment brings another set of sensations and experiences. The only way to put seeking to rest was to resolve it. I needed to practice more than ever before. Lingering on this experience was not going to help. While it was encouraging and led to some important insights—it was over.

~~~

I tossed and turned. Dreams of mirrors reflected past images of characters chasing me through hallways of blinding light. I also saw the ping-pong activity of my dualistic mind working away within a larger view of okayness. I sat up in bed, and returned to the gentle in-breath and out-breath, which helped me tolerate some of these unusual perceptions and vibrations.

When the retreat ended on the fifth day, everyone quickly departed. I went to the beach, feeling reluctant to leave the serenity of the ocean's embrace for the bustling city. I paced on the shore and sat, unaware of the time passing until it was pitch-black. I didn't want to drive, especially through unfamiliar territory, navigating alone on highways in the dark. This was before Google Maps. I only had a flip cell phone. And, more importantly, I felt pulled to continue investigating every single phenomenon that was arising. Every moment of contact with each footfall viscerally expanded my whole body with sensate awareness. I wanted more than anything to stay with the process.

But I needed to shift my attention to the process of driving and focus on steering along the highway. Before driving off, to bookend the event, I called Daniel Ingram and shared a little bit about my series of experiences at the retreat. He briefly stated that the intense opening was likely one of the typical stages one goes through on the path, a sign of strong practice, and that only time would reveal if it was abiding enlightenment because of the way things tend to progress. This was both reassuring and mystifying. Turning inward with integrity, I also assessed that I couldn't attribute the opening solely to Adya, but more to the seriousness with which I was practicing and the uninterrupted and supported space that allowed for that.

It was certainly more interesting and significantly more intense on a sensate level than any experiences I recalled. And, even though the top of my head was still buzzing with the vastness of space, it was not fully satisfying. *I knew that opening was not it.* The experiences were already fading memories, no more than the faint clash of ocean waves that crashed against the sandy shore in my rearview mirror. The moon's brilliant light, now engulfed in a haze of clouds, lent weight to this truth of impermanence as I made my way toward the airport in the dark of night.

Dive deep, O mind,
dive deep in the Ocean of God's Beauty;
If you descend to the uttermost depths,
There you will find the gem of Love...
Light up, O mind,
light up true wisdom's shining lamp,
And let it burn with steady flame
Unceasingly within your heart.[24]

---

24 Sri Ramakrishna, "Dive Deep, O Mind," in *The Gospel of Sri Ramakrishna*, trans. Swami Nikhilananda

CHAPTER NINETEEN

With Gratitude

I F THERE ARE NO BARRIERS, why not listen more? After my retreat in California, the kids told me how quiet I had become. I reminded them of things less often; instead, I encouraged them to examine the risks they were taking with schoolmates and their social lives. I was discovering how little truly needed to be said. I started to see how much I filled up my life with words that were spent on organization and orchestration. Orchestrating what? I wasn't even sure what I had been doing most of my life. I could only listen.

One day, I overheard Stewart exclaim, "What the heck?!" when he opened a box that came in the mail. I went to see why he said that, and saw him, eyebrows scrunched, gaping at the book, *I Am That: Talks with Sri Nisargadatta Maharaj*, which I had ordered because the library didn't have it.

Stewart's apprehension was evident in his gaze, his gray-green eyes evading mine as I tried to meet them.

"I know, right?!" I couldn't contain my enthusiasm.

His attention returned to the dishes he was washing, lips pressed into a thin line, head slightly bowed, revealing the grayed edges of his balding crown. How could I reassure him about a process pushing me forward that even I did not understand?

Nisargadatta's dialogues seemed interesting for about five minutes, but then the discussions in the book just annoyed me. I didn't want to read texts. I wanted to read my *self*. Silence was my new friend.

I worked in silence, drove in silence, sat in silence more and more at the Zen center and at home. If I couldn't sleep, I would sit through the night in silence.

The fever to go to any length with this process was paramount. I developed a careful balance between chores around the house, the needs of the kids, and work assignments. I couldn't even talk about it. Like an immigrant in a new country, everything was new—what I had felt, seen, heard, and said was gone. *Gone.* My head was on fire for the Dharma with every cell pulling toward *knowing directly here and now.*

How could I tell my friends what I had seen and how much my body vibrated day and night? My friend, Sara Jane, wanted to know about the retreat, so I tentatively shared with her that it was help-ful, and that the experience of the elephant trunk had come up. She smiled and said, "Not to worry. If you've gone crackers, I have just the thing!" while holding up a box of gluten-free crackers. Her enthusiasm for life affirmed my desire to playfully keep going. She also said that the sensation of feeling like an elephant sounded similar to Ganesha. At the time, I didn't know that he's a symbol popularly worshiped in Hinduism as a remover of obstacles.

There is nothing better than playfulness to offset fear, loneliness, and pain, so I hired a square-dancing teacher to come to our house for a hootenanny for my 50th birthday party. Having a caller shout out dance moves would simplify the social event for my husband and everyone.

Making preparations for the upcoming party pushed us all to apply extra effort to properly sort and dispose of construction materials. Even though we had no drywall up, our floor was bare underlayment, and we had no real kitchen to speak of, I went ahead. I figured if people used to have shindigs in barns, and since our house *looked* like a barn, why not?

The dance teacher showed up, and we rocked the house with a potluck and an old-fashioned, stomping country dance. I thought my old sponsor, Guy, was going to have a heart attack from having so much fun. We opened all the windows, and danced and sang. Allemande! Do Si Do! Roll Away to a Half Sashay!

As I looked around the room, a huge Love arose within me. When our guests asked me to speak, I felt like a ghost had entered my body and I wasn't there. It was like watching my own wake and feeling the privilege to enjoy it while still alive. I knew that the next few years were going to be tough. I was watching myself inwardly say, *Goodbye, I love you all. Thank you. I need to go on alone from here.* I do not remember what words tumbled out. Words could not express my heartfelt gratitude for all of their support.

From then on, I became more speechless, turning towards stress with more compassion at its root. Feeling my way into this rooted compassion lightened the inner pull of my mind as I leaned into the darkest and driest of deserts. A force drew me closer each day to an abyss of unknowing; I couldn't have stopped even if I had wanted to. Clearly, the way had been paved with kinship, and an unconditional movement toward knowing would arise in its own time. The fire for the Truth was my teacher. I signed up for another, longer Zen sesshin over Memorial Day weekend at the end of May 2008.

CHAPTER TWENTY

One True Desire

WHEN IT CAME TIME for my next sesshin, led by Steve Hagen, I asked him for clarification: "What is it that walks me in here? There is a desire to know Truth. If I didn't know that, and didn't feel willing to practice in line with that *one true desire*, then I would be an idiot coming in here. Right?"

He seemed a little taken aback by the earnestness of my question. After a pause, he affirmed that it was true. The Buddha had said it was okay to have one desire, and that desire was for the Truth.

There appeared to be a taboo against striving and exerting effort, so I was a bit irritated he didn't tell everyone that. Every Sunday we all chant to end all desires. That felt lopsided; why not chant about the one true desire we all carry within us? As soon as I heard that enlightenment was actually doable, that one desire blazed through me like a river of molten lava.

Devotion to mindfulness allowed me to accept fear more readily. With my years of recovery, there was less bleed-through or inappropriate behavior when a core belief of unworthiness came up. To practice skillfully and openly, I was compelled to recognize old patterns and *know* the pain with a sense of forgiveness, and try to replace unhealthy thoughts with feelings of goodwill for learning. At times, I also stopped and waited for an unhealthy desire to pass. Understanding and self-care were paramount. In spite of these challenges, I experienced long periods of peace after a sit, often extending for days.

At the Adyashanti retreat, I had tuned into a sense of privacy while sitting in the back among the hundreds of people gathered. As the upcoming Zen sesshin approached, where only a small group of us would be together all day long, I began to worry about difficult emotions surfacing. So, I asked Steve, "What if strong feelings come up for me?"

"We do not do that here," he said.

I inhaled, cautiously asking him, "Well, then, what *do* you do here?"

He stared back at me firmly, and with a tone of finality, stated, "We sit."

I didn't know what to say back. He seemed nonnegotiable. We all feel!

I realized that if my deep work were to come up in the zendo, if I started to cry, then so be it. If I didn't fit in, I'd find out. My intention to not cause harm allowed me to be open to learning. What is *is*, and that is *that*. The mind tries to control and monitor our external projections; it enslaves us when unaware. Done. I felt so done with that.

I spoke with Daniel briefly over the phone before my next sesshin, and he asked me, "Are you sure you are ready for all of this?"

"I am going to die," I said in an exasperated tone. "This needs to be resolved while I am alive now!"

He murmured deeply before saying, "I understand."

Being born as a human granted me an incredible opportunity to investigate my consciousness with compassion and find release from suffering. The Buddha recommends five subjects for frequent recollection throughout the day: first, that we humans age; second, that we can get ill; third, that we all will die; fourth, that we'll lose everything we love along the way; and lastly, that whatever we do, whether it is good or bad, we are responsible for the outcome.[25] Death won't bring the end of suffering.

Relationship stuff comes up when caring about other people. The environment at the Zen center often seemed stark. There was nothing to grab onto, which felt strange and also refreshing in some weird,

---

25   Ajahn Sona, *Life Is a Near Death Experience: Skills for Illness, Aging, Dying, and Loss.*

puzzling way. Even the teachers, Steve and Norm, appeared to struggle with knowing how to respond to questions. Being a spiritual teacher is the hardest type of occupation. It requires many skills and abilities. I knew they were only human, doing their best, but sometimes, I wished they would dispense with all the double-talk, relate to me as a human being, and speak in first-person like Adya.

It is painful to have doubts about the teacher when on the path. In the psychological model known as the Johari Window, we benefit from the observations that others make about us because there are things that others see about us that we do not see. However, in the realization of ultimate Truth, all must be seen by oneself. The inquiry arose: *In what ways does self-reliance help or hinder practice?* The fire for knowing Truth was my teacher.

At the beginning of each weekly class, the teacher asked us to hold questions until the end. But often, the time was up and the teacher ended class without discussion. One evening, I became so frustrated that I went upstairs to the zendo for half an hour to sit with irritating sensations. Reflections arose: If the Truth cannot be grasped with words, then it is in silence that it will be known. But, if the Truth is everything, then aren't words also an expression of Truth?

No. There was a call for gnosis, deep down in the body.

Later, I was reprimanded for using the zendo alone. It is only to be used when we are together. What is the middle way? The desire to break free from the isolation of aloneness was as strong as my wish to not impose burdens on relationships.

I recognized how my preferences had been impacted over the years because of the egalitarian environment of the Twelve Step recovery program, where everyone openly owned and shared their experiences. The realization that I had to stand in my own process more and more grew in my mind. We must face ourselves alone, and at times the path felt excruciatingly lonely. It seemed like in Zen they were basically saying, "Sit down and shut up." Okay. I did that. But I wrestled with it too. I decided that it was best to stay silent and continue to practice diligently.

We are alone, together.

Sometimes, Norm would drop the phrase, "You are Buddha."

Right, I thought. *Nice for you, but I do not know that!* Still, I paused, considered, and wondered, because I had a subtle sense just then that there was absolutely nothing wrong. It seemed all right to share in the practice with them because noticing what didn't sit right with me as an object for practice was like molding pure, soft gold into something usable. When I honestly and gently faced my fear, this transmutation happened at every sit.

The spring flowers brought up a more positive outlook for change and growth, but inside, I occasionally reeled into a despair that pulled me to a complete stop. At home, intense mood swings came and went. One night, as I walked downstairs and turned the corner, I held the banister with a thrill of joy for being alive. How to even categorize a feeling called fear when it sidles up with gladness to know the fear and then mixes with sadness or regret? There are never-ending mazes of interconnecting feelings. Just over a month had passed since I had come home from California, and already I eagerly began another, longer, silent sesshin at Dharma Field Zen Center.

At the beginning of the Zen sesshin, they put up fabric to cover the bookshelves and the bulletin board to prevent people from reading things. *Illusion of control*, I thought. Just as I saw the fabric over the books, I couldn't help but motion to the fabric and softly mention to Steve Hagen as he passed by me, "You have to let go."

He abruptly turned toward me and sighed, "But they don't," then walked on.

I was not talking about the practitioners. It was his decision to put up the fabric. Perhaps he was trying to help them keep it simple, but again, only they could do that for themselves. Maybe they could all benefit from working a Twelve Step program? The program continually repeated that I needed to let go. And if I did not let go, that affected the people around me. More importantly, I had to look at my own process, receive what was offered, and leave the rest. I needed to respect this tradition. I was not there to change them, but to wake up to Reality. First things first. Stay out of other people's stuff.

If pain emerged, I paid attention to its exact location in the body without letting thoughts roam about it. If a thought emerged, I'd gently notice "thinking" and then return to breath sensations as they arose in the body. I didn't rely on a technique, merely acknowledged its presence and paid attention because it was *there*. Keep It Simple.

We walked, sat, and ate in community.

Practice. Pain. Pleasure. Whatever. Know it.

On the second day, while I chewed and swallowed the peanuts from my little bowl along with everyone else chewing and swallowing, a wave of tenderness washed over me. As I surveyed our group, I felt the sweetest love for everything and everyone present—the cool floor, the walls, the space—everything zen. Out of the blue, they-we all looked sweet and innocent. I wanted to go around and kiss each person on the top of their head. *We are Buddha!*

Every day, I-we sat and walked in total silence from 5 a.m. until 9 p.m. My spot was right underneath an open western window where a lilac bush blew fresh blooming kisses. With each passing day, the smell grew stronger. I could sense its green shoots unfurling toward the sunlight. The constant aroma wafting through the open window tickled areas in my head and sinuses. Continuously returning to the breath at the abdomen brought tingling in my legs and feet and in the area behind my navel and groin. With each flow of the breath, I continued making a conscious effort to feel and recognize each irritating sensation that came into awareness as it happened, and I felt-knew every sensation passing away, to the best of my ability.

What came next caught me completely by surprise. While I sat perfectly still in the zendo, gently listening to Steve begin his Dharma talk, the most intense ecstasy of sexual union I had ever experienced arose. Invisible hands softly slid up my body and entered me. My body sat motionless while everything expressed love with one another. The flowers, all the men and women there, the air itself danced within *me and within each other*. We were making love fluidly and brilliantly, naturally holding and being held.

I quickly assessed that another "arising and passing away" experience was beginning. I wasn't going crazy. I could see that in a highly concentrated state, there was an inner dedication to be with the process; to look at any clinging within my body and breath, even if the breath was no longer the primary focus of attention. Fire shot outward from the front and back of my hips and stirred me into my kneeling Burmese posture on two stacked zafus. I closed my eyes, using my best effort to notice any subtle clinging to pleasant or unpleasant sensations in this process. The breath was low and barely perceptible; my posture was upright, and the body arena felt steady with light effort. The edges of the body became porous. Investigating any leaning in or pulling away from the experience was interspersed with interest in what was happening. Maybe that is what Steve meant?! *We sit.*

Then, another vision arose. I saw and felt a man, Siddhartha, having sweet intercourse with *me*. After that, with some surprise, as I looked at his erect penis, he detached it and handed it to me. That seemed perfectly fine as I took it from his delicate fingers and watched it grow out of *my* body while breasts and a woman's form morphed into *him*. The penis on *me* dropped away, and we became a golden sun that became a brilliant flower and the flower melted into the sky and the earth. The moon became a vagina and transformed into a full moon vagina that engulfed the sky. There was no focal point you could call *me*, only this raw perspective from this pulsating center above my groin climbing up the spine, arousing beautiful forms, some ugly and repellent forms, yet all interesting and new. An emaciated human corpse appeared, which brought a sense of connection with the trees, the soil, the bugs, and the animals. Awareness of being devoured while also consuming orally and through the pores arose and passed. This amazing constant coupling massaged every cell, infiltrating this natural aspect of human existence. It was like watching a wonderful dream. It's impossible to describe how much ensued and how little I was aware of time passing as I kept a gentle focus on the breath and watched this dream arise and pass away.

As this unforgettable experience began to dissolve, I lifted one eyebrow to glance around at others shifting uncomfortably from side to side, struggling to find any relief, painfully enduring the discourse, and thinking hard about every word Steve was saying while I was totally blissed out. There was no pain or outward movement; a perfectly still, naked intimacy—which, without question, rivaled a physical orgasm—for universal love with all. While I hadn't had any sexual openings at previous retreats, I knew I wasn't going crazy. I remained grounded because of the steadiness of my concentration.

Steve ended his talk by sharing that the Buddha had said it was okay to have one true desire—the desire to know the Truth.

One of the young students immediately shot his hand up, urgently asking, "What did you just say?! I thought we had to let go of all desires?!"

Steve replied, "No. You can keep one, and that is okay. It is the desire to know the Truth."

I felt my lips press into a tiny smile. He had listened to me after all. That one true desire helped anchor me into a controlled descent from the height of ecstasy, relaxed and supported by gently landing back to breath awareness as we bowed and stood together.

When the sesshin ended, as I put on my coat, one of the more seasoned practitioners, who also seemed to be finding more stability in his practice, whispered, "Your concentration appears more still." I nodded back and, in a soft tone, shared, "Things seem to be picking up and moving along."

He nodded assuredly, and while reaching for his coat, he softly suggested, "It would be good to research places to go." His influence touched me as a gift. I felt honored to momentarily connect with his sincere encouragement. I nodded back, receiving confirmation while I contemplated seeking assistance for the fire cooking inside me.

Another man remarked to me on our way out the door, "Tell me how you can sit for over two hours and not move an inch during the long Dharma talks, when only a few months ago you could not get settled?!" I stood on the sidewalk in front of the center wanting to tell him that when the schedule said "break time," I continued to feel into the body, and with every predominant sensation that came into awareness, I felt-watched it arise and pass away, and that somehow this continuity between sits brought up an ease for whatever arose.

But before I could say any of this, he had already slid into the driver's seat of his car. I watched him drive away, noticing that instead of feeling my bare feet on the smooth floor of the zendo, I felt the texture and pressure from the movement of my feet inside my shoes pressing on the rough pavement as each step took me home.

After the Zen sesshin, I reviewed a book about energy systems in the body and realized that my second chakra had experienced a crucial opening. The second chakra, a vital sexual and creative center in the body, is above the first chakra, about three fingers below the belly button. A continuous, pleasant smell can trigger openings, which might be why many Buddhist centers keep the use of incense to a minimum. Some people are also allergic to many fragrances that are in soaps, which is why participants are requested to use scent-free items. I threw out my perfumes and scented products decades ago, although I use a few drops of essential oils occasionally for health.

Scent can be distracting as it connects deeply in the brain and can sometimes arouse the sexual center. If one got caught up in an experience like this and didn't practice mindfully, the raw intensity could send someone straight to substance abuse, sex, or running from the temple down the mountain and into a cold shower. Much later, I heard about monks who, after taking their vows, would have a similar opening, then pack it in, disrobe, and leave the temple.

Many ideas get embedded into our psyches from our respective cultures. This energetic experience reinforced my own grounding in gender fluidity; it eroded some marginal suffering around the way I held my identity as a woman. Our bodies come with certain genitalia and preferences, but we do not need to be defined by them. Our relative ideas as interacting forms are limited when we identify purely as individuals. We are all inseparably connected in the vast universe.

Even though my sexual desire had already been diminished by giving birth twice and enduring two miscarriages, this experience attenuated it with wisdom. It left a lasting impression that revealed all these energies as not me nor mine. Knowing that our bodies are both beautiful forms to behold, as well as corpses that will soon decay, helped me see that while this body is precious, it is also not worth holding onto. It did not feel like an achievement but a deeper letting go of sensual perceptions and ideas.

My one true desire to know *that* which is not bound by any sense of experience felt closer than ever in my heart, and I knew... *This was not it!*

Chapter Twenty-One

Tending to Family

ONE OF MY home-away-from-home places that I visited once a month for a break from the house and kids was a local Thai restaurant that served a fantastic gluten-free lunch special. The waiter, Kyle, knew me by first name.

"Hi, Kyle," I would say, as I made my way to an open table.

"The usual?"

"Yes, but today, can you please keep the hot jasmine tea coming, okay?"

"Sure thing."

It felt luxurious to sit in the large front window, allow sunshine onto my lap, and eat a delicious brunch that filled me up for the entire day. First came the salad rolls, then the delicate mixture of steamed vegetables and rice noodles sautéed in a peanuty-salty-spicy-sweet sauce that only they could perfect. Oh. So. Good. And, hot jasmine tea, all for $11. Yum!

It was potentially a day for flan dessert as well.

I had so much on my mind, I could let it drift and roll around. How could I manage a longer retreat with the kids' schedules and the house reconstruction at this point in my practice? I really wanted to apply these new tools in a focused way for many dedicated days. A retreat allowed me to relinquish the role of parent and just be with myself. Returning home after retreat presented a stark contrast to retreat life where everything is in order, quiet cooperation imbues the space, and there is no need to cook or do anything other than bodily self-care, sitting, and walking peacefully.

There was a table nearby with five amiable guys in their thirties or forties chatting in a boisterous manner. They were served after me. I could overhear them talking about other men and relationships, clueing me in that they were gay. After I paid my bill and tipped Kyle, I spontaneously reached out to the guys at the table.

"Do you mind? I don't mean to intrude, but I just wanted to ask you something."

They stopped, and with a generous look gave me their attention.

"Are you guys gay?" I asked.

"Honey, you got that right!" one of them exclaimed, and they all laughed. "What's the matter?"

"Well, I think my son is gay, and I don't know how to help him meet other gay guys."

"What?!" They all exchanged surprised glances.

"How do you know he is gay?" One man inquired.

"He says he is bisexual, but I think he'd be happy with a man."

Another man chimed in, "The mothers always know."

They all nodded in agreement.

"Dear, do you know I was kicked out of my house at sixteen and my family will still not even talk to me?" another man shared.

A nod came from another, who added, "My family won't accept me."

"Wow, oh no." I sighed. "I just want him to feel happy and supported. But it seems so hard for young gay men to find one another in a supportive way."

"How old is he?"

"He just turned eighteen."

"He's already going to be great with a mother like you."

One man who hadn't spoken, asked me seriously, "How does his dad take it?"

"He said it makes no difference to him, so no worries there."

"Well, then, you are a goddess, and there is nothing to worry about—with your support, he will find his own way! You can trust him."

Kyle came by with another cup of hot jasmine tea and gently touched my shoulder, inviting me to the empty seat at the table with the guys.

We talked more about life and love. They shared ideas about how people meet now on the Internet, ways I had never considered before. I didn't even know much about social media platforms. I asked them how they met, and they said at bars, through work, or with a friend of a friend, and they all added that their families were not supportive or welcoming toward them.

They all wanted to give me a hug when I left. Wow! That made me feel great, but it also made me sad on the way home in the car as I reflected on all of the stupid estrangement in the world, especially among heterosexual men. Seldom are there opportunities to come together and be open about feelings, vulnerability, and challenges. All of this swirled in my heart with my wish for happiness for the three men in my life, each one unique in their own way.

This conversation was so helpful and exactly what I needed to help me let go. It gave me some latitude to discuss sexuality more openly with both of my sons. I didn't know where I fit on the spectrum of sexuality anymore either. Basically, it all seemed so much a part of finding loving, healthy relationships and friends who support you the way you are.

~~~

During this time, in raising teenagers, the gap between my own mindfulness practice and theirs created some challenges for us all. I talked more about taking better care of things, adding things to the grocery list, putting things back, folding laundry, tidying up after oneself, putting the recycling out front, and doing homework. They did more dishes, but their rinsing was not that great. I decided that the taste of soap on the dishes they washed was at least an improvement. They were growing and changing, but definitely not ready to fly off yet.

Sometimes, Preston would finish his homework, but not hand it in. How did he manage that?! He was only weeks from his high school graduation and in danger of not graduating due to one missing assignment. During the teacher conference, my body went into rhythm, and I started to sing a 1977 Paul Simon song about things that slip away. I asked his teacher to join me if he knew the lyrics. He pulled out his guitar. We both serenaded sweet, wonderful, creative Preston while he sat, bent over, head in his hands, cringing with pressed lips while the smoke of denial evaporated off him.

When we opened the door to see the faces of the other parents waiting, they appeared wryly amused, proving that I was not alone. The song said it all, but I had to insist, "What do you want? Do you want to graduate with your peers or what? Just because I am sitting in silence more does not mean that your goals need to slide. I am not the pusher for your life. Initiative needs to come from a deep well within, or a Higher Power, however you want to see it." He immediately made up the work and sheepishly handed it in. Parents are a large part of what encourages children. We do so much. We need to let go, too.

The teenage years are difficult for everyone. With my sons having immediate access to the Internet, I worried they were taking in more information than they could process. On certain occasions, in an effort to get them to stop and go to bed at night, I would actually crawl beneath their desks, unplug the computer's electric cord, and install a little luggage lock through the hole on the end that connects to the wall socket. Their glazed eyes stared at me as they jolted awkwardly and lumbered into bed.

Taking care of some things seemed like a struggle for them, but I had to relinquish some control. The results were not always reassuring. I often came home to a scattered mess on the floor, dirty dishes, piles of laundry, phone messages not properly written down, and the dog's mess in the yard. Softening my supervision helped them to at least trip over these things and see them more. When my younger son complained about how much dog poop sat drying out on the lawn, I felt we were getting somewhere. I informed him, "Picking up poop is your job now."

Stewart often retreated to our woodshop to take care of projects, leaving parenting entirely to me. He exhibited little concern for the kids, except when asked to help, but he generally showed up for supper or a science fiction show that interested him.

For decades I contemplated the Kahlil Gibran poem, "On Children," and painted it all over an old chair, often singing along in the true spirit of Sweet Honey in the Rock's rendition:

Your children are not your children.
They are the sons and daughters of Life's longing for itself.
They come through you but not from you,
And though they are with you yet they belong not to you.[26]

Overall, my kids did fairly well, partly because they were not into smoking, drugs, or alcohol. They occasionally walked, sat, or listened to Dharma talks with me. They got themselves up for school, had some interests outside of school, and got deeply involved in creative projects that enlivened them.

Their appetites amazed me when, after finishing a large takeout pizza in the car on the way home, they'd enter the house and shout out, "Now, what's for supper?" With their youthful metabolisms, they could always eat more and not put on weight. Planning another meal and making it for them was a big deal to take care of daily. Fortunately, they were making more things for themselves, even if it was mostly frozen pizzas.

As a carpenter, I assessed whether construction was good, better, or best. I used dumpster scraps of wood to set up backers for the edges of the drywall we'd eventually hang. I also decided to reinforce our floor trusses with a scissor-style design, girding the trusses one-third of the way and two-thirds of the way across all of them to reduce bounce and make the floor stiffer. In doing that, I spaced the wood pieces out appropriately, taking the plumbing and wiring into consideration. I also had to reset some wires to finish it. Our building inspector said it was better and that most folks don't do it. I also reinforced our three sliding door frames with plywood to make them the best frames they could be. They can end up being a pain if they are not set correctly. And I screwed in backers where I knew pictures would be hung. The majority of the time, we finished things better than they were before, and always strived for "best." Each task I completed helped me fall fast asleep at the end of the day.

Having just finished some major work upstairs, Stewart and the boys were able to move out of the garage and into the upper part of the

---

26   Kahlil Gibran, "On Children," in *The Prophet.*

house, while I kept my office in the garage for a bit longer. Stewart and I taught the boys how to attach ends to LAN cables and phone wires and install plates on finished outlets. I fixed desks for them that I had gleaned off neighborhood boulevards to set up computer workspaces for them. All of the trim work was going to wait for many more years, along with the kitchen.

The house slowly became habitable. The first floor of the house was gutted, but the second floor was mostly finished, so I could finally give the boys their own rooms for the first time in their lives. I added lamps and shelves to get them organized. They were happy to arrange their own spaces and set up their beds and closets.

The boys rode their bicycles around the neighborhood, putting up fliers I helped create for their "Two Brothers Yard Support" business. In a short time, they were receiving calls for odd jobs. The faster pace at which the kids skidded around felt a bit overwhelming at times after everything had been so simple for me on retreat. They often interrupted me to ask for guidance on how to negotiate with their clients. Tools and yard bags had to be provided by the customers; they were to show up and provide muscle, and as long as they continued scheduling and finding jobs, it worked out well for them.

Adjusting back into daily tasks and roles took me several weeks. There was an energy moving through me like the force of a diamond blade cutting through granite rock. Standing, sitting, walking, touching, writing lists, planning, organizing, managing one task at a time with breath awareness, transforming functions into peaceful, trusting moments. *It is what it is.*

The days passed into weeks as I continued to return to the zendo to practice synchronizing the mind and body in a more relaxed way. Many details had to be considered in preparation for my absence, so my commitment to a retreat started many weeks beforehand and continued afterward. The idea of retreat started to blur.

The retreat is right now.

CHAPTER TWENTY-TWO

Progress, Not Perfection

W HEN SITTING STILL and letting honesty work in and through me, I'd contemplate, *How can I feel so close and still not know?* An integral need to go further pressed into the core of my being and persisted in the periphery of my consciousness.

For decades, I went on retreats, sat alone in hermitages, and went solo camping. These were relaxing and spacious to some degree, but I wasn't reading novels or sunbathing; I was seriously contemplating prayer with breath awareness and looking into the fundamental nature of Reality. Deep openings kept happening, so why didn't I come home feeling refreshed and ready to get back into daily routines?

After these deeply expanded states, I instead came home feeling somewhat miserable and depressed, struggling to pick myself up and get back into rhythm with my family. I felt desperately inquisitive about what Daniel had said to me after the retreat in California, that there was "a way things tend to progress." This called for more investigation.

The instructions in Mahāsi's *Practical Vipassana Exercises* had been helpful, so I returned to his work and discovered *The Progress of Insight: A Treatise on Satipaṭṭhāna Meditation.*[27] As I made my way through the fifty-page book, my reflexes twitched with interest, just as they did when I revisited the Satipaṭṭhāna Sutta. Unlike the Zen

---

27 Venerable Mahāsi Sayadaw, *The Progress of Insight*, trans. Nyanaponika Thera.

center where I had been meditating, these teachings come from the oldest existing school of Buddhism, called Theravāda, which means "School of the Elders." The book lays out a series of Knowledges that practitioners encounter in succession when engaged in continuous intensive meditation. Mahāsi's teachings, grounded in the earliest Buddhist texts known as the Pāli Canon, answered many of my burning questions and revealed what was happening in my practice.

It takes time and a supportive environment to be able to gently calm the mind from the regular everyday way of thinking into deep concentrated meditation. But even in daily life, there was an inquiry happening, like when my son was in intensive care, not understanding a communication with my husband, or simply putting apples in the shopping cart at the store. I wouldn't just lightly ask a question; I would deeply bow to it.

As a stay-at-home mom, in an isolated situation, it's like I was practically on retreat for years when I was home alone for long periods of quiet. Then, as the kids came home from school, or a contractor showed up unexpectedly, there would be something to bring me back to the everyday tasks.

Periods of prolonged meditation on retreat provided a deeper profundity to the insights, which proved to me that I was centering appropriately as I moved through stages that clearly aligned with what Mahāsi outlined. So, while I began looking for the next retreat, I also started to find methods to work with these stages given the idiosyncratic ways my being is affected by the Progress of Insight.

The foundation for this practice is always first rooted in the purification of conduct through the precepts so that the mind can become tranquil, unfettered by harmful deeds. Starting with a beginner's mind, I followed the practical instructions of noticing the rising and falling of the abdomen, noticing/feeling what the predominant object of awareness was in the moment at the six sense doors. If I were on retreat, this practice would be continuous from the moment I awoke in the morning until the moment I fell asleep at night; while eating, while defecating, while drinking, while urinating—in all movements.

By this point in my practice, following these instructions was becoming easier. Stray thoughts arose and were immediately noticed. After several days of this, I could sometimes sense the noticing happening through the night. This deepening of concentration is what Mahāsi calls The Purification of Mind, allowing for the Progress of Insight to unfold. I found it helpful to visualize this process as a donut or rotating wheel.

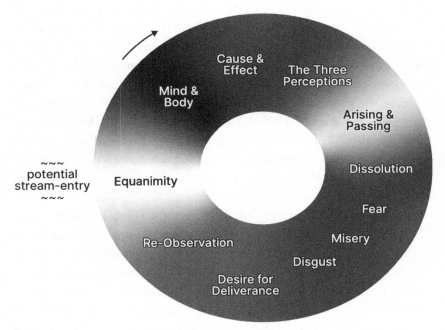

Progress of Insight Before Awakening

This process was truly delightful and very interesting. Standing at the sink and feeling a breath might seem boring to some, but to me, it was incredibly cool! Urinating, once a simple task to hurry through, now felt incredibly alive and relieving. What a gift of the moment! Gratitude swelled for this practice. It was good that I had delegated chores and organized as much as possible so that I could focus inwardly. How I moved in any direction, listening to the inner process and turning toward that felt more important.

Once I had developed strong concentration with the breath and the senses, I began to see thoughts and mental sensations arising and vanishing as observable objects, rather than merging with them. Being able to see thoughts and mental sensations from this detached perspective is what is known as Knowledge of Mind & Body. This involves recognizing the material process, such as the rising of the abdomen, and the mental process that observes it, nothing else. This refers to The Purification of View, because the "me" and "I" have taken a step back to allow for an objective analysis of what is happening.

Behind every action is an intention. First, there is the intention to scratch an itch, lift the hand, touch the nose, etc. I could see how the posture, leaning forward or back, was giving me feedback on what was going on in the mind. Staying with the flow ushered a shift into noticing the process of cause and effect happening in every moment within the mind and body, which is why this is called Knowledge of Conditionality. From the position that sees material and mental processes as not being me or mine, this Knowledge is so categorical as to eliminate doubt that what I am is anything other than a conditioned mind/body process continuously unfolding.

Every sensation has an initial phase of arising, a middle phase when it is present, and a final phase when passing. I would feel a mosquito land on my hand, notice the intention not to interfere, notice the tingling sting as it arose, and after it left, feel the pain slowly fade, etc. Each noticing would come with exquisite detail. Mahāsi called this Knowledge of Comprehension, and points to the Buddha's teaching that all phenomena are marked by three characteristics: they are impermanent, they produce stress, and they are not-self.[28] In the context of deep continuous practice, these are the three perceptions. Comprehending impermanence means understanding that what arises will not last. Comprehending stress means understanding the pain that comes from the noticing mind's clinging to what has arisen. Comprehending not-self means understanding that what is arising and passing here is not separate from everything else. This phase often felt tougher, with some sweating and shakiness. Occasionally, there was some ambivalence about staying with the practice. More precision in concentration smoothed out the sense of self being shaken up in the mind/body.

---

28 Ṭhānissaro Bhikkhu, "The Three Characteristics," in *The Buddha's Teachings: An Introduction.*

The next thing to happen is the Knowledge of Arising and Passing, which I abbreviate in this book as "a&p." My experiences of the a&p were powerful, sensate, and spiritual. After all this time, it was heartening to learn that these mystical experiences I had been having were indeed part of the path. At times, this involved fantastic images and sensations, almost as though inner expressions were letting off insightful fireworks, as had been the case during the sesshin with the blooming flowers or on Adya's retreat. Or, it could be a quiet moment, like when I put my hand on the door and knew the forest it had come from. I had to be careful not to get lost in the a&p lest I fall prey to the ten corruptions of insight.[29] Seeing that the wonderful sensations, insights, and other events are not to be clung to is a way to stay clear. Crossing the a&p is an important juncture, and reaching it more quickly than my previous cycle proved the need for rigorous sensate awareness, which felt very encouraging. The only way forward would be to continue noticing the rising and falling of the abdomen and the formations at the six sense doors.

The a&p is about the arising, creative, coming-forth of formations. As an a&p slowly faded, I'd usually be exhausted and need to rest. The mind was incredibly affected and wanted to cling to the experience, but try as I might, it was passing away. Then endings became more predominant. Like the final phase of the in-breath, or the final phase of the out-breath, a sense of dissolving and fragmentation was more apparent, which Mahāsi aptly named Knowledge of Dissolution.

Before I discovered the Progress of Insight, I didn't understand why I felt so tired when I was well-rested and had been taking good care of myself. It seemed like sometimes I was slipping away and believed my practice might be flawed. Finally, I knew this was part of the process and could focus on developing deeper concentration to move through the difficult sensations with more ease.

With so many endings being felt within, it seemed like there was a sense of self that got terrified of its final demise. Trembling and scary

---

29   Ajaan Lee Dhammadharo, "III. The Foul: Tranquility Meditation," essay, in *Basic Themes: Four Treatises on Buddhist Practice*, trans. Ṭhānissaro Bhikkhu.

images often arose, creating reactive feelings of shock and worry, which led to difficulty sleeping and sitting still. The concentration process was revealing the Knowledge of Fear. While fear helps us survive, fear is also a great teacher; it must be known intimately for release. Now that I knew this was normal, I could stay with the sensations and meditate through these states like riding a roller coaster. I do not like roller coasters, but this was the time to accept with compassion that I was on one whether I liked it or not.

Next would come Knowledge of Misery. Fear is incredibly draining, so I'd become tired and fatigued. In misery, everything would seem horrible and impossible. Longings to connect with others and to avoid this loneliness came up. This is because I value connection and feel supported by sangha. It's a natural part of my being and long-time practice to check in with others when things get tough. The comforting presence of another helped me through this phase. Restlessness predominated with the mind's commentary of self-pity and doubt. I would need to take care of the body and practice compassion for myself as the sensate field of awareness processed this insight.

When I'd look directly at the misery and feel no satisfaction, a shift into Knowledge of Disgust happened. Even with all the bubbling sensations of disgust in the torso, it can be interesting and helpful to see the stories that flow through the mind on their own. This state would also bring up some negativity, so simple acts like holding the door open for someone or offering a napkin would help me through this phase. By practicing kindness and being generous with others in the midst of this insight, I could turn to our shared humanity and the stress we all carry.

When thoroughly finished with disgust, the Knowledge of Desire for Deliverance would arise. For most of my life, my spiritual practice had strong devotional aspects. So at this phase, I would often be pulled into prostrations, kneeling on the floor and touching my forehead to the ground while lifting up the Dhamma in my mind and heart. If there was no space, I'd prostrate in my mind. I felt that this process had its own process, and that "my" will was being eroded on a fundamental level. There was a deep desire to go beyond any conventional viewpoint and open to Truth.

Having come this far along the Progress of Insight, continuously attending to the movement of the abdomen and the predominant arising and passing of sensations at each sense door, the endless proliferation of the mind became extremely irritating. Fear, misery, disgust, and desire for deliverance had taken a toll. The mind was operating at a high speed but required great skill to settle down or see anything in a clear way. I recognized this entry into Knowledge of Re-observation because of the restlessness coursing through the system, which seemed almost impossible to tolerate; perhaps *this* will offer an escape from formations, or perhaps *that*. My body/mind shook like a rock in a tin can, making it difficult to discern arisings and passings. My ears hissed loudly with so much noise from many senses of self, each clamoring for attention, including the sense of self that was seeking relief. An agonizing feeling of inner division brought up a heaviness in solitude, along with some waves of despair. Everything had to be given up, even despair! I could understand how many practitioners at this stage might pack up their suitcase, write a note, and leave the retreat.

It would be the worst of the worst for me, which is why I needed to rely on gentle and patient practices that had worked and listen carefully to any softening ideas to stay with it. Taking a shower and running water at the base of my neck often helped. Some gentle stretching or walking meditation was key in this phase. Opening to a larger view shifted attention to the periphery, such as seeing the sky or going to a place to take in the panorama, offering space for this raw re-observation to run its course. To maintain concentration, I needed very disciplined self-care.

Eventually, through rigorous and disciplined practice, my heart opened. This is why I prefer to call the second of the three perceptions "compassion for stress," because the heart can accept it all and work with it. In the heart's surrender came more patience for the process, and a shift arose into Knowledge of Equanimity. Sometimes, during this shift, I was reminded of the Buddha when he touched the earth on the night of his awakening. In that remembrance, I connected with the earth element to feel grounded. I recalled similar qualities of inner peace despite all the conditions around me. Usually, when these patient and kind qualities arose, I found myself able to function extremely well; difficult decisions happened with intuitive ease. But, this was a much deeper and more sublime sense of nonattachment and peace. Feeling into the low, medium, and high intensities of equanimity usefully informed my process.

All of these insights are impermanent and will fade, but if I was not aware, balanced, and focused, then I would have to start again from the beginning with mind and body and would miss the entrance for stream-entry I was seeking. I needed to pay careful attention to the state of equanimity. Knowing the subtle aspects of equanimity helped me let go of attaching to it.

The three perceptions appear like buckets of clear water for each formation that arises to dissolve into. It is through this insight that consciousness, as Mahāsi writes, "leaps forth into Nibbāna," which is a state that is void of all formations or conditioned phenomena. At this level of purification, the mind/body is processing at the highest ultimate capacity where several insights follow in quick succession. This is when concentration is of the utmost importance, unencumbered by outside distractions.

At first, consciousness will notice that unending stream of formations until there is a fruition, an apparent momentary blip in awareness, when consciousness evaporates completely. Wow! There are additional stages that Mahāsi describes in the book, the most significant of which are what he calls the "threefold knowledge of maturity, path, and fruition." This is followed by a period of review as this insight is absorbed on a profound level.

Mahāsi explains that the knowledge present after a fruition has "the nature of the knowledge of arising and passing away." So, returning to the practice after awakening, the intensive meditator can cycle through the Progress of Insight again with the a&p. It appeared that when one resolves to go on to a higher path, one goes back to the beginning at mind and body, but with skillfulness in meditation, the states and stages shift more quickly. The stages and insights also depend on continuous ongoing concentration. Using purification and concentration helps to let go of the self. I recalled how Adya likened it to how a rocket ship needs enough power to launch into space in order to get beyond the earth's gravitational field. I needed more dedicated energy to go deeper into the mind/body.

~~~

Unearthing this map or path of progressive insight was like finding a hidden compass. I'd been in recovery for a long time, accepting
difficult states in many ways, but the cycles kept returning, making me
feel eternally lost in the country on a cloudy day, not knowing which
way pointed north. For decades, I had practiced with contemplative
prayer using the "via negativa" process as taught to me by some
Franciscan nuns—"not me, not mine, not yours." I'd reviewed St.
Theresa of Avila's seven mansions and St. John of the Cross's Ladder
of Love. However, Mahāsi's map laid out terms I could easily relate
to because I had used the same words to describe my states during
and after retreats. Even if perhaps this was privileged information for
monastics, it brought up an ardent and wholehearted focus for going
the distance. I envisioned the countless nuns, monks, and lay practitioners who had walked on our earth and gone this way. I felt united in
sangha with them and with those practicing around the globe for inner
peace and clarity, giving me the courage to keep going.

And there is plenty to keep one going. In the Pāli Canon, the
Buddha refers to four major types of noble persons who have achieved
increasing degrees of liberation through the release of hindrances; the
first is a sotāpanna, or stream-enterer.[30] What did this mean for me?
Why enter the rapid and flooding stream? This metaphor was difficult.
But I saw that he was pointing to a willingness to face our delusions and
suffering at the deepest level in order to find release. How am I to know
that I am stuck in a cycle of suffering if I do not look into and feel the
pain of that stuckness?

The Buddha described the stream in this way:

"'The great expanse of water': a designation for the four floods:
the flood of sensuality, the flood of existence, the flood of views,
and the flood of ignorance. 'The near shore, which is dangerous
and fearful': this is a designation for [self] identity. 'The further

---

30 Ṭhānissaro Bhikkhu, *Into the Stream: A Study Guide on the First Stage
of Awakening.*

shore, which is safe and free from danger': this is a designation
for Nibbāna. 'The raft': this is a designation for the Noble
Eightfold Path..."[31]

Abandoning self-identity intrigued me. Cultivating my practice of
honoring the Noble Eightfold Path is likened to the raft that carries one
across the stream. I wanted to let go of any fixed views and experience
the agility and flexibility to respond to life with more skillfulness. The
self-identities of being an addict or codependent, counselor, teacher,
mother, daughter, sister, neighbor, artisan, woodworker, web designer,
etc., are to be abandoned so that each moment is met with Suchness.
To see how I hung onto these ideas in my mind and body was a form of
right effort and mindfulness.

The Buddha continues:

'Making effort with hands and feet': this is a designation for
the arousing of energy. 'Crossed over, gone beyond, the [noble
person] stands on high ground': this is a designation for the
arahant.

Discovering that there was a final realization, a further shore, an even
more profound knowing—crossing over, going beyond—seemed quite
incredible at this point. Human consciousness is capable of much more
than I had ever thought possible! Each of the stages has to do with
more subtle forms of clinging, which I have illustrated as an upward
spiral toward complete and total liberation.

These stages of liberation are often described in a yang way as
"attainments;" however, a yin way would be to say that one "receives"
this profound knowing. Either way, an enlightened being does not stop
knowing fear, pain, misery; rather, one develops a quicker and more
compassionate intimacy with Reality. With each pass through these
stages, one can develop more skill and wisdom in a state of review that
rubs away the hindrances that cause stress.

31　Saṁyutta Nikāya, 35.238, "Āsīvisopamasutta: The Simile of the Vipers,"
translated from the Pāli by Bhikkhu Bodhi.

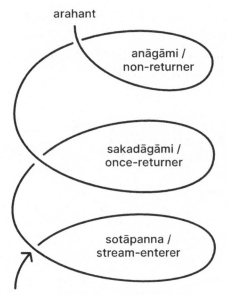

arahant

anāgāmi /
non-returner

sakadāgāmi /
once-returner

sotāpanna /
stream-enterer

Four Stages of Liberation

High levels of concentration were required to make progress in insight. In the Pāli Canon of the Theravāda tradition, there are varying levels of concentrated states of absorption called jhānas.[32] It is clearly stated in the suttas that the level of investigation for insight, especially in the fourth jhāna of equanimity, aids the opportunity for stream-entry—the release I was seeking. This is a profound shift in consciousness.

Given the abundance of teachings on the jhānas by the Buddha in the similes preserved in the suttas, the Vimuttimagga, and the Visuddhimagga, I'm only lightly touching upon this intricate subject. *The Jhanas in Theravada Buddhist Meditation* by Henepola Gunaratana was a great introductory resource.

These states are very difficult to describe because they are enhanced states of being. Extensive study for a beginning meditator can bring up overwhelm and/or paralysis in analysis, and I want to encourage actual practice. It is only through intensive meditation

---

32 Aṅguttara Nikāya, 5:28, "*Samādhaṅga Sutta: The Factors of Concentration*," translated from the Pāli by Ṭhānissaro Bhikkhu.

practice that I've been able to know these states. These beautiful states inscribe a deeply felt knowing into the mind/body that radiates peace and joy. With that in mind, below is my own oversimplified illustration of how I personally name the jhānas of form.

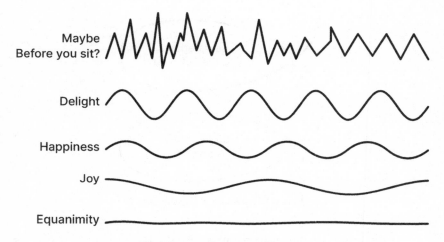

The Four Jhānas of Form

Finally, I could put a name to the sublime supportive energy I felt during a sit. I thought of it like riding a bike. I pedaled with the breath up the hills and down the valleys of experience; jhāna was the gear that allowed my mind to move through difficult Knowledges more smoothly. The natural interest and smoother vibrations that come with jhāna actually made it more fun to move through a difficult state because now the mind's chaotic dance is accompanied by a naturally curious awareness that gets deeper with each level of concentration.

Maybe Before You Sit: This illustration of energy is my slightly humorous way of empathizing with the difficulty a practitioner may have when beginning practice or before a meditative sit. It helps to have a relatively positive inward attitude toward oneself before getting deep into meditation. Otherwise, it will be difficult to concentrate well or develop the skills needed to get into the deeper states where there is liberation.

Delight: This is the first jhāna in which there are five factors. The first three factors, directed thought, singleness of preoccupation with the breath, and evaluation, produce the last two factors, rapture and pleasure.[33] For me, little bubbles begin to dance in my hands and feet and up my spine. My awareness becomes one with the breath, creating a synchronized connection between mind and body. The breath energies permeate my being, soothing tensions into a resulting tranquility.

I notice the breath's nuances, whether it's short or long, and then discern various qualities such as heaviness, lightness, coolness, or warmth. I pay close attention to any sensations of tightness, examining their precise location, gradation, spatiality, and form. I also notice any emotions that arise from exploring these qualities.

Happiness: This is the second jhāna where there is no longer a need for directed thought or evaluation, as the rapture and pleasure increase with a sense of refreshment and ease.[34] The happiness here is comparable to the amazing moment when I first saw my babies after giving birth, but ten times more profound; infused with a deep and natural appreciation for each moment of awareness. Focus on the object as it's touched becomes more precise. The edge of my attention softens around pleasant, unpleasant, or neutral. It involves refining the focus of my attention to energetics as they happen and unifying the foreground and background of Awareness.

Joy: A great depth of openness and interest permeates every cell of my mind/body. The breath is stable and barely perceptible as a point of focus, with a deep centering and stillness in the moment. There is a deep reverence for life. The hindrances are fully at bay. Past or future thinking does not disturb the quietude. During continuous practice, when focused and balanced, eventually, even the pleasure from this refined joyousness starts to feel coarse, and a natural interest arises to let it go and see what is also present in harmony.

33　Ṭhānissaro Bhikkhu, *With Each and Every Breath*

34　Ajaan Lee Dhammadharo, *Keeping The Breath In Mind*

Equanimity: This is an incredibly beautiful state of mind, one that is easily suffused with a lightness of being. For me, there is no higher happiness than equanimity. It starts out light with the mind easily able to negotiate anything. The rapture and pleasure have faded to stillness. There is natural curiosity, seeing what is coming and going with total ease. It gets deeper as attention steadies on its own. The Buddha described this as being completely covered in a white cloth.[35] It is a fully focused inward state of being for a yogi. For me, it seemed to take about ten days to move through the Progress of Insight stages to get into this jhāna.

After experiencing the jhānas, it seemed so unbelievable and surprising that at first I couldn't even call them by these names. This is because these mind/body states are not associated with any greed, hatred, or delusion. Having been a child of an addictive system, it took me a while to reassign positive feelings to these terms: delight, happiness, joy, and equanimity. It's okay and highly functional to enjoy these states of being. They imprint wholesomeness on the mind/body. These beautiful states of being are enveloped in innocence and peace, and are available to all of us. Jhāna practice is encouraged and supported in Buddhist literature as a way of learning to live as a wise and compassionate member of our human family.

At home following a retreat, some challenging vibrational energetics emerged vigorously. The departure from a once quiet and supportive environment that allowed for smoother meditative jhāna practice made for a rougher ride. Hindrances became blatantly apparent. Therefore, walking and gentle self-care had to be increased more than ever. I just needed to keep riding it out, abandon "my" ideas and stay with the process. There was something happening that wanted to be free and liberated. This deepening cycle of progress, not perfection, kept rubbing away ideas of "my self."

A progressive path is not about becoming perfect. It is about everything moving through naturally on its own. This validating research

---

35 Aṅguttara Nikāya, 5:28, "*Samādhaṅga Sutta: The Factors of Concentration,*" translated from the Pāli by Ṭhānissaro Bhikkhu.

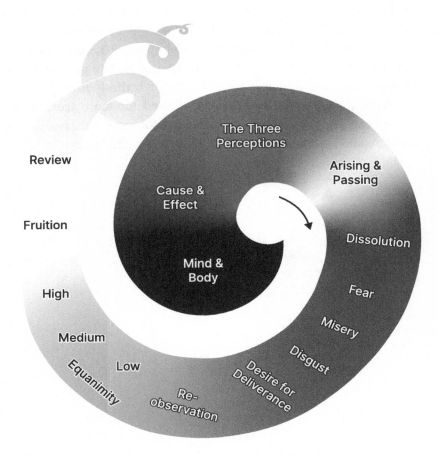

Progress of Insight After Awakening

made it seem all the more doable at this point. After stream-entry, the cycle unfurls into an open spiral, as illustrated by the diagram above.

Connecting with the Progress of Insight map helped release judgments about these various stages. What I was experiencing was not wrong, but a natural part of the progressive path. For instance, I now knew it was normal to experience exhaustion after big energetic openings. So, there were appropriate times to take a bath, nap, and rest. Even when the stages were hard, the state shifts between each Knowledge increased a sense of patience and faith by providing nourishing insight into *all things arise and pass away.* Some may not feel like their practice aligns with the Progress of Insight, and that's okay. I was amazed by how precisely it applied to my process.

Being in the role of a parent, I had important karmic responsibilities for my children and myself. Reviewing the five powers helped me apply self-care practices for going through these difficult states. Following through with compassion allowed for more trust in the varying energies to be addressed. When tensions arose, the body/mind felt more and more drawn to an unfathomable depth of Love.

CHAPTER TWENTY-THREE

Five Alive

We want to take the easy way, but if there's
no suffering, there's no wisdom. To be ripe for
wisdom, you must really break down and cry in
your practice at least three times.

– Ajahn Chah[36]

I N EARLY JUNE 2008, I looked around and did a few searches at night for a longer local retreat. I stumbled across a blog connected with Dharma practice where someone mentioned an upcoming retreat only a few hours away. Something compelled my fingers to click on the link. I wouldn't even have to take a plane!

This longer, ten-day retreat would fit perfectly right after Preston's high school graduation, and although it was unfortunate that Stewart was recently unemployed, he would be around for the kids. Registration had closed, but I applied without hesitation anyway. I knew nothing about the teachers, only that they were affiliated with a local Theravāda sangha. Amidst all the arrangements, including my son's graduation, I'd hardly have time to get ready.

A few days later, I received wonderful news—they had room for me at the retreat, and they even offered a small partial scholarship! Feeling

---

36 Venerable Ajahn Chah, "Suffering," in *No Ajahn Chah: Reflections*, pp. 122.

grateful to be registered and granted this support, I eagerly shared the news with Stewart, Preston, and Forrest. I suggested that we all visit the retreat place together, so they could see where I would be and not worry while I was away. They agreed, and I began preparing us with some organization and teamwork. I informed Stewart about the various household projects that would need attention and ensured that he and the boys had solid plans to watch over our beloved dog, Ruby.

I remembered Stewart's parents lived nearby, so I asked him to call them. They kindly invited him and the boys to stop by for a visit on their way back home. I thought perhaps he'd enjoy the country air and take in some of their kindness since he was struggling to find work.

After taking care of a million things for the kids, making sure our Ruby had her crate in the car, and checking that we had enough full water bottles and lunches for everyone, we were on our way.

Upon arriving, Stewart took Ruby to go pee on the grass while both strong sons walked ahead, carrying my bags up the steps (there was no ramp) into the old monastic school building just south of Red Wing, Minnesota. I paused to look up at the two towers shouldering the old entrance where the Ursuline Sisters once passed through to teach girls and practice Catholicism. Over the years, it eventually turned into an interfaith retreat center. Nestling within these sacred walls, I was honored to practice in a place that seemed to hold a heartfelt wish for all humanity to know Christ.

In Christ we all walk.

I was fortunate to have my own room upstairs in the corner, since that was my preference. We sat on the bed and I hugged the boys under each of my arms. With a firm tone, I told them that I needed to stay there for ten days and that it was all for the best. I would be home soon. I tapped the mattress and asked them to help me move it onto the floor, where I was usually most comfortable. They jumped up, feeling useful, and began to help rearrange my room.

When we said our goodbyes, I sensed the boys would miss me, but I also knew they didn't have much going on at the time. Neither one had a job or classes, giving them a chance to consider their own changes. They could relax and enjoy themselves without the pressures of school and with less supervision. Now that it was summer, they had their yardwork business to focus on. They were getting older, becoming grown men. These ten days apart would give them a chance to reflect on their own paths and spend more time with their father.

~~~

After supper on the first night of the Theravāda retreat, the teachers outlined the rules for silence, keeping to the precepts, and other instructions. The chanting of the precepts had an enlivening effect on me with my love for the Dhamma and my willingness to be there with the community of other practitioners.

The retreat here had a few differences compared to the zendo back home. Some participants set up lawn chairs in the hall. The teachers maintained a clear boundary by not eating or sitting with us. Unlike our collective, circular walking meditation in the zendo, here we did walking meditation outside on our own, while a few engaged in tai chi behind the trees. The freedom and individuality were new to me. Despite this, attendance at all meditation sessions and Dhamma talks was expected, making it stricter than Adyashanti's retreat.

I reviewed my boundaries to see if I was out of alignment, and vowed to mind my own business and practice as best as I could. Sitting in the back near a window provided a refreshing view of the large open field. I didn't bring my own chair, and they had many cushions available, so I chose to sit in a Burmese posture with a zafu and zabuton, the way I did in the zendo.

The two teachers took turns meeting with students every other day. They had to meet with more than forty-five other practitioners in just a few hours, so the interviews had to be, at most, ten minutes.

I was supposed to meet with one of the teachers right away. I didn't know what to say about my practice. I had been sitting zazen and was often losing contact with the body. The teacher looked at me quizzically when I said that I had recently come across Mahāsi. The teacher exclaimed, "Mahāsi!?" Then he quickly closed the interview. I wondered whether that meant I should not have mentioned him.

It is better to prepare a little and research the teachers before spending time on a retreat. I immediately feared that he didn't know

Mahāsi or his work or that it was against their way of teaching. As I walked away from that interview, I resolved to not let it be an issue and to continue my practice. There is only the here and now, after all.

On my walk, I happened across a maple leaf and placed it in my sweater pocket. Later, I pulled it out and saw the five tips on the leaf as a representation of the five aggregates that make up this human existence.

1. Body/form: seeing, hearing, smelling, tasting, touching
2. Sensation or feeling: the inner vibrations of any contact, pleasant, unpleasant, or neutral feelings
3. Perception: mental conceptions of contact
4. Volition: intentions toward any contact
5. Consciousness: the root sense base, or mind, contact with any mental or physical object

I kept it very simple by allowing interest in any of the five aggregates to emerge while filling the body with comfortable breath energy. I'd notice the moment of contact, automatically, *as it was arising*. For instance, when I saw something, I'd notice that I was only seeing. I would not form any notion other than seeing. If I saw a tree, I would not say, "Oh, what a beautiful tree." I would just notice seeing, and feel behind the eyes, noting the sensations as pleasant, unpleasant, or neutral. Hearing a sound, just hearing. Tasting and smelling, just tasting and smelling. For painful sensations, I needed to raise more energy to breathe in ways that provided comfort and support or dissolved the pain. This experimenting became deeper and deeper as I awkwardly steered little by little a way to Stillness.

There is a great deal of fun and flexibility in noticing. With a wandering mind, it could be that the mind needs to be given a little more space and friendliness mixed with grounding in the earth. With each noticing, balance in my concentration improved.

As the noticing increased in tempo and consistency, I could feel cause and effect in the eye organ itself; then a *knowing* of "seeing" happened. As the moment of touch happened, the *knowing* of touch was happening. Noticing became more rapid in the torso with each moment of contact, whether pleasant, unpleasant, or neutral. This also kept any mental fabrications to a minimum and allowed me to continue to investigate the raw details of being alive, moment by moment, at a faster pace. It brought to mind the spontaneity of playing patty cake as a child, or playing a computer game—just going with the flow and letting the mind work along in the environment. I was noticing each and every detail as it passed through the aggregates. Everything was just occurring at a high rate of speed and I *knew* it as it was occurring.

~~~

The weather was a splendid 70°F, sunny every day, raining occasionally at night. It was a gorgeous place to be, and the food was delicious. The entire area was quiet, with no planes overhead, and the staff was generous in spirit. This place and the uninterrupted time for practice were huge blessings, allowing the mind to stay focused.

Each evening, the teachers took turns giving a wisdom talk, which also inspired me to deepen my concentration and commitment. The talks increased my faith in our teachers' guidance because I was finally getting to know them. More importantly, glimmers of understanding thrummed through the body as vibrating energy, and the place of bodily contact was seen directly. The equanimity in their wise words whirred perspicaciously in my whole system while I stayed with breath awareness.

Ideas floated through the mind/body and the hindrances vanished. How could I hold onto the idea of a cup being a cup? It is also earth, wind, water, and fire in the temporary form of what we refer to as a cup. The idea of a cup is a concept, and sometimes it seemed like concepts themselves were bad because of the way folks carefully couched their questions to the teachers.

One night, when they asked if any questions had come up, I spontaneously burst out asking, "How is it that concepts seem to get a bad rap in Buddhism when they are so open-ended?"

Everyone laughed. The teacher said, "They aren't bad when we really *see* them."

I nodded, laughing along.

~~~

Stepping out from the meditation hall, I was greeted by the sight of dozens of people walking in slow motion across the open field in different directions. It brought to mind an old film, *Invasion of the Body Snatchers*, where replicated human beings were following in a hypnotic state to the demands of the alien invaders. I could hardly take it. I giggled a little while walking to the labyrinth, where it at least seemed to make sense to walk in a weird, going-no-place way.

We followed an alternating schedule throughout the day, beginning with a fifty-minute sitting meditation at 6 a.m., then moving on to fifty minutes of walking meditation, and continuing this pattern until 10 p.m. There were ten-minute intervals for going to the bathroom or getting water, during which meditation persisted.

And, why not? I was there to do just that. With ten days ahead of me, I had more time to explore my practice. I didn't have to drive anywhere, cook, clean, or take care of the myriad details at home. I was there to practice being in the moment, so I did it happily with everything I had in me. Any added effort was also a source of investigation; each moment of contact was interesting.

The willingness to sit with discomfort and balance bodily care helped to increase concentration, which felt rich and wonderful. It didn't take long to shift from seeing "what is mind" and "what is body" to the stage of cause and effect. The itch and the intention to itch followed, and the motion to itch came after in quick succession. I could also feel the entire process unfolding and see the mind moving along quickly.

As I stayed with the bare sensations *just as* they were happening, some irritating tension changed into stabbing pain in my back. I considered whether I was getting into tougher territory, like the three perceptions before an opening such as the a&p. Even the experience of "wondering where I was in the process" was just noticed as a thought passing, letting any ideas of assessment go for the time being.

I simply couldn't stop noticing! The mind cruised along speedily after three silent days with a natural tendency to see points of contact *just as* they were arising, staying present with them, and watching them pass. I could see how, as much as I tried, I could not hold any point of contact in the mind. The mind had its own agenda. Trying to hold on was futile—already going, going, gone. We do this all the time; we don't know how much we are doing it until we sit still and really pay close attention.

All events simply passed through consciousness. The three perceptions of all phenomena became incredibly clear. They presented with Awareness over and over again. I continued to practice steadily, even during meals, walking back and forth to my room, and resting if needed.

On the fifth day, another big opening occurred. I could not identify with anything as *mine*. When this sank into the body, the pounding pain in my back changed into exquisite rapture and clarity. I found myself tuning into the sounds of the birds chirping and settling on branches outside the hall near the window where I sat. The sounds vibrated through the belly and outward, *birds=us=nature*.

I could see that all of my suffering was not "my" suffering but rather the result of many causes and conditions that were not totally "my" fault. I faintly heard the bells ringing in the background. The sit had ended, and the other practitioners stood and went outside. I sat transfixed in the same spot, taking in and learning much of what I had always wanted to know.

In attempting to hold a mudra, I noticed a little leaning on my right wrist. I'd straighten my posture, notice the intention to change the posture, then feel the movement while changing the posture.

After meditating for over three hours, I rose for the supper bell, and knew I had crossed the a&p again. The state shifted into seeing endings, which felt tiresome and irritating. In the past, I tended to overexert myself whenever this happened. But this time, instead of pushing too hard, I let myself explore the grounds and enjoy a hot shower. Broadening my awareness and eating the salads at lunch helped me settle back into balancing faith and wisdom with energy and concentration.

The hours flashed by, and it was nearly time to see the teacher. I was five days in and had had another mystical experience (a&p). And, *that was not it.* The meetings needed to be brief, useful, and somehow to the point. I wasn't sure how anyone could even help.

Because it appeared I'd said the "wrong" thing when I mentioned Mahāsi at our first meeting, I felt apprehensive about sharing this type of discussion with someone I hardly knew. Divulging the details of my sensate experience seemed like revealing my most intimate encounters. How could I help them understand the way I was practicing? I knew at least some validation or connection would help. I went back to my room and pulled out my notebook and colored pencils. I drew two quick sketches—one of the pain in my back and the other of me falling off a cliff.

When the interview started, I knew it had to be short, so I pulled out my journal and showed the teacher the drawings. She brought her hand to her mouth, gasped, and said that this was not at all what her teacher would accept on a retreat. Ashamed, I put it away quickly in my tote bag and slid it under the chair. I didn't know what to say. I had recently crossed the a&p, and could have told her that, but didn't know if she understood the Progress of Insight or supported that kind of assessment. I touched into knowing that I was passing through a deep state of fear while sitting with her, so her response wasn't especially helpful, given the contracted state I was moving through.

SUFFERING
real +
all ILLUSION

I sat there stunned, noticing the sensations of shame and fear. She looked down, hesitated, and fumbled to try and mediate the situation. "Is that how you feel? Is that what you have been feeling?"

"Yes," I said, nodding shyly. "Yesterday, early on there was back pain, and today..." With some reluctance, I showed her the picture of me falling off a cliff. I didn't mention the a&p, or the deep mystical event, because I thought she would think I was crazy, and she already had some reservations about my way of sharing. Isn't a picture worth a thousand words? I felt awkward and strange and wanted to leave, but I was also practicing breath awareness while sitting there. I saw the misunderstanding between us. I wondered if she thought that I was just sitting around ruminating in my stuff. I wasn't an expert at labeling these states, although I wasn't a kid either. More than anything, I sensed some kind of cultural barrier, and didn't know how to cross it.

We both sat together waiting for words to come, and then she said, "All of these ideas or insights are like butterflies. We may touch them, but then they go."

I agreed with her on that, and nodded while looking into her kind eyes, sighing in relief at our meeting in the moment. I knew that any holding pattern was exhausting. The drawings were a way to communicate, not hold onto any ideas.

The whole process, the entire retreat, seemed unbearable at this point. I went back to my room, skipped the next sit, and fell into a deep nap as if I were magnetized to my bed. I woke up an hour later and pushed myself up. I worried someone might have noticed my absence and would be coming to check on me because in Zen, everyone is almost always together. So, I quickly got right back into the schedule. I really didn't want to cause a disturbance for anyone else there. As I walked to the meditation hall, I remembered how exhausted I had felt at home after having a deep opening at the last retreat.

Over the next few days of going through fear, misery, and disgust in total silence, I left the teacher a brief note sharing my concern about proper communication. I wanted to learn more about reporting during an interview. An hour after leaving the note, I regretted doing it and then worried about that. I could only continue to see the mental fabrications in the mind and how little they mattered as they passed away.

The WiNDs of change
6-17-08

She did not respond to my note. I am glad she left it alone and trusted my process.

As fear moved into misery, a deer tick showed up on my arm, and I carefully removed it. This brought up more fear and concern about getting Lyme disease. But the next thought was that if I were to contract Lyme disease, then I had better practice extremely well because I would need it. Later in the day, all thoughts related to this were gone as I dedicated my practice to feeling into the sensations connected with the thoughts, breathing in and out slowly and long.

As the mind and body clung desperately to ideas, the only relief was the continuous, hard-core practice of watching sensations dissolve up close. If I stopped practicing, I would suffer more pain. When including nurturing activities and doing them mindfully—like drinking extra water, showering, stretching, taking my vitamins, cleaning my room, and enjoying pleasant moments such as the view from my window—only then could I withstand the agony.

Still, as I grew disgusted with feeling miserable, I also felt hopelessness arising. My feet wandered off into the woods, Mother Earth present with each footfall. I sat on a stump, and with a deep exhale, started to cry out for deliverance from the agonizing storm that was striking at my spine, my mind, and my heart. The surface seemed so unreachable as hulking waves of hopelessness crashed through my body, its brisk tide luring me into despairing depths. And yet, in that hopelessness, there was a deeper desire for the Truth rising in me from the storm. No way was I going to break the silence and interrupt this precious time to practice, even though I wished for someone to comfort me. This aloneness pierced my heart with a profound knowing to *face my suffering, turn toward the tide and not look away,* just as this body birthed each of my sons; no one else could do it. I had to push. I had to do the work.

On the eighth day, while walking outside, I suddenly remembered I was due at the top floor of the monastery for my meeting with a different teacher. Quickly, I went to my room for a piece of paper and a pen. Even though it wasn't "right" to bring paper or a drawing, I did it anyway. I laughed inwardly at all the hundreds of job interviews, doctor's appointments, and school-teacher meetings I had gone to over the course of my life. Ordinarily, I carried a small notebook, pen in hand, and had a few questions jotted down, which made me feel prepared. *Was I holding on to this process?* I didn't know and wasn't sure; it felt instinctual.

Outside the room, as I waited for the interview, a clear reflection arose as my pen touched the paper. I quickly drew five cannisters, like buoys, that each connected via a line. There appeared to be something happening with respect to the five aggregates and how they arose and passed away on this vast ocean of experience. When we see a line of buoys and one begins to bob, the next one bobs, and they are all bobbing, and as *a wave moves, they all move.* I sensed this happening inside and throughout the entire body. It felt very interesting.

When the teacher invited me in, he asked me how I was. I shrugged and mumbled, "Not too great." I just stood there awkwardly holding my slip of paper, slightly down to my side, kind of hiding it behind my leg, not sure if it was safe.

He looked at me, nodded, saw the slip of paper I was holding, and asked, "What have you got there?"

I tentatively showed him my rough drawing of buoys connected by ropes floating on an ocean, describing how each barrel appears like a bundle of different things, or like the aggregates, and when one moves, the others tilt and rock in tandem.

He smiled broadly and said, "Yes, that is true!"

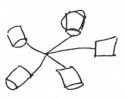

We looked at each other and paused for a deeply connected moment over this fact. I felt heard, and it affirmed the way I was practicing.

I said a little more about how the eyes just see, the tongue just tastes, the ears just hear, the skin makes contact with touch...and as my stomach growled at that moment, the stomach just growls. Hearing lights up from sound, feelings arise, perceiving lights up, the intention to eat or not eat, and consciousness *knows!*

He smiled and nodded, giving me direct eye contact.

The short session ended serenely. I considered what was actually happening as I walked: touching heel to floor, intention to turn the corner, stepping as I turned the corner—all these aspects were seen as they were happening. Practice continued.

The aggregates arose and passed away in amazing wonder.

I continued to walk around like a blinking Christmas tree.

~~~

The Buddha once pointed to people who were collecting sticks and leaves for a fire. He asked the monks if they felt concern or attachment to those sticks and leaves that were going to be burned.

"Of course not, they do not belong to us," said the monks.

The Buddha replied, "In the same way, monks, give up what isn't yours. Giving it up will be for your lasting welfare and happiness. And what isn't yours? Form... feeling... perception... choices... consciousness isn't yours: give it up."[37]

~~~

On the last day, I came back from breakfast, continuously noticing each detail of contact, and suddenly I felt a subtle shift. The body felt lighter. As I looked around my little room, I could see that all thoughts, *all of them*, were just thoughts.

In this beautiful movement into equanimity, I happened to pick up my notebook and glance at my few drawings, and they were simply drawings. They didn't have any ideas stuck to them; they had space around them, much like a chair—not separate from the space around it. I pulled up the shade to see the sky—*magnificent sky*. I was okay with not knowing. Everything appeared incredibly open and transcendent.

I needed to investigate. Taking "me" outside, I walked quietly and slowly down the back hallway. All felt okay. I could see a feeling as just

---

37 Majjhima Nikāya, 22, "Alagaddūpamasutta Sutta: The Snake Simile," translated from the Pāli by Bhikku Sujato.

a feeling; it wasn't me, not mine, and not my soul. It was calm, unlike the a&p, which had more coarse energy—this state was smooth and tranquil, like cutting through the clouds on an airplane and seeing the clear landscape below. This was a new level of insight, natural to all of us, penetrating perfect serenity into every pore.

I had to wonder: *Was this enlightenment?*

Then those thoughts vanished.

All of the five aggregates were alive. I could see no separation from all beings. I was enamored with the state. I *knew* a deep, relaxed openness with all: the background, the foreground, and the expansive panoramic level of awareness and confidence.

The retreat was ending. Being enchanted by this state of equanimity left me unaware of time. I walked slowly toward the hall and pulled out the five-pointed leaf from my pocket, and a sense of perfection suffused my entire body and mind as I stood there in the open field.

When I arrived at the meditation hall, I was late, and the group had formed a circle, each person sharing one by one what they had learned or found helpful from the retreat. Spellbound, I didn't know what to say. I felt concerned about breaking silence. I wanted to stay in this timeless, peaceful state forever. I was the only one there who didn't speak.

It was soon time to pack up with a new friend who had offered me a ride home. Halfway back, we stopped at a Dairy Queen, took our treats to a place by the river, and started talking. I felt like I was going to burst whenever I spoke. The mind's break-neck speed felt incongruent with how slowly things appeared to be moving.

A conflict in *believing* the things I was sharing also became distinctly apparent. Most of us connect through our stories and what our lives look like—married, two kids, etc.—instead of what we know to be true. I knew that what my life looked like was only a tiny part of what was truly happening, and I wondered how much this could change my view of life. That "noticing" told me the state was fading, as all phenomena do, and I was off into the content of life and not the underlying truth. And, in the work of driving home, some irritating sensations began to emerge around the edges as this beautiful state faded away.

CHAPTER TWENTY-FOUR

Re-Entry

RETURNING HOME from the sweet silence in the country to the pandemonium of the bustling city was a real shock to the system. Noticing operated so quickly that every detail in life seemed enormous. And while the warm June air invited us to open our windows for the summer breezes, it offered little relief as several of our neighbors seemed to have declared a construction marathon.

The south-side neighbor was busy rebuilding their deck using a pungent, oily stain; the north-side neighbor was constructing a garage with a high-pressure nail gun and receiving frequent truck deliveries; and the neighbor across the street was engaged in a major landscaping project involving a constantly beeping backhoe.

The road in front of our house was a construction zone, with trucks and loaders constantly hauling pallets or dropping rocks. All the frenzy of activity, in addition to the steady airplane traffic we tolerated throughout the year, created an indistinct barrage of noise. I used earplugs just to walk around the house, and then I'd startle in shock when the kids tapped me on the shoulder to get my attention.

When I went back to sit in the zendo, my ears hissed like a prairie full of screeching cicadas. Adding to the discomfort, a distinct bump on top of my right wrist that had appeared on the last day of the retreat shot burning prickles down my arm. Being right-handed made it tough to handle my drills and other carpentry tools. And yet, amidst all this, my attention gravitated toward inner spaciousness. I couldn't help but see my resistance and feel into sensations as they vibrated through the body, observing any pulling away or leaning into the process. Overall, it felt as if I was going from a more contracted state to a more expanded state, and back around again.

A few days later, I visited with my recovery friends. During our discussion group, after a woman checked in, I found myself wondering aloud why she was working her program without a sponsor if she was going off her meds. Everyone stopped and stared at me, and I realized what I had said was inappropriate. It was just a thought, but it was also none of my business. I apologized to her before leaving.

Sure enough, I had what can be called "yogi mind," where the usual social filters and perceptions are weakened. The space between my thoughts and my speech had suddenly shortened without inhibitory control. If I were in a discussion and simply had a thought, *watch out.* I didn't even know what I might say. But I was responsible for what I was saying. All this brimming awareness of what was happening inside couldn't help but make me feel awkward.

Everything seemed intense. I was moving through another dark night, just as the Progress of Insight predicted. And, how could my sponsor help me? I was certain that I was in territory he knew nothing about. It occurred to me: Perhaps I need a place like a monastery, a place where they carried out this work, where you speak mindfully as needed for tasks and duties? Perhaps people there would know how to honor others in various states without the psychological accoutrements?

Speaking inappropriately can create a lot of troubling situations. I'm continually trying to improve in this area. The Buddha talked about right use of speech, and its importance, laying out five conditions— saying things at the right time, truthfully, beneficially, with kindness, and goodwill.[38]

One of the teachers from the retreat had given an excellent talk about this. He spoke about the qualities of enlightenment, which include generosity, wisdom, kindness, and compassion. Speaking honestly

---

38 Aṅguttara Nikāya, 5.198, *"Vācā Sutta: A Statement,"* translated from the
Pāli by Ṭhānissaro Bhikkhu.

gives me clarity for love and acceptance. I always felt that when I spoke from my heart, I didn't run into trouble.

This talk humbled me because I realized how much more there was to learn. As someone who is more introverted, I can be more plainspoken at times. Also, for the first twelve years of my life, I was mostly mute due to not being given the time and space to express myself. Many times, visualizations came to me instead of words. Using nonviolent communication techniques didn't always work out; it's a moment-by-moment skill to listen and respond. All of this made me want to just keep it simple.

Sinking into my chair in the garage, I adjusted my posture and granted myself an hour of stillness to meditate. As reflections of my retreat experience came up, I was beginning to notice how various senses of self can cling to various states and identities. In some of my deep process work, I felt how I had in part been feeding a sense of self conditioned with hopelessness. However, in that hopelessness, there was a reaching out for Reality. By frequently noticing in silence without distractions, for a longer time frame, there was a field of Awareness underneath. The practice itself fell back into consciousness, and I saw how each sensation was just happening, and that I couldn't help it or stop it. Phenomena happened so fast that I felt like everything was already done by the time I saw it. And at the same time, I could affect sensations, perceptions, and intentions with experimentation during practice. My practice was becoming more tolerable due to my interest in these phenomena arising and passing away. Touching into compassion felt softly reassuring. *What was this "I" that saw this?*

Seeking support, I called a relatively new friend I had met on the Internet, Vincent Horn, who was open to discussing practice. During our talk, I opened up about some of my retreat experiences. In response, he shared that many yogis generally need much more practice before they can cross the a&p. I guess with my long-term contemplative practice and maturity gained from my recovery work, I was cruising right along.

Vincent also mentioned that my practice sounded quite similar to the Progress of Insight, which normalized things for me. I asked him how long one could normally sustain high equanimity, since it was a point of entry for true abiding enlightenment. He recalled that a monk once told him it was about three to four hours maximum. On my drive home from the retreat, the state was indeed fading after about that long. So, I had missed out on the point of entry by not staying with my meditative process. I had been ripe and ready for a truly deep change, but it had been time to leave the retreat. *Hard lesson.*

That state of high equanimity was incredible, and I became fascinated by it. I needed to be very cautious around this clinging and let it go. This was the most important assessment. The best way to get to that point of high equanimity again would be to work my way through sustained contact at every sense door, along with becoming aware of any clinging to sensations with application of right effort at every moment of contact. But, I did not want to get hung up on the details, I'd understand the finer qualities of these states as I continued to investigate. All in all, the retreat offered a great bird's-eye view of what I had been going through for decades!

I heard about a place in California called Spirit Rock that offers a range of retreats, including a two-month option in February-March and a one-month for either February or March. Both options seemed fabulous, but the one-month was already a big stretch for our expenses and the waiting time was seven to eight months. That felt too long to wait! Plus, they relied on a lottery system, so I wouldn't even know if I got in for some time. Still, I went ahead and applied for whichever one I could get into, and for a scholarship, just in case I didn't find any other options.

I reached out to Norm, and told him that I needed to go further. He listened and understood that I had been practicing diligently.

He had been curious about what I was studying, so a few weeks prior I had left a printout of one of the Mahāsi books for him to review.

In my next meeting with him, I asked, "Did you get the little book of Mahāsi's I left for you?"

"Yes," he said.

"Isn't it cool, the way he talks about meditation?"

"Well, that is not what we do, though. That is not our practice."

I wondered about our differences in how we each practiced. "Did you read it?" I asked him.

"No, I don't practice like that."

While I appreciated his honesty, I was a bit taken aback. If someone gave me a book I wasn't going to read, I would return it to them and say, "Thanks, but no thanks."

He was usually more curious, so I wondered why he seemed uninterested in the pure gold I had uncovered. I shyly asked if he had heard of the Satipaṭṭhāna Sutta,[39] where the four foundations of mindfulness are outlined: Contemplation of the body, feeling, consciousness, and mental objects. He said he was aware of the sutta, but preferred to practice with the koans and the Diamond Sutra.[40]

I perceived that Norm was happy with his life. We can be different. As I stood up at the end of our meeting, I found myself humming the chants from the retreat.

Norm asked me, "What are you singing?"

"The Triple Gem Refuge chants in Pāli from the retreat."

At that point, inclining towards the Theravāda lineage, while being regularly exposed to the teachings of Dogen in Zen, created some slight cognitive dissonance in my relationship with the Dharma Field practitioners. Since Zen was founded about 700 years after the time of the Buddha, I felt safer taking the Theravāda path and using the original words of the Buddha. When I first read the Satipaṭṭhāna Sutta, there was this peculiar feeling that I had come across it before, possibly in a previous lifetime. It had an elevating effect on my faith in the practice. The Buddha's encouragement to be aware of the nature of the breath, whether it's long or short, and knowing it, struck a deep chord in me. He also spoke of experiencing the whole body and knowing pleasant, unpleasant, or neutral feelings with the breath. This harmoniously aligned with my somatic background. Also, the Sutta on the

---

39 Majjhima Nikāya, 10, "*Satipaṭṭhāna Sutta: The Foundations of Mindfulness*," translated from the Pāli by Nyanasatta Thera.

40 Dhyāna Master Hsüan Hua, *The Diamond Sutra: A General Explanation of the Vajra Prajñā Paramitā Sūtra*.

Seven Factors of Awakening expressed values and qualities that I had been cultivating in my Twelve Step work for decades. The whole Pāli Canon, recorded over 2,500 years ago for us all to see and read—truly a treasure of the greatest magnitude. There were even stories and poetry of women and mothers who had taken vows with the Buddha and had become highly enlightened!

There wasn't time to waste. I began integrating these early teachings into my routine right away, and I kept an eye out for teachers with this training and understanding. It also just felt incredibly fun and amazing to imagine the Buddha walking to different towns, receiving alms, and sharing what he had learned with others. This made him more of a human being in my heart even though he was supremely enlightened. I had to stop myself from reading sutta after sutta, and get back to meditation in daily life.

CHAPTER TWENTY-FIVE

Clearing Skies

THE RETREAT IS RIGHT NOW. I carried this wisdom into my daily life. With all of the interruptions at home, taking care of the house and kids, and my website business, I paused frequently to work with difficult sensations.

With my suffering already reduced by ten percent, I knew more intensive practice would be worth it. My family's well-being is interconnected with mine, as we all live together and influence each other's happiness. So, every small improvement in my own state of mind would have a positive ripple effect on all of us.

A gut feeling told me that what was said about stream-entry was true: there could be a deeper shift in consciousness. After all, many insights had been happening gradually for decades, and I'd been getting into some astonishing concentration while on retreat. But I knew *it* hadn't happened, and I certainly wasn't interested in deluding myself.

From what I had been studying from Buddhist Theravādin elders, some from Burma and Thailand, they said it usually took Americans, with all their greed and clinging, about three months to attain stream-entry with continuous practice. Wow! That was very interesting to me. I inquired more about this and read that it takes longer because the hindrances need to be worked with skillfully.

In Theravāda Buddhism, the stages of enlightenment are related to the removal of hindrances. With my challenging re-entry back into the city, I was dedicated to learning about these aggravations of the mind with right effort and mindfully applying the antidotes. Observing a hindrance arise, then inquiring into the resonant antidote, offered a gift of reflection that supported my devotion to practice. It helped to see that the solution was already inside. A faith arose that called all of this to be held in an open way, *not my will but Thy will be done.*

Gradually, I learned to recognize these five primary hindrances with more of an open, compassionate attitude.

The first hindrance, **compulsive sensory desire or craving**, creates a sense of lack. The antidote I apply involves first recognizing the compulsion and then nurturing a gentle sense of acceptance, which reduces resistance to it.

Sometimes, I really want to eat a particular food. I realize it will only be temporary yumminess. I'm better off not wanting it and feeling free. Learning to be more relaxed around my desires reduces thoughts of scarcity. I can still have a few bites without overeating, or I can set it aside, giving myself time for the compulsion to subside.

The second hindrance, **hatred or ill-will**, encompasses feelings of aversion or anger that can turn inward, manifesting as depression, or outward, expressing themselves in destructive behaviors. I prefer to first stop and feel the discomfort and unpleasantness these emotions bring. It is very unpleasant, which makes it easy to want to let it go. Breathing in deeply and waiting a few minutes for it to pass prevents harm. This is an important practice for working with expectations I am not aware of beforehand.

Sometimes boredom is a form of aversion, wanting the moment to be more interesting than it is. Not wanting what is happening is pushing reality away, preventing me from seeing my options in that particular moment.

This hindrance ranges from mild irritation to intense hatred. I need to admit to being angry or depressed and know it. It is often accompanied by the idea that someone or something is to blame without recognizing the many causes and conditions under which things happen. I need to look at if I'm holding a distorted view of myself and listening to old negative voices, to observe changes happening within, to understand that it is passing and not solidifying the ideas arising.

Anger can also be transformative when the initial impulse is recognized. I can take in the context and clarify a boundary to express myself assertively.

The third hindrance is **stagnation**. It's like my energy pools into a vortex and keeps swirling around, going nowhere. A drowsy or dull affect can occur, which I find often connects with the fatigue that follows an a&p experience, amplifying the "this isn't it" feeling. I find that overeating, being lazy, reclining in bed too much, or sitting too long causes stagnation.

To address stagnation, the Buddha recommended pulling on the earlobes. Sometimes, I have to make myself move. I like to splash water on my face, focus on the in-breath, stand up, do walking meditation, increase my circulation with yoga or qigong, be with folks who are expressing good energy, or find something creative or useful to accomplish. I also enjoy lying on the floor and moving my body authentically, stretching through muscle aches in my own way.

Activities like going for a walk, riding a bike, and taking hot showers (due to my cold climate), or cold showers to wake up my system all provide a refreshing boost. Listening to podcasts or Dhamma talks during a walk can be uplifting. Reading courageous stories or memoirs, and watching inspiring films, can be helpful. The simple ritual of having tea in the morning with the rising sun and walking with the setting sun in the evening brings me joy.

On occasion, I notice the mind wants to shut down and go to sleep; a part of me doesn't feel safe. So, I need to enliven mettā practice right away when I first feel drowsy and remind myself of the kindness inherent in the practice; this will raise energy.

The fourth hindrance is **agitation and excessive energy**. In the old texts I read, agitation is often called worry and flurry. It involves unpleasant feelings alongside a jumpy mind; my breathing becomes shallower, and my shoulders stiffen up. My mind can be overactive, like a washing machine drum swishing with soapy, sloshy, gyrating thoughts.

To address agitation, I need to do calming activities like resting, stopping, sitting, and focusing on the out-breath. I love listening to Dhamma talks from teachers who express equanimity because they transmit a calming presence. Finding a place to do standing meditation with a view of the horizon or the sky opens my mind.

When agitation is arising, it is not the time to do reflective insight meditation or engage the thinking mind. It's better to do calming meditations. If agitation happens at night, interrupting sleep, it is best to focus on lengthening the breath and feeling the feet, wiggling my toes, or giving myself a simple foot massage to draw the energy down toward the earth. That way, balance can come in and rest can resume.

The fifth hindrance is falling into **doubt**. There are doubts about what the best options are in life, and then there are deeper fundamental doubts in the Dhamma. There can be anxiety and doubts about oneself and whether one can learn and grow. Doubt can lead to forgetfulness, dull states, and feeling stuck.

There can be too many ideas arising at once and too many decisions to make, which can feel overwhelming. When working on our house, I often confer with building inspectors to facilitate decision-making because there are various ways to solve problems that I may not be aware of. I often spread out tasks, giving myself time to choose options. It always helped to slow down and allow space to reveal what's best for a situation.

I appreciate my sponsor and wise teachers and value their encouragement to help release doubt. I am reminded to trust the process, increasing my faith and patience for learning and unlearning. For each of the hindrances, the resistance to accepting things as they are depends on the level of concentration. When I feel resistance lessen and compassion grow, faith in my practice reduces doubt.

As I reflected on these insights in my practice, I felt intensely drawn to how doubt in the Dhamma would be completely removed upon stream-entry! That would be fantastic! I read that full enlightenment is the removal of all hindrances; the end of the seeker. That seemed awesome! A deep faith was pulling me into the process of investigation into all phenomena, like I had been pushing a boulder up a hill for most of my life, and now the boulder was coming down the hill after *me*.

Superstitious attachment to rites and rituals, which is connected with doubt, appeared to have already been removed. However, there were still forces moving through rituals that can only be understood by those who animate them. Some of these forces take the form of spiritual communion, serving as an alchemy that dissolves an individualistic view.

The Fourth Step of the Twelve Step program encourages us to "Take a searching and fearless moral inventory of ourselves." So I ran to my bookcase and pulled out my journals. Flipping through the pages, I noticed that while I had named a few of these hindrances differently, I had been investigating them in my written Fourth Step inventories for decades.

In the Seventh Step, "We ask God to humbly remove our shortcomings," I often felt the shortcomings, or hindrances, had been like clouds in the way of Truth. Recalling that the clouds would pass by or disappear as I became more peaceful and relaxed helped me feel more confident about my practice. With gratitude for knowing which cloud was arising, I could relax and tune into what I needed in the moment.

Being aware of the hindrances at a sensate level was a deeply sensitive skill. How could I become even more aware? I needed more concentrated meditation to shift through the jhāna phases. I felt some delight growing in meditation, so stream-entry seemed possible. When I meditated and the factors of enlightenment were supported, I felt the hindrances disappear. Wow!

My studious review made me wonder about any teacher's depth of understanding. How does one know how deeply one has gone in practice? These were privately held secrets and rarely discussed (although, St. Theresa of Avila had outlined her stages as mansions and wrote about them in her journal). In Buddhism, the paths were described in several texts that I was just discovering. In Zen, there are ten oxherding pictures showing a path of insight.[41] The stages were well-trod paths in deep contemplative communities. I also knew I was not skilled enough in areas of carpentry to perform certain tasks. In looking at a wood carving, one could tell how advanced the carver was in their craft. In looking at a spiritual teacher, it would take quite some time and mutual understanding to know how deeply they understood. Given

---

41   Daisetz Teitaro Suzuki. *Manual of Zen Buddhism.*

the moral misconduct among many teachers, I had to question whether all of them were enlightened or how deeply the hindrances had been uprooted.

We are each ignorant; as Jesus said, "Forgive them, for they do not know what they are doing."[42] I felt I had to forgive myself over and over again and begin again. Many desires were attenuated from working a program for twenty-five years and parenting at this point. I simply wanted to practice with my whole mind and heart and gut with more clarity.

~~~

One afternoon, while I reviewed the house to-do list, and delegated certain tasks to Stewart, he asked me out of the blue, "What are you going to do now?"

"I have no idea. Well, except one."

"What is it?" he asked.

"I know this sounds crazy, but I am thinking of going to the heart of where this stuff is being practiced, where they do it the old-fashioned way, so I can be with a teacher who really understands what I am going through. And I can practice continuously, full throttle, non-stop."

"Yeah, where is that?"

"I think it is in Malaysia."

"Wow, that's pretty far."

"I know. What's cool is that the cost to meditate there is next to nothing; they offer it for free for their own citizens. They charge foreigners a small stipend of only $2.50 a day for the first two weeks and that's all!"

"Wow!"

"How can we possibly afford the airfare?" I asked.

"Let me go check." After a few minutes, he returned and said, "There are a bunch of open flights going to Asia for the Olympics, and they have some good deals. By using the points I accumulated from flying for work last year, you can fly there and back for $800."

That was the last thing I expected to hear!

---

42 Luke 23:34, NIV

"Don't you need the points?"

He replied without hesitation, "No. Because of the restrictions, they don't help me buy tickets for when I like to fly." He sighed, adding, "These spots using frequent flier miles fill up quickly, so I should book it before it disappears."

"Wait! You don't even have a job right now. No. Let me sit with it and go over all of the terms. I also need to check the kids' calendars and contact the Meditation Center to see if they have space. Can the ticket be refunded?"

"No, it would cost extra to get a refundable ticket and can't be done using these points."

I paused to notice how much I desired that special ticket; I might lose the seat as I considered it, yet it was such a big decision. Something told me I'd already been preparing to go.

"I think I'll have some sort of job in the next month or two," Stewart tentatively offered.

I paused. "Aren't you worried about me being gone so far away?"

He seemed surprised. "Oh?" With a polite smile, he replied, "Well, I go away often for my work. Isn't it your turn?"

A confusing mixture of relief, sadness, and gratitude washed over me from his reply. Not answering my question answered a question I'd been wary of calling attention to—how little he worried about me. We had become accustomed to long periods of separation with his work out of state. He never called me when he was away; he never said he missed me or us. He often wouldn't tell me or the kids when he was returning home, and he kept to himself.

On one level, this type of spouse was ideal for me because he didn't place any demands on our relationship, giving me the space I needed to further cultivate my practice. Sometimes though, I wanted to know how much I mattered to him, and how my practice affected him. When I asked him about this, he just blinked and said things were fine. He seemed quite neutral. And while he didn't object, I had still been doing the majority of the parenting.

"Are you okay being here alone with the kids?" I asked.

He was already on the stairway when he responded, his words coming slowly, "We'll be all right. Let me know what you decide."

All of a sudden, the idea of flying to Asia to sit in a Mahāsi Meditation Center for three months felt like a radical departure from my everyday presence and long history in my community. It would be best to leave after the kids were back in school in September. Forrest was starting high school, and Preston was starting at a local community college with a scholarship for the first semester's tuition.

I talked with the kids about my leaving for a longer retreat. We would still be able to spend time together over the next few months with biking and ushering at a local theater. I brought out the globe and showed them, for their sake as well as my own, that I would be on the other side of the planet from where we lived. I couldn't go any farther than off-planet to practice! Forrest had his priorities in mind; he was already over six feet tall and still growing. He asked me, "How am I going to eat?" I told him he would have to learn more about cooking. I would teach him.

I sat down and figured that up to this point, perhaps, since I am a slow learner, I was most likely an average American, and would probably need the entire three months that was recommended. I could be back in time for Thanksgiving. That would at least give me enough time to cycle through the stages several times and practice working with the hindrances for release.

If it didn't work out as I had hoped for attaining stream-entry, there was still the retreat in March at Spirit Rock the following year. Or maybe I could ramp up practice at home by arranging things in a more secluded way over the winter.

The journey would involve four legs of travel. Minneapolis to San Francisco. San Francisco to Tokyo. Tokyo to Singapore. Then, finally, I would fly from Singapore to Penang, Malaysia, an island off the west coast of Malaysia.

In three days, after reviewing the details of what the trip would entail, I asked my husband, "Is the ticket still available at that low price?"

He checked and said, "It is!"

"I'm ready." It was time. I knew it. I simply had to go where there was wise support as soon as possible.

What a relief to have this planned. I'd completed plenty of silent retreats alone in hermitages but not made the kind of progress I was making when I was with a teacher and community. I would leave in early September after the kids had completed their first week of school.

I met with Steve at Dharma Field and told him, "I'm leaving for a long retreat." He hesitated, so I asked him, "What is it?"

He said, "I don't want you to abandon your kids."

I simply stared at him. If he had gotten more acquainted with me, he would not have said this.

I moved on. "I was wondering if you have any advice or a note for my new teacher?" I thought it might assist my new teacher in understanding my practice and help create a connection. But, just as the question slipped out, I could see how silly it was. Each moment presents itself fully. My new teacher would immediately see what he needed to see.

"You do not need anything from me. You are free," he said.

I pondered this. *We are free.*

And, I was free from whatever he thought about how I raised my children.

He bowed and said, "Good luck."

As I returned the bow, I wondered what he meant by "luck." I thought it had more to do with right effort, mindfulness, and concentration, along with luck.

I appreciated his expression and concern. Enough said.

Over the next few days, I started a list of things to do in preparation for my trip. I hadn't been out of the country since I was nineteen years old. I needed a careful budget, my absentee ballot, passport, immunizations, and more.

My sponsor just about had a heart attack when I told him. He also asked me if the place was safe. I nodded. Life is uncertain but I trusted the process.

He murmured with assent while we both sat with the quiet space of the room.

CHAPTER TWENTY-SIX

Graceful Preparations

T HE FIRST THING I had to do to prepare for the trip was teach the children to cook for themselves. They knew how to make sandwiches and heat frozen food, and they had assisted with several meals, but the kids needed to know more, and our makeshift kitchen in the basement would be sufficient. I helped to refresh their memory with a simple variety of easy, healthy recipes they could prepare for themselves. But, just in case, I packed the freezer with frozen pizzas and vegetables. I figured they would get to the vegetables eventually.

As I practiced at home and continued with mindfulness in everyday events, there were some improvements in communication, functioning, and life in general. Minnesota winters hit hard, starting as early as October, bringing heavy snow, icy streets, and teeth-chattering sub-zero temperatures. It was tough on everything, so I took charge of shutting off external water valves, organizing materials, and gathering items into proper storage.

There would need to be a system for taking care of Ruby, so I made laminated "pooped" and "peed" index cards that could be put out to communicate between the kids and Stewart when she had gone outside. To stay on top of things and prevent costly problems, I put up calendars to mark important dates, and taped up notes around the house as reminders.

It would be a challenge for Stewart to manage the house and supervise the children. Or I should say, "be with the young men," who did not

206

need quite as much looking after anymore at ages fifteen and eighteen. Or did they? I compiled lists for Stewart outlining clear instructions to check in with the kids, open the mail, take care of the house, and focus on a few projects. Doing this helped him function better and alleviated some of my concerns, but my decision still seemed risky in many ways.

I felt sad and a little guilty that I would miss Forrest's sixteenth birthday in late September. It would be difficult for us both. There was no making up for what has passed. Sometimes, we need to make sacrifices for the greater good. What is *is*. I was called to go.

I stopped in to talk to our neighbor friends Marge and Jeff, letting them know I'd be away for twelve weeks, and asked if they could keep an extra eye out for Stewart, the boys, and the house. They both chimed in, "Yep, always do."

Since I needed a more efficient communication device for traveling to accept emails, I bought my first used touchscreen phone online for $200. Little did I know that I would spend twenty-six hours reprogramming the thing so it would accept our cheap family phone plan. Once we got it to work, I handed down my old flip phone for my sons to share when they were in need.

Preston was called up for jury duty right after he turned eighteen, and Forrest had more yardwork to carefully schedule. Because the kids made $15 an hour (twice the minimum wage) from their yard business, they had enough savings to buy their own audio devices and computers. Stewart continued to look for work and had regular phone interviews. I hoped that he would get a job in his field within a month or two, but it was uncertain due to the recession.

Before I would leave in early September, I had to carefully consider which immunizations to get: hepatitis B, yellow fever, dengue fever, tuberculosis, and any other diseases that could be contracted in the area. The hepatitis B vaccine shots gave me migraine headaches like I hadn't had in years. The mosquitoes carry a risk of malaria, but I decided to not buy the malaria vaccine pills due to the expense, choosing instead to bring a good repellent as a potential deterrent. I also saw my Eastern Medicine doctor for a general checkup, and went to the dentist.

After seeing an acupuncturist three times and getting no relief for my wrist pain, I saw a hand surgeon who diagnosed that I had a ganglion cyst on the top of my wrist pressing down on a critical nerve. He said that folks sometimes get them from holding paperback books awkwardly when they read for hours in the same position, cutting off circulation, but I hadn't been doing that.

We discussed how it likely happened at the retreat when I unknowingly leaned on my right wrist while holding a mudra with thumbs touching. He held a heavy hardcover book and initially suggested slamming it down on my wrist to dissolve the bump! No thanks! But then, setting the book back on his shelf, he said the best option was surgery, which included cutting to the bone and scraping it clean. I scheduled it right away, and asked him to remove a sliver in the palm of my hand too.

Unfortunately, the earliest they could schedule me for surgery was only ten days before leaving the country. I'd need to cut the stitches myself when I was in Malaysia. The doctor said it would heal in a few weeks. (That wasn't true for me—it took over twelve weeks to heal, and an entire year for full flexibility and strength to return.)

Out of gratitude for my close friends, I invited them to a tea party at the Lake Harriet Rose Garden. I set up a card table and chairs. We all sat together eating a lovely gluten-free strawberry shortcake I had made with lots of whipped cream. We also sipped iced tea on that marvelous early afternoon with the roses in full bloom. It felt really special to be together; to see and smell the beautiful blossoms with dear friends.

Each of us went around and shared various events that were changing in our lives. They all surprised me with a necklace they had worked on together by each making her own unique strand of fringe and combining it into a necklace. Wow! It touched my heart. I felt happy to be loved and supported in going forward.

We are alone and not alone.

~~~

The summer flew by as I strolled back and forth to the zendo, immersing myself in every half-day or full-day sesshin available. At home, with the help of my family, I completed several inexpensive projects with mindfulness—hanging drywall, putting up reused cabinets, and pouring a cement pad for the future air-conditioning condenser. After a decade's worth of effort, I finished my beadwork picture. With the school year approaching, I made sure Forrest and Preston were organized and had new notebooks and backpacks ready to go. As quickly as the sawdust scattered, they were settled into their fall school routine and kissing me goodbye at the airport.

Then suddenly, with my bag, ticket, and passport, I was flying halfway around the globe.

CHAPTER TWENTY-SEVEN

Willing to Go to Any Length

IN THE SINGAPORE AIRPORT, I had to wait seven hours overnight for a small plane to take me farther into Malaysia. My head and shoulders drooped heavily from the lengthy trip. I needed to rest. I settled onto a small couch in a quaint coffee shop, and soon, a friendly Malaysian woman took a seat beside me.

"When is your plane?" she asked.

"Not for seven hours."

"Where are you from?"

"The U.S. In the Midwest."

"Why are you so far from home?"

"I am here to practice meditation."

"Oh, you are coming here to pray? That is beautiful."

"I'm so tired I can't hold myself up."

She paused. "Just put your head down here, and I will watch your bags for you. I am leaving in a few hours, but you can rest now."

Seeing her gentle, open expression, I shifted to lie on my left side, avoiding pressure on my wrapped right wrist, and gratefully collapsed into a much-needed rest.

After three hours, a light pat on my arm roused me, and then she was gone.

Feeling somewhat refreshed, I sat up and practiced centering prayer with awareness of the sensations of being alive, moment by moment.

Finally, I boarded the little plane, which took me onward to Penang Island. The other passengers spoke English and were hospitable. The view of the coastline, dotted with islands in the deep blue-green sea, was nothing short of breathtaking.

I collected my bag at the claim area. Per the protocol, I prepaid for a taxi to the hotel and went out to the line of drivers, taking the first one in line. The driver, dressed all in white and wearing a turban, took my bag roughly and drove me to the hotel, swerving around bicyclists and pedestrians right and left.

Glancing out the window to my right, I saw a man driving a tiny motorcycle, with a toddler seated in front of him and a woman situated behind him, carrying a bundled baby strapped to her back. They had no helmets. I knew having this many on a motorcycle was illegal in the United States.

As I rummaged around in the tattered back seat of the cab, I discovered there were no seat belts. I quickly reached up and tapped the driver on the shoulder to ask him to slow down, but this only made him press harder on the accelerator, pushing me back into my seat. Maybe it was a mistake to touch him, perhaps an intrusion, especially from a woman. Still, I tried to get him to slow down, but my plea only increased his speed even more! Not once did he turn his head in my direction. I prayed that my life would be spared long enough to get to the meditation center. My one true desire to know the Truth wasn't going to help if I died first!

The hotel overlooked the shoreline on the northeast corner of the island, facing the mainland, which I could barely see on the hazy horizon. Thin, spirally trees lined the busy avenue in front of the hotel. On the other side of the road, the beach was muddy before the white, mirror-like ocean. I paid my driver and tugged my luggage to the front desk only to discover that they couldn't find my reservation. They were kind enough to stow my suitcase while I visited the enormous shopping mall next to the hotel to find an international phone card and check the details when calling home.

Eventually, after five hours, the hotel staff found the missing communication for the room and I got checked in. These mishaps were a common occurrence during my travels because the discount hotel websites sometimes did not forward my receipts.

Each day at 3 p.m., I fell over in bed as I meditated, utterly exhausted, and woke up around 1 a.m. I had booked the hotel for three days before going to the center to recover from jet lag. Because it was a monastic center, the schedule would be extremely strict; I wanted to enter rested and prepared to slip right in without any fuss. But I was not so young anymore, so I extended my stay another two days at the hotel, for a total of five days of peaceful and silent practice in my room before I finally started going to bed at 8 p.m. and could sync with the time change.

Coming from a cold climate, I found the heat a huge shock. Temperatures during the day were at least 100°F and incredibly humid. The cool air-conditioning of my room, the nearby shopping mall, and restaurants with available WiFi offered a welcome respite as I adjusted to the weather. I was able to use my first cell phone, which we had bought on eBay just before I left, to send texts to my family, and I sent emails from the hotel's computer to let them know all was well.

The swelling and pain in my right wrist from the recent surgery had intensified. I cut the tops off some white athletic socks, soaked them in cold water, and wore them as cool compresses to protect the sutures and keep the wound clean. Often, I had to stop and use my awkward left hand instead.

This injury, however, turned out to be a blessing in disguise. In meditation, rather than hold a mudra with my thumbs touching, I comfortably let one palm simply rest on top of the other with my thumbs relaxed. Because I use my hands so much for work, they are somatically tied to my being a "doer"—a carpenter, a cook, a cleaner, a mother, a fixer, etc. This facilitated letting go of roles and resting in *simply being.*

On my second day at the hotel, I met Jamel, who would be my main taxi driver for my stay in Malaysia. He was much more relaxed than my first taxi driver. He dressed in casual clothes, spoke English, and understood my request to drive slowly. His car also had seatbelts. He drove a gray Proton Wira, which didn't have any decals on the outside as I am accustomed to seeing on taxis in the U.S. After taking me on an errand, he gave me his phone number and invited me to call him whenever I needed a ride.

When I awoke on the fourth day, I looked out my window to see several dozen workers in bright vests walking down the beach and along the street, picking up litter and emptying garbage cans. When I asked about the excitement around the hotel at the front desk, I learned that they were preparing for an event called the Mooncake Festival. The harvest celebration dates back over 3,000 years to China's Shang Dynasty and is held every year on the night of the full moon between early September and early October.

In the hotel lobby, some thin boys had been diligently mopping sections of the floor. I'd seen them working hard each day. I pictured my sons spending hours pulling weeds in the heat all summer long and saving every dollar. I carefully stepped to the side of the wet sections so as not to undo their work. Then, as one of the workers was still cleaning an obviously damp area, a boisterous party of tourists in designer clothes and gold jewelry strolled over his efforts, pausing to take a group selfie. Their blatant disregard made my jaw drop as they proceeded toward a large SUV taxi waiting outside, leaving a trail of heel impressions on the wet floor.

Isn't there suffering in blatant avoidance of seeing what is right in front of us? I considered the stark contrast between the number of wealthy and impoverished people in the world, and why that might be the case. I thought, What are the multimillionaires and billionaires doing to help our world? It was too much to bear. I needed to let go for the moment by offering loving energy to the boys mopping the floor. It took another minute of reflection to also offer kindness to the rich tourists.

As I stood gazing out the large lobby window, a beautiful young woman joined me to view the street activities. She introduced herself as Jenna, from London, and she was working as an evening singer in the hotel bar. It was curious to me that a woman would come so far, not knowing anyone here, to perform.

While walking around the area, our attention was drawn to stages being set up with ornately decorated cloth. Meanwhile, actors dressed in beautiful silk robes and headdresses were rehearsing for small productions as part of the festival.

We strolled down the street to a small restaurant for lunch, soaking in the bustle of excitement all around us. When we arrived, I was amazed by the vast number of aquariums against the restaurant's inner wall, housing a diverse assortment of live fish and mollusks. I stared at one tank with a single enormous fish that could barely turn around, the container just large enough to hold it.

When I ordered nothing but a bit of egg and rice, the waiters appeared disheartened that I had chosen one of the premier seafood establishments on the coast of Penang but hadn't requested any seafood. I shrugged off their complaints, simply content to be spending time with someone friendly.

As we began to talk, Jenna asked me what I was doing in Malaysia and was shocked to learn I had come this far to meditate. I had to pause at the thought too. After all, this was the second time someone had expressed surprise at my journey since I had left. *How could I explain to her the longing I felt in my core to awaken?*

I explained that it was simply much more affordable to go to Malaysia for twelve weeks. Retreat places I had researched in the U.S. cost about $100+ per day plus lodging, compared with $2.50 per day here! Ten-day Goenka retreats are less expensive, but I didn't think I'd comply with the strict body-scanning technique. At many retreat centers, I was presented with a lengthy scholarship form to fill out, and coming from a poor background, I felt chastened by that process. (Although, I did move forward and ask for a scholarship from Spirit Rock; I had not heard back from them yet.) I especially needed to go to a welcoming place that was flexible to the length of stay.

I thought it was brave of her to come alone so far from home to sing every evening for people in a bar. She too talked about needing to make a living and wanting to do what she enjoyed. She said she was finishing her short term contract and was paid more for a singing gig there than in London.

We chatted for a while about other things in the company of the tilapia and the geoduck and then parted ways. I never spoke to her again, but was grateful for her company. Walking back to the hotel, I noticed throngs of people filling the street and sidewalk. The street in front of the hotel was blocked off for the parade that was about to begin. Mooncakes were for sale all around the area. I wanted to taste them but discovered they were made from wheat.

I weaved amidst the people, enjoying the festivities. The mayor and other dignitaries were in attendance, watching the parade's pomp and stateliness. At one point, several strong male performers competed to balance huge wood poles with enormous triangular flags on their foreheads, chins, lower jaws, and shoulders. Another group of men lifted the motionless figure of a dragon puppet, bringing it to life, which gave the illusion of a dancing dragon.

Once the sun had set and the last light had drifted from the hazy horizon, magnificent fireworks lit up the faces of the Malaysian people, with hundreds of candlelit lanterns floating upward to the moon. I was touched by a family of four who lit four small candles under a bench on the sidewalk and made their prostrations. Then they blew out their candles and gathered them into a box the mother had stored in her bag before they left. The whole ceremony with the community was uplifting and made my heart sing as I made my way back to my quiet hotel room.

~~~

The next morning, I called Jamel, and he was available to take me to the Meditation Center. The only prior arrangement I had made was an email with a volunteer staff member confirming when I would arrive. We had a little trouble finding it because he wasn't familiar with the area. Our eyes eventually landed on a beautiful, tall structure with a crimson-red roof and elaborate turrets. As we approached the center, a mural of the Buddha teaching five disciples on the front of the building came into view.

We looked across the yard at another colorful building, a Thai monastery, and noticed several monks passing by. When I opened my wallet to get some ringgits to pay Jamel, he put his hand up, refusing to accept any money for the trip.

"Why not?" I asked, extending the money towards him.

A cautious expression washed over his face, and he murmured, "Hmm, you powerful yogi."

I laughed with surprise and shook my head, "Well, not yet, at least."

He leaned firmly on the trunk of his old gray sedan, unamused. "You meditate; maybe I not take it."

I paused, matching the seriousness of his expression, then remembered that I had inquired about him and his family. "But, you have five children. Would you take it for them?"

His demeanor shifted. Jamel put his hand on his heart, and smiled, gladly accepting it. He insisted that I call him when I was leaving or if I needed anything. Then he drove off.

Standing there, feet touching earth, I breathed deeply with happiness to have arrived.

I hoped there was still space for me. Places like this go back to ancient patriarchal times; generally, they had room for men. Today, if there were limited spaces available, a male monk or male yogi would definitely be given priority over a nun or female yogi. Because things change day by day at the center, would there be enough room for a woman?

I stood at the doorway, my heart already taking refuge in the shining triple gem: the Buddha, the Dhamma, and the Sangha. I tuned into the desire that had brought me to this place, the intent to go on this journey, the energy to practice, and the inquiry. And in the next breath, I felt all of that wash away. I was here.

There arose a new readiness and willingness to do whatever it took to extinguish my *one true desire*. The next step was to walk through the door.

Malaysian Buddhist Meditation Center

CHAPTER TWENTY-EIGHT

Time for Awakening

A WOMAN VOLUNTEER welcomed me and directed me to place my suitcase at the rear of the building before entering the front office to pay my fees and complete a brief form. As I turned the corner, two monks in maroon robes came down the steps. The older monk eyed me carefully as the wheel of my bag snagged on the rough sidewalk, slipping from my fingers; my water bottle dropped to the ground with a crunch. The younger monk, who couldn't have been more than eighteen years old, bent down to retrieve the bottle and handed it to me.

The volunteer ran quickly ahead and opened a door to a small room with three cots. She said I could leave my bag there temporarily, and then, facing me, she firmly stated, "The teacher will decide if you can stay."

After I filled out the form for the teacher, Sayadaw U Thuzana, she read over the rules of the center, and asked me with seriousness to sign the form. Right away, the young monk popped into the office, took the form from her, and left with it in hand.

I was expected to wear white at all times. Those who wore all white were full-time yogis. The yogis wearing black pants with white shirts were part-time practitioners and were not staying at the center. I wanted to change out of my long blue shorts and blue shirt, but she insisted I head upstairs—the teacher was waiting to meet me.

She instructed me to leave my sandals on a shelf outside the entrance, where many dozens of sandals had been stored. I walked upstairs to the second floor where I met a thin man with bright twinkling eyes, large ears, and a wide smile. Wrapped in burgundy robes, he sat on a wooden chair at the end of a long hall. He was the one who had looked at me carefully when I arrived, and was holding the form I had filled out minutes before. In front of him was an older woman in pink robes, her head cleanly shaved. She sat on the bare hardwood floor in a Burmese posture, her legs folded to one side.

He motioned for me to sit on the floor in front of him.

Humbled, I kneeled and bowed. He bowed in return.

"Constance?" He glanced at the piece of paper and said my name in a long, drawn-out way as if he were singing it.

"Is that how I say your name? Constance?" He made a "z" sound at the end. I liked it, so I said yes. He introduced me to the older nun beside him, and said her name, Achara.

I nodded and waited. The beautiful old parquet wood floor felt hard and cool compared to the carpeted floor in the hotel where I had recently practiced.

"Where are you from?"

"I am from Minnesota in the United States."

"Where is that?"

"It is in the middle of the United States at the top."

"And, you have children?"

"Yes."

"How old are they?"

"They are fifteen and eighteen. No," I said, putting one finger up. "One is almost sixteen."

"Oh, they are big now!"

"Yes, I have worked hard with them. They do well in school."

He paused for some time.

I took in his presence, his kind eyes, his soft voice.

Breathing. I noticed breathing in short and out short.

I almost cried, my voice cracking. "I have waited so long for this opportunity to practice."

"Well, Constance, have you seen the arising and passing?"

"Yes, well, er ... that's for sure!"

They both laughed, looked at each other, and then turned their attention back to me.

"When was this?"

I hesitated, as there had been so many. My mind focused on the one in April, and so I said, "In April."

"Then, you must understand what it is to practice well, and to keep practicing."

I nodded.

"Constance, what do you want?"

"I want to *really know* the Dhamma. I need your help. Can you help me?"

He nodded affirmatively, adding, "Constance, now you must set aside *all* of your worldly concerns."

He nodded to Achara. She bowed three times, and I bowed too. This indicated the interview was over.

"Achara will show you to your kuti."

After the interview, I was relieved and thrilled to receive a key, and therefore be accepted at the center. Achara pointed at my key, then at the row of kutis—small huts about four steps up from the ground, made out of half-inch plywood about six feet by seven feet in size. My key was for a kuti farther away from the main building. I found it and put my suitcase inside, grimacing at having to heft it up the four steps with both hands, aggravating my sore wrist.

I looked inside and there was just a wooden cot with a metal frame. She said to go into the main building to get my mattress and blanket. I visited the office and was given a mattress, which consisted of two inches of well-used foam, pressed flat as a pancake, and wrapped in a thin sheet. The "blanket" was just two bed sheets sewn together, so I asked for another. The pillow was square, just large enough for my head, and only an inch thick. Fortunately, I had a small travel pillow with me, and a two-inch thick, short inflatable camping mattress for my bad back, so I placed that under the mattress. I didn't need my back to go out this far from home.

Before I had time to unpack, Achara was at my door motioning for me to follow her right away. She then paused, gave me a quick once-over, and said I must change first. So, I put on my white yogi clothes, and we headed upstairs into the hall. When we passed the second floor, I saw several monks doing walking meditation. Achara looked at me, shaking her head strongly. I took this to mean that these were the monks' quarters and that we must always pass through quickly.

We went on to the third floor where I'd do both sitting and walking meditation. It was a large and beautiful hall with hardwood flooring and tall ceilings. Being a carpenter, I recognized it as rainforest wood, a rare variety, and that it would hold up well in this humid and rainy climate. The windows all around the hall had screens, but the mesh was two inches square—designed to keep out birds, not mosquitoes. The evening sun cast long shadows across the room. Two wings on each side flanked the hall where there were a few rooms toward the front of the building that faced south.

The Buddha altar was situated at the far end of the room. It displayed a large golden Buddha in a seated posture surrounded by fresh flowers. She said this area, nearest to the altar, was for monks only. Male yogis sat behind the monks, while the nuns sat behind the male yogis. Female yogis were meant to stay at the back of the hall. That was fine with me. Per my usual habit, I found a place in the back, inside one of the flanking tiers where I found a common white plastic armless chair by the wall.

She said that the teacher wanted to see me again, and that I should wait right there until he was ready. She also showed me where there were floor cushions in a shelf area on the other side of the room. If I wanted to sit on the floor, I could use their cushions, but a chair was okay to use as well. I chose a few cushions for the floor and placed them next to my chair to try alternating between both options. How nice it was to be able to use a chair if I wanted! I sat in the chair to take in the whole space and began meditative practice right away.

~~~

It had been really helpful to have five days to rest and get into a schedule before going there. I started to feel into my breath energy right away, realizing the precious gift of time to practice wholeheartedly. I noticed breathing in short and breathing out long, and some tiredness arising, but before I knew it, energy arose, and at 9:30 p.m., they all began chanting in the ancient Pāli language, led by the voice of my new teacher into a microphone. The monks and nuns echoed their beautiful prayers throughout the hall.

At each hour, a clock near the stairway chimed. At ten o'clock, there were ten chimes, which I heard one after the other, indicating it was time to go to bed. No one rang the bell; it was apparently set up digitally to chime every hour, but I never heard it ring between ten o'clock and four o'clock, perhaps because I was asleep.

When I returned to my kuti, a short older man came up beside me and bowed.

"You can call me Uncle Choo. If you need something, you ask me, and always lock your door."

"Thank you, thank you so much." I bowed back to him.

In a flash, out of the corner of my eye, the brightness of the moon caught my attention. I gazed upward and pointed, "See that?!" I exclaimed.

"Oh, yes." He stood and gazed up with me.

The moon resonated in my belly, and I felt something tingle from my finger up my arm and into my heart. I reflected on the entire planet and all the beings and how I was halfway around the globe. It felt the same in some way. Then it made me think, as my finger pointed, to not mistake the finger pointing at the moon for the moon. This was something I had once heard in a poem by the Zen poet Ryōkan Taigu at a Dharma talk back home.

I bowed good night to Uncle Choo and the moon, and all beings on this lovely planet. He disappeared into a small portable trailer near my kuti. At once, I felt at home there.

I began unpacking my bag under the one long, fluorescent bulb in the room and noticed there were no drawers or places to store personal belongings. There were also no curtains, so I switched off the light to put on my pajamas and sighed as I slid into my makeshift bed. Then I started to worry about the mosquitoes buzzing around my head. My eyes were drawn to the large holes in the window screens, which caused me to get out a small roll of duct tape I had brought. As I placed several pieces over the holes, a slight uneasiness arose at the thinking sense door. I dismissed it. Slipping back under the covers, a curious tingling sensation lulled me to sleep.

In the middle of the night, a rumbling motor powered on and off at irregular intervals behind my hut. I tossed and turned. Since I had drunk so much water that day, I had to get up anyway to find the closest bathroom.

After carefully locking my door with the key, I wandered out into the pouring rain in the dark. An assortment of old wooden cots and tables were stacked up around the building. Passing a large mound of rocks, I nearly tripped over a shovel and tried to avoid slipping in the mud as I weaved around a couple of wheelbarrows.

Three enormous toads lounged at the foot of the door to the bathroom, one sitting on top of the brick that held the door ajar, and two more to step over in order to use the toilet. They looked old and fat, their heavy jowls blowing up and down. They sat there staring at me, their huge eyes just inches away from my feet, seemingly ready to leap at any moment. I greeted them in my mind, "Hey, how ya doing? Let's be still, all right?"

When I finally got back into my kuti and settled into bed, I noticed that the fluorescent lights under the main building's overhanging eaves were shining directly into my eyes. I got up again and rearranged the cot perpendicular to the door to avoid the lights. They had given me tangled netting to hang over my bed for mosquitoes. I untangled it and tied it up, but I kept pulling on it because the cot was too short for me. I had to sleep at an angle and bend in the middle.

Why did he tell me to always lock my door? I thought it was safe here. These were the unwelcome thoughts of my first night. What a lot of stress. Being human involves so many desires and wishes for satisfaction.

"Time to rise, 4:30 a.m.," alerted an unvarying tone through the wall of the kuti. The timely robotic announcement of my neighbor's talking clock became a reliable alarm since mine had broken during travel. As I rubbed my eyes, my bladder similarly intoned, "Time to pee."

It was time to freshen up, brush my teeth, and get to the upstairs hall to meditate. I took my vitamins and one gentle essential oil pill to aid digestion and support my immune system. The faucet's water had a metallic taste; I remembered I should only use it for brushing my teeth.

The night before, the nuns and yogis had filled their water bottles in the meditation hall from a five-gallon water dispenser. So, I brought a little bag that contained two empty water bottles to fill, and some toilet paper, just in case.

As I stepped outside, it was still very dark. A dewy, pungent zing filled the air, cooler, around 80°F. The faint stirring of the other yogis guided me to the early morning sit from 5 to 6 a.m. Some nuns sat under umbrellas with veiled nets, which they pointed out to me after a rather buggy session.

When 6 a.m. arrived, one of the cooks rang a large antique bell that hung outdoors adjacent to the building. It made a resonant "thunk" sound. One of the nuns took my arm and led me to the end of the line to demonstrate how to line up on the first floor of the main building, then walk across the parking lot to the dining hall for breakfast. We stood there until my teacher led the monks downstairs. The single-file line was always monks first, then nuns, then male yogis, and female yogis arranged at the end. We had to put on our sandals as we exited the building, so I learned quickly to prepare ahead of time by placing them on the other side of the building, ready to slip on as we passed toward the kitchen.

We glided into the dining hall, our hands in a prayerful gesture against our chests, and lowered ourselves onto stools around a circular table near the kitchen area. Since there were only a few male and female yogis at the time, we shared a table, but usually the male and female yogis would have separate tables. The nuns sat at their own table about six feet away from us yogis. The monks sat on a raised dais on the other side of the kitchen wall in a large room with space for volunteers and visitors to sit on the floor in front of them.

The appetizing smells of cooked rice, spiced meat, and fruit filled the air. I salivated and felt the pain in my stomach. I hadn't eaten since lunch the previous day. Meals were only served twice daily at 6 a.m. and 11 a.m.

Before each meal, the monks chanted prayers and blessings in Pāli for about twenty minutes, an ancient language I barely knew at the time. We were to sit and continue to meditate during all activities, meals included. The smells from the kitchen stimulated saliva and sensations of swallowing for the quickly cooling food. The monks, at the top of the hierarchy, were definitely given vegetarian meals, and some of the nuns made special arrangements to obtain their own vegetarian food. The center relied on donated meals, so the yogis were given what was left, which included fish, meat, and occasionally tofu.

There was a circular turnstile platter in the middle of the table full of plates and bowls of various dishes. I waited to learn the ritual in silence. We each took a serving of rice first, and then the rice bowl was taken away. After that, we could reach for whatever was available on the platter, and turn it toward the left when we were finished.

I had never seen many of the foods before. Not knowing what they were, I had to guess which ones might have wheat. I took things like a small amount of fish meat or some chicken, a few vegetables, and fruit. The fruit was incredible. There were huge slices of ripe red fruit I had never tried before, and I enjoyed each bite. There were many delicate cakes too, but I suspected they were wheat-based, so I did not touch them. The food was deliciously spicy. I had to mix my rice with some of the sauces that came with the meat to temper the heat. I gladly accepted what was offered.

When we all finished eating, we left in the same order we had entered. This kept the process orderly and silent. As I walked along the cool tile floor, I tried to keep from scratching the mosquito bites on my ankles. I hadn't realized they were biting me under the table, having been entirely focused on eating. I made a mental note to put on my thick athletic socks from then on before going to the dining hall.

After breakfast, at about 8 a.m., I returned to my kuti, noticed my odor, and wanted a shower. In the early daylight, I could finally see the way to the bathroom. When I stepped inside, I saw there was nothing separating the shower from the toilet and sink, and I wondered whether the toilet and sink would get sprayed by the shower. But I just accepted that this was the way the bathroom was built. The water was so cold, but I accepted that too. With the tiled floor all wet, I had to be especially mindful of balancing. I ended up getting my white clothes kind of dirty. I moved slowly, albeit awkwardly enough, to continue to note the sensations of cold, wet, slippery, caution, care, touch, and tight small breaths while I bathed.

I noticed that the female yogis washed their laundry after breakfast. I found a bucket and put in my sweaty set of white clothes to soak
in some soapy water. There was a clothesline outside my kuti and
I planned to finish the washing later, perhaps when my wrist didn't
hurt as much. I was not taking anything for the pain, not even aspirin,
because I wanted to know each and every sensation as it was arising.
Whenever it became too much, I simply took care to use my other hand
or stop and let it rest.

I followed the schedule, alternating one hour of sitting with one
hour of walking practice back and forth while going along with the two
other female yogis. Being able to alternate between the floor and the
chair prevented any back or knee trouble from arising. When I needed
to use the bathroom, I watched where the other female yogis went on
the other side of the hall near the water dispenser.

During one of the sits, two cats—one white and one gray—careened
around the corner at the top of the steps, skidding several feet onto the
smooth wood floor. They arched their backs, wrestling, biting, hissing,
and swatting one another. I found it amusing to watch the showdown.
The gray one raised his front paws and pounced onto the white one,
then both raced rip-roaring around the hall before launching down the
steps. I simply noticed energy arise in the periphery of my experience.

The lunch ritual proceeded similarly to breakfast. We were to line
up about ten minutes before the bell and walk mindfully into the hall.
I followed the nuns, who turned off their ceiling fans before we walked
downstairs. I put my sandals outside the doorway to the dining hall
and returned to get in line.

There were a few more volunteers to help cook and clean, and the
chanting seemed longer. I hadn't taken much rice from the bowl during
breakfast because I didn't want the bowl to be empty after I took from
it, so I was hungrier at lunch. In keeping the silence, I didn't want to ask
for more rice either. There were quite a few foods that might have had
wheat, so I kept my portions small.

After lunch, I realized that even a tiny crumb from my meal would
lead to an ant procession up my leg and onto my lap. They formed an
orderly line seemingly out of nowhere. Leaving just a single dirty tissue
lying around could attract millions of itty-bitty ants into my room.

After seeing this, I carefully put any refuse in the covered bin immediately. From then on, I kept my kuti very clean.

The evening came quickly and I returned to the chair I had chosen the night before in the meditation hall to watch the movements around the room. The nuns and female yogis were all spread out and had their own spots as well. I assumed the monks and male yogis did their walking meditation downstairs in their own space since they did not do it on the same floor as we did.

I noticed the faint, pleasant sensation of the air current from a distant fan that swiveled in my direction. A few of the nuns had turned on ceiling fans from a bank of switches on the wall before they sat. Looking up, I saw one fan that would provide a more direct flow of air to my spot. I went to read the faded piece of paper on the wall indicating the switches and tried to ascertain the switch for the fan closest to my spot. Through some trial and error that involved turning off a couple of the nuns' fans, I eventually discovered the correct switch, noticing the sensation of bashful whimsy as they all slowly turned their heads in my direction, like antennae detecting my movements. When I turned the switch off before leaving, I made a mental note of its location for the next day.

As I continued to happily notice the sensations of cause and effect cascade across the bodily field and then pass away, I knew that practice was progressing well, and that was all that truly mattered.

Later that evening, a young monk, whose name I didn't catch, bowed toward me in the hall after dark and said it was time to see the teacher, Sayadaw U Thuzana. He led me to a simple room next to the meditation hall with windows that faced the front of the building. The teacher sat under the windows in a low lawn chair about a foot from the floor. He greeted me with a bright smile and welcomed me. I bowed and sat in front of him on the floor.

"Constance. I forgot about you last night. You were waiting to see me. I am sorry."

"Oh!?" I hesitated. "I forgot too."

I really had. As soon as I had been told to sit and wait in that spot the night before, I began immersing myself in the sensations of being alive, moment by moment. I was just being there. There was so much to take in.

He smiled and seemed to like that.

He handed me the yogi booklet and showed me the precepts printed on the page.

I took refuge in the Buddha, the Dhamma, and the Sangha three times, then recited the eight precepts—all in Pāli to the best of my ability.

"I want you to go and listen to a Mahāsi tape with meditation instructions and continue your practice. Is there anything else you need?"

"What do I call you?"

"Sayadaw."

I repeated it phonetically, saying, "Sy-ah-door."

He nodded.

"The water tastes funny."

"We have water for drinking up here in jugs. Only use this water. The water here is not potable but okay for washing."

I nodded. "I am so far from home. I didn't realize how far I came."

"Constance, you are just here."

I nodded again, and as I breathed in, I could see what he was saying. I am just *here*, no matter where I am. There is nowhere to go but here.

"Constance. Continue."

This signaled the end of our meeting, so I bowed, and he bowed in turn.

I walked out of the room and returned to my chair.

I am just here, rang in my ears...*how open...how comforting.*

The next day during walking meditation, I walked back and forth, turning and walking back the way I came, feeling heel to floor, pressing, feeling pressure and knowing it, shifting weight and knowing it, lifting foot and knowing it, turning and knowing it. It was a passage of timeless awareness and flow. The heat of the day gave way to a soft coolness in the hall.

After walking meditation, I stopped and drank eight ounces of water, then went to the bathroom where a teeming troop of tiny ants had claimed the toilet, hence the hand sprayer next to the toilet. I prayed for the little beings as I sprayed them off the seat. When urinating, I noticed the relief of pressure, the smell of urine; the touch or smell was contacted with the mind, knowing it.

After lunch, an afternoon rain shower soaked the clothes I had hung out to dry. It didn't matter though. I squeezed them out again, and brought them inside my kuti thinking they might dry overnight.

The night brought a storm like I had never experienced. Droplets beat harshly against the tin roof and thinly walled confines of my kuti. The torrents of rain, thunder, and lightning sent shivers through me, and I was grateful to have asked for two blankets in addition to my small travel blanket from my suitcase. It was the rainy season, and *I was in a rainforest.* Even though it wasn't cold by Minnesota standards, it was startling in comparison to the afternoon heat. I noted the sensations of hearing, the pounding vibrations of rain against the little hut, and before long, I was fast asleep.

Soon enough, it was time to rise and begin again. *Constance, continue. You are just here,* echoed in my mind as I stepped up the stairs and past the sign that read "ATTENTION: You are now entering intensive meditation area. Please be quiet." The area had already extended everywhere, not just the meditation hall.

~~~

One day passed into the next as I adjusted to the schedule. By watching closely, I learned to find what I needed: laundry soap, mosquito nets in the evening for sitting and chanting, cushions to sit on the floor. On the fourth day, much like at the retreat with Adyashanti, I hit a hard spell of intense contractions as I noticed every single thing falling away, unable to grasp or cling to any image, thought, sound, smell, taste, or touch. For a brief moment, I was aware in the background that I was entering the three perceptions, making further progress as I observed the arising and passing of all phenomena in a balanced manner, while also maintaining a light focus on the object of breath at the abdomen.

In the afternoon, after lunch period, I could feel this state beginning to fade. With the air especially muggy, I chose a spot on the cool tile of the main floor to meditate. During my sit, I passed through a sublime, illuminating, and strong a&p event. I knew it was critical to stay centered and not cling to the vast and powerful awareness that was being known. It was a heated experience, and yet, that too was another thought, and an inner resolve arose to continue. For four hours, I delved into deep, painless, focused practice as this great opening unfolded.

In the evening, I felt a penetrating exhaustion, followed by irritating sensations as I drew nearer to dissolution and fear. The mind still clung slightly to the previous experience, so I continued relaxing into the sensations of Being, moment by moment.

There was definite momentum.

~~~

Every other night, the teacher's assistant invited me to see the teacher for a ten- to fifteen-minute visit. I had been given a yogi book when I arrived that listed the rules and how to report to the teacher. I committed to following all the rules and instructions to the best of my ability.

He smiled when I asked him how he was, in my usual Minnesotan way. He said he was well, and swiftly steered the conversation in my direction.

"Constance, how is your practice?"

"I have seen the arising and passing away."

"Oh, when was this?"

"Yesterday, downstairs in the afternoon." Then, I shared a few details about my current state.

He nodded, considering this, and said, "Constance, continue," signaling the end of the interview.

It was up to me. I was practicing and simply had to keep going. I didn't feel like I was relying on him. I wasn't sure what he could say that would help anyway. And, because this was a Mahāsi center, I knew that what I said would be understood.

On the fifth day, as we walked back to our kutis after lunch, one of the other yogis approached me. In hushed tones, her lips barely moving, she said, "My name is Gho. What is your name?"

"Constance."

"There is a kuti open, number four, closer to the main building. I think you might want to take it."

"Oh, how do I do that?"

"First you must put your bucket on the step of kuti four, then go and find the teacher and ask him if you can make the change." She walked on ahead, then turned abruptly to face me. "You are not supposed to dry your clothes in your kuti; you must use the place at the end of the yard under the overhang. They will not get wet there."

Apparently, I was being noticed. I felt a little embarrassed to have broken a rule about where to hang my clothes—it seemed practical to take them into my room to dry. I had seen the place where others hung their clothes, but I assumed it was only for nuns due to the nuns' robes that hung there.

I returned to my kuti and considered what to do. I didn't want to interrupt my practice by finding the teacher, or cause a ruckus by moving my things across the long yard to the other kuti. She had probably heard me splashing through puddles around the construction materials in the yard as I dashed to the bathroom at night in the frequent downpours. The kuti she suggested was a lot closer to the bathroom. What a gift! It seemed a wise thing to do. *Would this break up my focus?* Then I heard a little knock on my door. It was Gho.

"You had better move or it will be taken."

Okay, I thought. That settled it. "Where do I find the teacher?"

"He is on the second floor in room number ten. You must knock and then wait. He rests there after lunch."

I nodded, then set my bucket on the step of kuti number four and headed upstairs. A certain heaviness became apparent in my knock on his door, revealing the tiresome energy emanating from the stage of misery. Making a conscious effort to calm myself while waiting, I told myself, "For gosh sakes, Constance, just stay with this process. *Breathe in a nourishing way.*"

After about five minutes, he came out and I asked him if I could move to another kuti. I stood there, knowing: standing, pressure, feet touching wood. Breathing in, breathing out. If he said "No," it would be easy then. I would just stay where I was. I had nothing to lose.

He considered it and looked at me, then walked gracefully and with intention to a desk drawer in the hall. He pulled out a key and gave it to me. I bowed and thanked him.

When I tried to open the kuti door, the key didn't work. In my nervousness, I remembered the number incorrectly. I had to go back up to apologize and ask for the right key. I was tempted to forget the whole thing, but now it was in motion. I saw Gho watching me out of the corner of her eye. When I went back up he was just as graceful as before, and we exchanged keys. I was feeling tight, scattered, worried, and my back pain was increasing as I moved silently.

After I got back to my old kuti, I began gathering up some things from my bag, being mindful not to twist my wrist. I made four or five very slow round trips, sparing myself the effort of repacking my entire bag and the potential strain on my wrist from lugging it all at once.

I stayed gently aware in each movement: walking, left, right, left, right, lifting, putting down, opening, laying out, wiping, touching, breathing, in and out, stopping, pausing. I reassured myself, *no need to rush.* It felt weird to bring time into awareness while in a timeless state. Everyone would understand that I was changing kutis. Reframing the undertaking with openness helped me pause frequently, and *be with* the entire process mindfully.

On my last trip to round up the last of my things, a young man and woman arrived at the doorstep of the kuti next to my previous one, and kissed goodbye sweetly. She appeared reluctant to part with him, her grip tight on his arm before he left her standing there.

I approached her to introduce myself and welcome her to the center. In some fragmented English, she said her name was Semry, and that she was from Thailand while her boyfriend was from France. They had come to the center together, but she appeared quite hesitant about separating from him by the way she had clutched at his shirt.

I was in the midst of intense meditation practice, dedicated as ever. I let her know I was moving to another kuti, and I'd be with her in practice. After she stepped into her kuti, I fetched a bucket over by the hose area and put it on her step.

The new kuti had a little wardrobe in it, but there was no means to hang my toiletry kit. So, I used my little travel screwdriver to fashion

a hook in the stud with a drywall screw from my travel kit. I spotted an old small table in the furniture pile by the construction area and cleaned it. With slow, mindful movements, I watched the mind like a centaur to guard against anything negative, and stayed with feelings of gratitude and happiness for the whole moving process.

Setting up my new space took several hours—carrying belongings, organizing the room, and doing my daily wash. But now, I had a side table to set my watch, vitamins, tissues, and the necklace my friends had made for me. Plus, I had a place to hang my clothes. It was nice to be closer to the bathroom. The window screens had fewer holes; I covered them with duct tape. The bed was the same as before, and the building lights still shone in, but it was already a vast improvement. I was also right next to the older nun, Achara, and if anyone could keep me on track, she would. Considering everything, this was the best place I could possibly be for practice.

Gho approached me after I had finished moving and motioned for me to follow her. She pointed out the hot water button outside the bathroom, demonstrating how to turn it on by clicking the switch on the wall and pressing down the duct tape over the wire holding it in place. "Remember to turn it off here, after you're done," she added.

"Oh, there is hot water!?" I whispered in astonishment, while feeling the thrill of moving upward on a Ferris wheel.

She nodded and smiled slightly with pressed lips. "We usually take turns in the afternoon. I go around 3 p.m."

I nodded. I had tried to shower, but several times when I went out, someone was in the bathroom, so I would go back to meditating upstairs. I thought it would be useful to have a sign-up sheet, but that meant I'd have to initiate something, and speak, which was not allowed. I went once in the evening and was swarmed by mosquitoes, but during the daytime I didn't notice them as much. She was doing me a favor by providing at least one clue when *not* to take a shower.

"What is wrong with your wrist?"

I peeled back my bandage and showed her the black stitches on my swollen wrist.

"Oh, that is painful. Too hard to wash clothes."

I nodded.

"Just put your clothes in a bucket outside your kuti and I will arrange to have them cleaned for you. It will not cost much."

I nodded.

She had already made one good suggestion. I told myself to go with the flow. This was generosity, and I gratefully accepted it.

Over the next few days, I continued to go to my spot and use the fan high up on the ceiling for some subtle relief as sweat rolled down my body. I leafed through the *Progress of Insight* I had brought with me, but it was useless to me now. Each moment must be fully met. I simply had to continue. At least I knew I wasn't going crazy, that this was all part of the process of dismantling a solid, seemingly separate sense of self.

During my meeting with the teacher, he asked me as usual, "Constance, how is your practice?"

I looked at him and pleaded, "I cannot hold onto anything!" while I lifted my left arm and reached out to grasp at the air with my fingers. As my fingers closed, his gaze shifted from me to my hand, and then he met my eyes once more.

"Hold onto what?" he asked, his voice steady and calm.

I looked quizzically at my empty hand with a growing sense of nothing to hold onto.

He nodded and smiled serenely, as if to indicate, *This is a great relief.*

I was not smiling. "I can only see the ends of things; all is vanishing."

He nodded again to this truism, "Constance, continue," which signaled the end of the interview and prompted me to get up, allowing him to start the beautiful chanting at 9:30 p.m., as he did before bedtime every night.

I went to find a mosquito net and sat for the chanting, just "hearing" the echoing choir of monks and nuns and yogis reverberating sound waves through the body in a flutter of vanishing sensations.

The entire world as I understood it was crumbing. I had to sit or stand or walk and *directly watch* my suffering and the desire to end it as the cause of suffering. Compassion for this seemingly separate sense of self, caught in this loop, was the only way to continue.

A considerable amount of my hearing attention throughout the day went to two men in the yard constructing a new brick and stucco building next to the kutis. The sand against the shovel, the mixer pouring, the scraping of the trowel against the bricks, and the turning of the shovel in the wheelbarrow as the sand and water crunched and softened into a usable mortar sent vibrations of the knowledge of "hearing" reverberating throughout the body. It seemed to simultaneously distance the sensations of misery and disgust and bring up joy in the mind. It actually felt fun. I welcomed each shovelful of sand as it echoed in the yard and bounced in waves around the body and the room. Even the slight anticipation of the next shovelful "crunch" was delightful to *know.*

Each day, as I passed by the construction on the way to and from my kuti, the walls of the new building grew a little higher. I remembered the footings I had mixed and poured for my own house, and the years I had spent watching construction around our neighborhood. Remembering, remembering, seeing, seeing—memories floating by the screen of Awareness.

I wasn't watching in the same way anymore. There was a watching happening on its own, and the sounds all around the building were felt and known within the body.

The full moon waned, the rains fell, and the sun rose again, the heat penetrating through my thick white cotton clothes, and another day flowed into the next.

I discovered a rhythm and found "my" time to shower around 4:30 or 5 p.m., after all the other yogis had finished. The pleasant sensations of a hot shower each day added to the happiness I felt in the practice there.

At times, an edginess arose, then grew to an almost unbearable intensity as coarse vibrations and a deafening hiss assaulted my senses. The mind questioned what was happening and whether I could endure it.

I needed to move. As I walked towards the front of the building, the nods and beautiful smiles from each passerby uplifted my spirit. Basking under the sun's tender rays amidst the vibrant flowers gradually eased some of the coarseness. Though, even as tight and painful sensations began to rip through my system, just as they had on my June retreat, there was an underlying happiness amidst it all.

My son, Forrest, and I had taken tai chi classes together during the spring season at Dharma Field from a wonderful old gentleman; I wanted to practice. The teacher said it would be okay for exercise, but only in the morning while it was still dark, in the parking lot, way over to the side, behind the bushes, away from everyone else. Doing some wellness body movements helped ground my energy each morning.

On the seventh day, while watching the women volunteers collect the plates and bowls after our meal, a sudden wave of gratitude washed over me, mingled with a twinge of guilt and a desire to help out. I was also developing a growing curiosity about some of the foods because I had been inhibited in my choices of what to eat.

After lunch, I broke the silence and asked one of the cooks to tell me if certain foods had gluten. They spoke to each other quickly in Malay. I didn't understand, and just bowed and walked away. After the female yogis had passed around the corner on the way to our kutis, Gho approached me.

"The cooks do not speak English. What is your question?"

"Some of the food may or may not be made with rice or corn flour. If it is made with rice or corn, I can eat it, but with wheat, I cannot. I was wondering if they could point out some of the things that are okay for me."

"Oh, you are allergic to wheat," she nodded pensively. "Tomorrow at lunch, I will point out for you."

"Oh, thank you!"

That evening, my pulse raced, and the vibrations became more irritating. There was a horrendous pain in my back that didn't respond to anything I tried. The teacher's young assistant monk tapped me lightly on the forearm to indicate I was being called for a meeting.

When I entered the teacher's office, he asked, "Constance, how is your practice?"

"I don't know. I don't feel well. I feel I should be helping more around here. All of the women who do all the cooking and cleaning in the kitchen are so kind. I feel I need to help out."

I was used to Zen where volunteer work was part of the daily practice. At sesshins, we worked for a couple of hours each day cleaning the entire building. I was also used to these chores at home. I hungered for work, and I didn't even have my own laundry to do. It seemed beyond luxurious. Even my roles were not there.

"No," he replied, "You must understand that they know you are practicing. You must accept."

I looked into his sparkling eyes and knew he was right. I also realized he knew I was not reporting to him the way a yogi is supposed to report to a teacher during intensive practice. I was getting lost in the content.

I looked at him firmly and stated, "Okay, this is the deal. I can accept it, *if* you will personally go to them and let them know how grateful I am for every meal and all of their work so that I'm able to practice. Will you do that?"

His eyes widened, and he said, "Yes, Constance. I will."

"You promise?"

"Yes, Constance, continue."

Our meeting didn't calm my senses. I still felt scratchy, nervous and agitated, but he had said "Continue," which signaled the end of the interview.

I stood up, and looked at him once more from the doorway and nodded. He looked up and nodded slightly too. I returned to walking meditation, and in an hour, it was all forgotten. The feelings of unworthiness upon accepting the many gifts of the volunteers had changed into pure gratitude once he had agreed to send them my message.

But then a new set of concerns and old tensions surfaced, and I had to simply continue knowing all of the sensations as they came and went. The practice itself was the only solution.

The next day at lunch, Gho subtly pointed with her spoon to indicate what was or wasn't safe to eat. If I reached toward something that had wheat, she'd shake her head. I took a little colored gelatin cake I hadn't tried before, and some breaded chicken as she nodded. Later, she told me she had checked with the cooks, and the breaded chicken was made with corn starch. I noticed a few things I hadn't tried before, like sweet potato cubes in coconut milk, and I started to enjoy the meals immensely. I had to be careful not to take too much, because that was wasteful, and not too little, so I would be sated until the next day.

Meals had pleasant sensations of taste and fullness, relief from hunger, and they had unpleasant sensations such as my underwear's elastic cutting into my bottom on the hard plastic stool. All of these subtleties were important to *know* as they arose and passed away because it was important to move with Awareness.

In the evenings, a volunteer presented each of us yogis and the nuns a coffee mug filled with green sludge. It tasted like roasted broccoli, Brussels sprouts, and spinach, and it had an unpleasant odor. Since there were not many vegetables in our meals, it was prudent of them to offer this rich drink, probably high in vitamins. I drank it while I sat in my chair. Then I returned the glass to the tray, and the volunteer picked up the glasses. One evening, I watched my teacher take his mug and drink it in one long swallow. His teeth were green afterward. He breathed in deeply and wiped his mouth with a napkin. *Movement.* He handed the glass back right away. I didn't like the taste enough to take it all at once.

My proximity to the bathroom made my 2 a.m. visits easy. The old toads became a familiar sight each night as I entered. I wondered where they went in the daytime. But that was just another thought arising and passing.

Each night, I laid aside my yogi clothes to change back into the next morning with a fresh change of underwear. I slid into bed, going out like a light. The rumbling sounds and lights from the adjacent buildings no longer influenced my sleep.

Acceptance flowing.

~~~

The only Dhamma talks took place on Saturday nights, and they were open to those in the yogi program from the local community. At the end of one of our meetings, the teacher told me that I would attend the Dhamma talk and go downstairs at 7 p.m. When I arrived, a smiling volunteer showed me to a cushion that was set up for me, and the other yogis as well. We sat on the floor, facing the monks, who were seated in a row of chairs in front of a big Buddha statue. My teacher entered and sat down in a chair to the left of the monks. He spoke in English with a Burmese accent. An interpreter sitting to his right, also using a microphone, repeated what he said in Malay for the community.

The Dhamma talk was interesting because our teacher gave the same instructions that Mahāsi had written, seemingly word for word, to the part-time yogis. To understand the underlying intention of my teacher while *knowing* the breath, the pause between each breath, and each moment of touch at the predominant sense door felt peaceful and brilliant at the same time.

He continued, slowly and carefully delivering a sentence and letting the interpreter share it in Malay. As I listened to the interpreter, I noticed the different waves of sound from the microphone moving throughout the body. There were about fifty Malaysians, a mix of men and women, as well as a few adolescents, dressed in white shirts with dark pants or skirts. They listened with deep respect and stillness that fed into my love for the Sangha. A blissful state of gratitude swelled within me as the words sang through my body from our shared presence, each in-breath receiving a pearl of loving wisdom from the translated instructions.

On Sunday morning, the center was full of families with children. We sat in front while the monks completed the ancient alms round ritual. As they walked through the group, we each placed rice into the monks' and nuns' bowls. There was a short Dhamma talk in Malay, this time without an English interpreter.

After the community gathering, we ate lunch, and then I returned to my room. There was a knock on my door, and Gho had a volunteer with her. They looked me over and handed me a set of yogi clothes to try on, then waited outside my kuti. The shirt buttoned down the front and had two patch pockets, but was too small. The pants were simple with an elastic waist, but the hem stopped just below my knee.

When I opened the door again, they looked at my long legs, shook their heads, and measured my body with a string, tying a knot to mark the length. They said they would have to add on to the pants. I felt tickled as they checked me over with such kindness. When certain practicalities needed attention, speaking was all right.

Gho had noticed how frequently I checked my clothes on the clothesline. Before I had left home, the only white clothes I could find were made of heavy cotton fabric. It was like wearing a wet rug on my back in that steamy weather. It took three days for my clothes to dry, and when I asked about them at the office, they said they hadn't dried yet due to the humidity.

The next afternoon, Gho brought me a custom-made pair of pants that fit perfectly! Then, she led me upstairs to try on larger shirts.

I said to Gho, "Thank you, this is very kind. And, thank you for pointing out the gluten food at meals."

"Sure. Sometimes I still don't know for sure what is and what is not gluten."

"That's all right. I was probably a glutton in a past life, so I'm allergic to gluten in this life."

We both laughed.

The new shirts had handy pockets for my key and tissues. With the new pants that Gho brought me and a pair of white pants that my friend Ruth had helped me make at home from an old tablecloth, I now had two sets of clothes that were light, wrinkle-free, easy for me to wash, and would usually dry in only a day's time. I simply had to rotate them and wash a set each afternoon. It was much simpler to do my own hand-washing, even if it meant being careful not to overdo it with my wrist. I soon found a scrub brush that saved my knuckles too. I donated the white cotton clothes I didn't need for the teenage yogis. The very next day I saw two young guys wearing my old shirts.

On Sunday afternoon at three o'clock, we sat in an air-conditioned classroom while our teacher gave a lecture regarding one of the suttas. All of the monks, nuns, yogis, and even some part-time local yogis, joined the class. Semry, the new yogi from Thailand, sat next to me, and we both shivered. I didn't know it was going to be air-conditioned, but I didn't dare interrupt the process to get a blanket. I simply noticed the specific sensations of coolness, tension, and pain with nourishing breath energy. Time evaporated. I had a notebook and pen with me but did not feel the need to take notes.

I stayed present with the pain reverberating through my spine and any effort seen as tension, and noticed the exact moments of contact with pain as the mind touched the exact space in the body, its shape, intensity, duration, and how it left or passed away. Frequently, I experimented with pleasant breath energy to counteract the pain.

Sayadaw Thuzana gave a wonderful exploration of one of the Buddha's teachings in English. There were no questions, nor was there any interaction with him. Everyone continued to practice and listen. What struck me was his innocence and openness to what he was saying, as if the words flowed from a place he had just discovered.

Still, there wasn't a single thought I could hold onto. The effort to do so brought suffering. Knowing the simple sensations of each moment and each breath continued to bring a sense of ease no matter what arose.

On the morning of the eleventh day, I was suddenly overwhelmed by a deep sense of distress. Pain arose in the middle of my chest. More despair than I thought I could handle was wreaking havoc in my mind as I tried to stay focused on the breath. I had done everything I could to deal with any aversion or clinging, and tried various ways of breathing and noticing it arising and passing. I tried bringing up feelings of goodwill for myself, the others practicing, and my family.

It was a day of walking and sitting while meeting my suffering moment by moment. I had to take care of myself. I had only been sleeping about five hours per night. After lunch, I tried to rest in bed, thinking I was just overwrought and tired, but I felt trapped and claustrophobic in the kuti. Lizards skittered and darted across the window screens. Breathing in and out was short. I checked the Progress of Insight and knew that this was the stage of re-observation, and that it was kicking my butt. I wanted out, to leave as fast as I could, but I also knew a deep process when it was arising.

Later that afternoon, after washing my clothes, I felt as though my entire world was crumbling and I might die of grief if it wasn't released. I sat on my cot and put some toilet paper in my pocket. I didn't have any particular plan, except to maybe find a private place where I could feel more openness and escape the claustrophobia.

Leaving the kuti behind, I slowly walked around the side of the building to the grounds in front, noticing as I went. I already felt better being on my feet. Moving towards a different area of campus, I came across an old temple with a beautiful Buddha statue surrounded by blossoms. While carefully walking around the temple, I saw a few stools stacked up against the opposite side of the veranda.

I glanced around; there didn't appear to be anyone using the space. I took one of the stools, gently turned it over, and set it down. As I was doing this, I noted and felt: lifting, placing, setting. Then I took out my toilet paper and placed two small rows on the stool so I would not dirty the bottom of my new white pants.

I sat down mindfully, first bowing, then feeling the bending of the legs and the pressure on my stiff bones as I lowered myself onto the hard stool. It was such a relief to have a place to feel my way into the pain openly, and I noticed the perceiving of relief.

Is this deep process still coming?

Yes. It was still coming. It started coming like a tidal wave. I pressed my hands on my knees and started to sob silently. I did not make any noise. This was not my preference, but given the situation, it was more important to just let it come, even if I had to repress the body around the sound. I did not want to draw any attention to myself or raise any worry. I wasn't forcing it to happen. I was just allowing it to be. A light breeze caressed my wet cheeks, my heart pierced by love with the anguish coursing through. I simply leaned forward gently and let it unfold. Only Love could serve my practice in this open space of being.

Several waves came, each wave pushing out the last.

Wet tears dropping, plop, plop, plop, stinging salt, wet, touch, clench, tightening, releasing, breathing in, opening, sighing, pause, exhale, clenching, tightening, squeezing eyes, dropping, stringy mucus, blowing, wiping, wet, water, air, fire, release, touching, sad, heaviness, fear, sinking, wet, water, cleansing.

I looked up. Seeing, seeing, seeing. No one was around.

Sigh, breathing in, breathing out.

I waited, wondering whether there were any more emotions that needed release. I had run out of toilet paper and needed to blow my nose, so I took the tissues beneath me and noticed "touching." All mental perceptions started flowing more freely, thinking, thinking, and the thought came. *I am just here.*

After several honest, surging waves, surrendering prayers, and long, steady breaths, this cavern of inner tumult felt less gut-wrenching. Awareness cut through like a light piercing the clouds. Onward came a true, honest, clear opening in my heart. I gathered up the scraps of toilet paper and held them in my hand. I looked down at the puddle of tears on the cement, smiled, and noticed smiling, knowing a new softness. I picked up the stool and replaced it exactly as I had found it, feeling the changing patterns and pressures of touch, putting, standing, walking, left, right, left, right, with each step.

I walked back around the building as if I were gliding, and a kitten grazed past me as Gho suddenly came out of the bathroom. She looked at me as I passed, and asked, barely audible, "Where have you been?"

I said, "I don't know if I should tell you. Umm..." I pointed in the direction I had come from.

"What were you doing there?"

I hesitated. "Do you really want to know?" She nodded, so I said, "I have been crying."

Her eyes widened with surprise. "That is not the practice," she said sternly.

I regarded her with ease, suddenly knowing it didn't matter; the whole exchange couldn't have been more perfect. The Buddha did say to go beyond sorrow and tears. It was a lofty goal and one that may happen, but until then, if crying worked, then it worked. Most of the canonical texts were written by men. Who is to say how a woman may find release from suffering?

I calmly said, "I suppose, but I feel better now." A small smile grew across my face.

She looked at me, surprised again, and said, "Hmm, you need to tell the teacher."

I felt glad for the interaction because it helped me feel that the state had shifted. It hit me that there had been a transition into equanimity. I knew this, because my thoughts had a spaciousness around them. And I had known this state before—this was low equanimity; it would progress if I nurtured it in jhāna. I took a wonderful hot shower, washed my hair, and put on a fresh set of yogi clothes. This state was only going to last a few hours. I resolved to continue practicing gently and diligently.

Before heading upstairs, I sat on my cot to revisit a small printout of the Mahāsi map, and then put it away. It did not help at this juncture. It was more important to be with all phenomena arising and passing to the best of my ability. I was practicing for the benefit of all beings with as much generosity and clarity as I could muster.

As I walked up to the third floor, a sharp, steady awareness carried each step. I sat carefully in my chair, continuing to focus in closely. I noticed a broadening out of awareness going further and deeper. The breath was too slow to notice. Standing, walking, then drinking water in a flowing ease of movement like everything was happening in ordinary perfection.

When I sat again, there was a light skirmish in the mind, but skillfully fought, cool and calm on its own. A vision arose of "my" head falling off, rolling away...There lay a dead body, and yet all was well. I noticed *seeing* when this appeared and stayed focused on being; right here, right now.

I noticed a subtle tendency to sit back and enjoy the state, to see it as perfectly ordinary, but instead I automatically concentrated interest in the torso.

Now hear what happened next.

An intuition moved me out of the chair. I stretched my spine into a cat pose before settling down on the floor with my legs crossed lotus style. The breath calmed, barely perceptible, the posture perfect. I continued to notice any sensation that predominated awareness. If there was seeing, I noticed the exact image and its felt nature, the knowing within the sense door, and its location in the body at a high rate of speed. An image would appear, and I would know it passing, and then see it leave in a certain way. I saw it happening with ease. The mind was moving very quickly on its own.

There was a natural curiosity about "there" or "here."

What can be over there that is not here?

All sensations at each entrance became exits. Perceiving was also open; the intention to awaken a moot point because even the intention to practice was irrelevant. Consciousness was alive and moving, and the knowing of it happened on its own. I felt an inner sense of "yes" to what was already happening on its own.

Then, there was a blip-poof-gone—all stopped. Then, a crystal-clear afterthought:

Not later. Now.

I opened my eyes and looked down at my hands, then turned my palms upward. I looked at the open palms again and thought, *Only now, right now*, and blanked out for a second. The next second felt as soft as the previous one.

I looked at my hands once more.

Ahh...that was it!

It is difficult to talk about in the past tense because time is irrelevant. It is happening now, right now, all the time! It was not an experience because "I" was not there. And, these words cannot fully convey the "no-thing" thing that I had been searching for. My heart had stopped beating the blood of a prisoner and now flowed with that of a free human being. I finally understood my humanness on our terrestrial plane, unified with our vital earthly life force, but also limitless, interwoven, branching outward to the cosmos and beyond.

On the heels of the fruition came review. A hole opened where everything passed through. The top of my head began taking in a huge download of information with energy pouring down from the heart and out through my toes. I looked at my chest and knew that a profound shift in identity had occurred. This openness softened the edges of the body as "me" or "mine."

Time flew in the evening. I wanted to share this with the teacher. I walked softly and drank the green sludge with gratitude in one swift gulp. There was a sense of wonder as fresh as a baby seeing for the first time. The effect was incredibly simple and beyond satisfying.

A monk I'd seen before entered the teachers' office in plain clothes. He had a long meeting, which meant that female yogis would not have time with the teacher before chanting. But that felt okay. It was *all so okay.* Serenity flowed. The universe, in the form of the expression that is "me," had aligned with itself and found harmony in chanting as our shared expression of the Infinite.

Late that night, I walked downstairs, looked around and smiled. I knew that the Buddha was smiling with me and always had, just as all those who had walked a path to Truth. Heck, even with those who hadn't, because, as Norm said, "You are Buddha." Although I was far from being a Buddha, I finally understood what he might have meant; Knowledge was alive in us.

No wonder the Buddha said you can have one desire: to know the Truth. Once you understand the truth of suffering, the desire defeats itself. I slid into bed that night and knew, *All is well always. Wow!*

CHAPTER TWENTY-NINE

Verify

THE NIGHT AFTER STREAM-ENTRY was full of insight and review. I saw how rites and rituals were like dances, shows, or expressions of the infinite, and that *the infinite is in everything already*. They were a form of cultural, personal, or familial expression, but not necessary on the path to knowing the truth of who we are.

I could see that rituals served as a way to practice in an orderly fashion with instruction. The instructions to see were apparent in every way. Anywhere I looked, I started to say to myself, *Duh! How could I have missed this?*

I slept deeply, reviewing and downloading this huge pulsating realization that everything was in everything else and unfolding continuously and underneath, within and without, a perfect peace. But even these words cannot describe this *knowing* through and through. What perfection the Four Noble Truths truly are!

~~~

A long black arm with sharp claws made a grab for my face, like a ghostly shadow. My eyes flashed open, startling me upright, as if I had suddenly avoided an attack.

My body rocked like a garbage truck rumbling down a pothole-riddled Minnesota side street. Rubbing my eyes with sweaty palms in the pure darkness, I blinked to see the time: 3:34 a.m. It was no use trying to go back to sleep, so I got dressed. Pulling out a small calendar, I marked "F" for fear.

I suspected that if I had stream-entry, I would start cycling in a different way. The identity view had already changed irrevocably, but with the coming dark cycle and knowing how my imagination could run rampant, I wanted to be sure and verify it. I would have to see how I cycled. Even though time is not the focus during intensive meditation practice, occasionally tracking changing states helped me investigate.

The big black claw replayed like stop motion frames in an old movie. I became aware of the need to drop it and move on. This was a dizzying state where mind and body quickly reviewed and edited concepts, but it was all a mirage. With the spatial kinetic awareness of roll, pitch, and yaw, as well as up, down, front, and back, a new velocity blasted through different energetic centers. Sleep cycles did not always include familiar oblivion, which brought up more inquiry.

What is this force that defies comprehension?

The next day, I followed the schedule again and practiced steadily into the evening until I was lightly tapped during my sit to see the teacher. Upon entering the room, I found him standing at the bookcase and pulling out a yogi handbook.

I swallowed hard. Though I had incredible news, it hardly seemed important now that I sensed how much further there was to go. Since I hadn't seen him for a few days, he wouldn't have known how my practice had developed. However, I intuited what he wanted.

After a mutual bow, we both settled onto the floor.

"Constance, have you seen this?" he asked, handing me the booklet.

I nodded and set it down. He wanted to be sure I was going to report to him in the way a yogi should report to a meditation teacher. His forehead was shiny with sweat, his eyes looked tired. It was best that I get on with it.

I spoke slowly with intention.

"Yesterday, I noted all of the sensations as they were arising and passing. The mind struck quickly and immediately upon the sensations as they were arising. An ease upon which all sensations could be seen arose, and the mind quickened along with it. The pain eased in the body and a firm posture was easily held."

He sat up, his face opening toward me, and leaned in to hear over the sound of the evening street traffic coming in through the windows behind him.

"I noticed every object appearing and disappearing."

His eyes widened.

"Impermanence presented clearly, and I started to wonder whether a sense of self was here or there. I also recall a question about here and now."

I paused.

"I stayed focused and interested in all sensations and saw each sensation passing when suddenly I looked down at my hands—and the ears—all senses stopped."

He looked at me with great interest.

"It was a cessation that I only know in looking back, then a huge review of all of the Buddha's teachings in perfection, all kinds of doubts vanished. The review lasted almost all night until I saw a big black claw early this morning and felt fear. This morning felt like a block of ice appeared in my upper back and shoulder. It appeared like a piece of wood, then it changed shape."

"Was all calm when this happened?"

"Yes."

"How was your posture?"

"Perfect. Firm. Painless."

He nodded in assent and smiled at me in a new way.

"How was the breath?" he inquired.

"Imperceptible, not noticeable."

There arose glimmers that this was a new beginning. I looked down, taking a deep breath. "There is so much more I must learn now." I knew what had happened and was already moving on, but he was just taking it in.

"Yes. Constance. Please continue."

"What do I do now?" *I had achieved the goal, but now what?*

He looked at me pensively. "Constance, you must just keep on practicing. Continue."

At this point in the interview with him, I was already moving quickly into a state of disgust, and he was right, the present state needs attention.

~~~

Stream-entry washed the dust clean, but my toes now touched the dark mud and the deep, chilly water below. A brisk energetic undertow stirred within a conscious awareness that I needed to get to the other shore to be completely unbound. A new ability to work with ideas in an openhearted and clear-minded way whirled through me with a significant level of force, far more than before.

There were some ideas that stream-entry would make life easier. However, it was more than clear that the Noble Eightfold Path was the raft to help me across the stream, and I needed skills in real time like never before.

I felt heartened to see that working with gentleness, developing more humility, right effort, mindfulness, and respectfully learning to surf these waves of intense contraction and expansion that formed around ideas of the self were all elements of being a skillful meditator. Little by little, I could practice with the ebb and flow of Life. I was being practiced whether I liked it or not. There was no escape from *knowing* Truth in every fiber of my being.

Mindful moment-by-moment practice saves the mind itself and helps to verify reality each second. As I listened to the evening mettā chanting, the mosquitoes made their entrance into the hall surrounding my umbrella netting. My ears turned toward hearing and feeling the swooshing sensation as bats swooped down to snatch mosquitoes. When attention drifted off into fanciful ideas, bringing attention back to the body was the obvious task.

Do I want to live in some dream world or Reality?

I wanted Reality.

And Reality wanted to consume any ideas of "me."

During the next day of continuous practice, I hit re-observation again. It felt like a huge foot on my chest. I could barely stand breathing; the pain in my upper back pressed through to the front of my chest like a crushing vice grip. I simply sat and walked through it until it suddenly shifted, as if a rock had been lifted off my body. I felt lighter and knew I had moved into equanimity again. Then came another shift, a blip moment, and a review phase followed with more wisdom.

The teacher moved me up to the beginning of the female yogi line, which gave us a little more time to discuss my practice in detail. He was primarily interested in the physical symptoms. Had I felt the stopping again? How did my belly feel? How was my posture? What states had been occurring? What knowledge arose in the review phase?

One evening, shortly before I went in to see him, there was the little cessation again. He asked me right away, "Constance, has it happened again?"

"Yes, just now, a few minutes ago. I feel like a new washing machine or like I have been rebooted." I shrugged—it seemed normal, albeit new.

"How was the posture?"

"Firm, very still, quiet."

"Constance, continue."

And on it went; practice continued.

~~~

Until now, I hadn't messaged anyone, not even my family, from the center. However, I made the choice to text two awakened yogis from the U.S. I informed them about my stream-entry. I hadn't expected this permanent shift in consciousness to happen so soon, especially on the eleventh day of my stay at the monastic center! My return trip wasn't going to happen for quite some time. They both texted me back and advised me to verify the attainment of stream-entry and continue practice.

At this point in my practice, it was a relief to not have the hindrance of sleepiness. One yogi who sat near me in front of a floor fan kept bobbing forward, her bangs sweeping the floor like a metronome over and over again for hours. She seemed asleep. We each need to learn from our own processes, but how can we learn if we are ignorant? So, the next day, on our walk to our respective kutis after lunch, I softly mentioned this to her. She was stunned and had no idea she was doing that. She quietly thanked me for telling her.

One evening, as I sat in the hall during the Dhamma talk, I couldn't help but feel a motherly love for the wonderful monks who rose at

4 a.m. and were nodding off in their chairs. Playfully, I began to wonder about which ones would fall asleep first. Usually, the one with the long chin would drop first, followed by the youngest, then the oldest, the intense one with pursed lips, the one with the furrowed brow, the one with wandering eyes, and finally the fidgety one. It felt sweet, like the Dhamma talk from our teacher was a lullaby. As each monk drifted off to sleep, appreciation bloomed in me for them, the center, and all the different ways that the Dhamma is expressed.

When I saw the teacher next, he asked me how things were going, and we both continued to review my practice in detail, the cycles, and how they appeared in the body. He asked me how I liked the Dhamma talks. I told him that it might not be a good idea to have the monks falling asleep in front of the community when they were trying to wake people up.

He and I laughed and laughed.

During the next Dhamma talk, the monks appeared to make more of an effort to sit upright and stay awake.

He asked my opinion about another monk who gave a Dhamma talk, and I said I did not resonate with him. He appeared to have evoked guilt and fear among the children by prescribing rigid obedience to the precepts. It reminded me of my early childhood in Catholicism where I often set aside what the priest was saying so that I could weather the vehemence of the sermons. Would this monk's strict lectures distance the children from the Dhamma? He listened to me carefully.

Sayadaw U Paṇḍita, my teacher's teacher, referred to as Saya G for Great Teacher, was soon to arrive and would be staying and teaching at the center for a week or more on his way south for a routine visit to see his cardiologist. I heard from Gho that many months earlier, when he was initially taken to the hospital in the midst of a heart attack, he calmly described to the doctors the sensations of pressure, swirling, tightness, tingling, and the precise movement of these sensations as he sat on the gurney.

His presence was a huge honor to the community; many workers came to clean, fix things, touch up paint, check the plumbing, and set up a room for him on the first floor. One of the two bathrooms for community use was cleaned and given a fresh coat of paint, a new hot water heater was installed, then they put a sign on the door that said, "Monk"—which was set aside for him and his male attendants, or sāmaṇeras. Given his recovering heart condition, I felt fortunate to practice with him, and happy to see him being provided for.

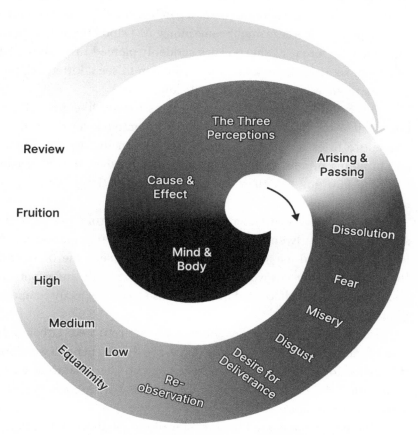

Progress of Insight After Stream Entry

Cycling through states came quickly in the following days. I continued to place a little abbreviated mark on my calendar to indicate the fruition review phases, and I could see over time that they happened faster. What had taken ten days now took about two to three days, and then cycled around again, with more wisdom and a deeper resolve to align with the Truth: Accepting impermanence, realizing there is no separately existing self, and *knowing* compassion for all suffering, which automatically extends to all beings.

More and more states of expansion and contraction spiraled every two to three days. One day I noticed that, due to the heat, I rarely got any sunshine and might need some natural vitamin D. So, I walked in front of the building where there was a patch of sunshine between some bushes; perhaps a breeze might come along. As I stood there, letting the sun touch my forearm, sharp claws suddenly pierced through my left pants leg, scratching my knee. I looked down to see a kitten gripping onto my thigh, escaping her siblings below.

Misery quickly turned to happiness as I stood like a tree for an hour while various kittens occasionally leapt onto one leg or the other. The entire litter whizzed around my feet, pouncing across my toes, and fumbling into my heels. In and out of the bushes, they alternated hanging onto one leg, then the other, and sometimes both legs in unexpected leaps.

Wow! Such a swift switch into happiness from the grip of a stressful pattern. Even the tingling sensations of anticipation for the leaping claws had me standing in joy. Had you seen me there from the window, the bushes would have hidden this comedy underfoot, and you would not have discerned my delight as I stood perfectly composed in meditative wonder.

However, the pain in my chest and heart returned. Other times when I was in such pain, I was called in to see the teacher and wondered if I needed to attend to a deep process. I had no idea what to do except *stay with it*. He could see I was in distress, as I'm sure my shoulders were tensing up more.

One day, as he passed by during walking meditation, he stopped and asked me about it. This was unusual, as he normally didn't take time for yogis during the day. I pointed to my chest and winced. He nodded with concern and compassion.

Still, after quite a while, I thought I was dying. I almost felt I needed to go to a hospital. But even these thoughts cascaded along so fast that they did not stick. The light of Awareness continued to pull inward, and concentrated energy took care not to create a dramatic event, but compelled me to investigate.

The teacher sometimes added, "Scrutinize, Constance."

I decided to go to my kuti and lie down for some relief in my shoulder and the stabbing pain in my chest. After I got inside my door, I pulled out my little notebook and stared at a blank page, continuing to note the sensations of holding a pen and the act of sitting in a general sense—the weight, the shifting, and the stress of seeking an answer. I questioned whether I was somehow holding onto the state. Suddenly, I saw a belief in the mind and wrote it down:

I am an abandoned daughter.

The words spilled out onto the paper, my eyes drawn to the words *and* the space around them. It wasn't what I expected, though I hadn't known what to expect either. It was true in the past and continues to some extent in the present. I felt this sorrow had haunted me all of my life. The mind and heart ricocheted back and forth within the sanctuary of Awareness.

Withdrawing from the note, I resolved to try walking meditation, and let myself inquire into this belief with compassion. Walking is like oiling the rusty gears around the body that habitually stick. The monks and nuns know this tried-and-true method and do not avoid mindful walking. In due time, all of that tension faded into bliss and gratitude.

The center became busier than ever with visitors for the great teacher, Sayadaw U Paṇḍita. I was very fortunate to be present with him for his traditional Dhamma talks based on the teachings of the Buddha.

At the end of Sayadaw G's last talk, he said, "Please forgive me if I have hurt or harmed you. I forgive you if you have hurt or harmed me." This struck me as a powerfully liberating request and invitation for the whole community. What would it be like if we did that with each other every day?

One day Gho approached me happily and suggested I go see him. She had been working with him since the early 1980s and had a deep love for him.

"How?" I asked. "He seems very busy."

"If no one is at his door, there is a space and you can ask to go in. Think about what you will offer him."

The only thing I seemed to have was my practice, but then I remembered I had some extra vitamin powder packets. I went to my kuti, brought back three packets, and went to his door.

I peeked inside, and the nun, who also acted as his interpreter, signaled for me to enter and sit. I entered and bowed three times, which hurt my left knee. Some nervous energy tingled up my spine at meeting this great teacher.

He asked me a question in his native Burmese tongue, and the interpreter asked, "Where are you from?"

"United States."

"Why do you come all the way here?"

"I needed a good place to practice."

"What do you have there?"

"It's a vitamin drink, for your health. It is good to take for your immune system." The interpreter handed the packets to him.

"What flavor is it?" he asked, studying the packets in his hand.

"Lemon, but it does not have much flavor. It is only good for you, like practice."

He smiled at me. "Do you have a question?"

I inquired, "What do you do when you have an old belief and it hurts and you aren't able to shake it off or see it as delusion?"

He answered in Burmese, and the interpreter said, "Note all that is happening, moment by moment, note the arising and passing..." He went on in a typical Mahāsi fashion, expounding on the noting practice.

I focused my eyes on his lips and strained my ears to see if I could decipher any words for myself. The whole scene was remarkable because his assistants were in such nurturing company with him. While he sat on a large chair with a high back, like a throne, there was one man waving a fan at him, one man massaging his legs, and the beautiful interpreter speaking and moving with total grace and ease. The company surrounding him evoked a sense of pure intent and loyalty.

I started to move into posture for bowing because I thought it was the end, or time to leave; I didn't really feel met in that moment.

He lifted his handheld ceremonial fan, holding it near his face, and peered into me. I felt like I vanished for a moment. Then he stopped and spoke again before I got up.

The interpreter said, "Wait, there is one more thing."

He stared at me thoughtfully, and spoke. The interpreter translated, "Be careful who you keep company with." Then the teacher waved his hand and the interview was over.

Breathing in and out in short breaths within the upper chest chamber, I reflected on his message. My family is the primary company in my lay yogi life. We each have very different lives. It was a good reminder to be aware of others. There are mirror neurons, and we are subtly influenced by everyone around us. I must stand in my own shoes and *know* what is on my path. Hearing this somehow shook me to the core, for there is no separation; even beliefs are like company we keep.

A persevering attitude arose to continue with the practice despite the pressure that, while reduced, remained in my chest. After walking and sitting in meditation more that afternoon, and knowing it was time for my shower, I went back to my kuti. There was a belief. What was it? Some idea was bugging me in the midst of a compassion for this tension.

What were some options? Exercise might have relieved some tension, but that was not allowed. My kuti was so tiny it was hard to do yoga or stretching. I tried some deep, relaxing breaths. I wanted to go for a long walk, but the plot of land is small, and that felt too distracting. I looked again at what I had written: *I am an abandoned daughter.* I sat and stared at it, asking, *Is this true?* This idea tugged hard, still squeezing inside my heart.

I stretched out on my cot and let the feelings come. Quietly and free from obstructions, the heart softened, the pain vanishing into swift-sliding memories of being a lonely seven-year-old, hearing adults arguing, and a girl seeing her father leave the house for the last time, never to return. I looked out my bedroom window at his smiling face as he turned back, lifted his fedora hat, and waved up at me. My parents were divorcing. He had left for good. He never wanted to harm me. I knew in that moment that my life would never be the same.

I held that little girl in my grown-up arms. I understood her grief. She could not help her parents come to an understanding. I realized that the abuse I experienced at the hands of my mother was part of her story. I didn't need to believe it. The heart gave compassion a way home. I knew that memory was not me, that my Spirit is untouched and cannot be harmed.

I was careful not to make a noisy disturbance through the thin wall of the kuti. After some time, maybe an hour, an insight landed like a butterfly brushing its wings.

I am not an abandoned daughter.

I am free.

And I am neither. And, neither either.

Pure, open heart, fading into Awareness with illumination.

After my shower, I returned to the hall for walking meditation. I stood near my chair, looking around to see everyone engaged in their own mindful movements; walking in collective stillness.

The wood floor and spacious area felt glorious, like the jazz dance studios I used to dance in when I was younger. All of a sudden, I spontaneously slid into one long low drag, then another, my hips and arms broadening out as I chasséd across the smooth wood floor, softly dragging my toes behind as a jazzy rhythm jived through me.

When pausing to enjoy a drink of water, I turned around to see Semry across the hallway, rocking back and forth and cupping her mouth with both hands to muffle her laughter. Her eyes twinkled with delight; then she mouthed, "Thank you! Thank you!" We both giggled with joy.

Before long, a new cycle of sadness arose. I gently wept while slowly walking among the flowers around the outside Buddha statues. The mental thinking processes started to disentangle from the sensate emotional feelings, and my processes became lighter; my breaking heart had a new kind of suffering that wanted to go deeper into the spectrum of consciousness.

At my next meeting with the teacher, in his compassionate way, he asked me about my day and my feelings. I was reluctant to tell him because it appeared that weeping was anathema to the practice, but in keeping with my need for honesty with him, I shared, "I was crying, but is that wrong?"

He shook his head, "No," then nodded kindly, "If it works."

"How do I stop this vulnerable process when it is already happening?"

"You will know. This will change."

His affirmation helped me relax around him and the sangha and removed my background worry about having tears, which laid bare my love for them-us-all.

~~~

One day during meditation, I noticed three nuns working together to lift a five-gallon jug of water onto the dispenser. With six hands grappling and trying to hold it, the jug passed back and forth while they clumsily aimed for the top of the dispenser, which was too tall for them. As they frantically clutched at the jug's slick sides to prevent the water from glugging out onto the floor, they each slid and fell. Then, with wet splotches all over their pink robes, they tried again, lifting but then quickly lowering the jug back onto the floor again. One of them ran into the nearby bathroom, got a rag, and started wiping up the puddles underneath their bare feet.

When they tried for the third time, I got up, walked over, and spread out my arms for them to stop. They stood back as I assessed the situation. I went to get a stool I had seen by the far window and lifted the now half-full jug onto the stool, placing it as close as possible to the right of the dispenser. Being tall helped with this task. I stood in front of the dispenser, crossed my arms, bent my knees, and clasped my hands firmly around the jug. Lifting and uncrossing my arms, I turned ninety degrees to flip the bottle and carefully direct the spout to fit straight into the dispenser hole. All settled with one fluid motion, and no more waste of precious water. There were big smiles all around!

Soon after this, the nuns would tap me on the shoulder and nod toward a jug already set on the stool, just waiting to be flipped over. Over the next few days, I noticed dozens of full water jugs sitting on the first floor. When I asked the office about this, I learned that they needed a volunteer to carry them upstairs. So, I sat in the first-floor public meditation hall in the afternoon after lunch, and soon enough, a strong young man stopped by the center to pay respect and offer dāna.

Shortly after he made his prostrations and got up to leave, I approached him, gestured to the line of jugs, and asked him to carry at least some of them up the steps to the meditation hall. He checked his watch, grimacing at first, but then, he hoisted a jug onto his shoulder and briskly ran it upstairs like it was a handful of leaves. With quick strides, he raced up and down, lifting one after the other, eventually bringing up all twelve. Relieved, I returned to sitting in the upper meditation hall.

At this point on the path, I couldn't help but look around and see what I could do to help. It made me happy to flip over a full jug when we ran out, and the nuns were considerate of my practice—they also asked some of the monks by showing them a jug they had already put on the stool. A gentle flowing current took place with the water that poured into my practice.

The air-conditioning in the Sunday classes and the cool air from the evening rains soothed my skin but chilled Semry's, so I brought a thin blanket with me to cover her. On my third Sunday at the center after class, she touched my shoulder with tears dripping off her chin. Her eyes pleaded with me for help as I handed her a tissue from my pocket. Because I practiced so closely with her, I knew she'd had a long and peaceful sit two days earlier, so she was likely going through difficult, contracted states following that.

Wanting to support her, I asked if she spoke English. She shook her head, saying she spoke some but her boyfriend, who had brought her, spoke it better. From what I could tell, it seemed like he wanted to practice intensively and remain focused in his practice when I saw him doing walking meditation, but she was clearly deeply distressed.

I stood with her and stroked her forearm, trying to comfort her while she wept big droplets onto her shirt. We could only pantomime and try out a few words. She trembled and moaned with sorrowful eyes. I wasn't sure how to help her. I suggested she go see the teacher but she didn't know how to find his room.

Since I could not tell her all of the directions in English, I just walked there with her. I also thought her boyfriend should know the troubled state she was in, so I asked a monk passing by to invite him to the meeting with the teacher. I stood with her for a few moments until her boyfriend came, and we all strode upstairs where I encouraged her to knock on the teacher's door. After he came and sat in his chair, we all sat down and bowed three times to our teacher before starting.

I told Sayadaw that she was struggling and needed some guidance. I turned to get up to leave, but he signaled for me to stay. He then began to instruct her in mettā meditation, which is a reflective loving kindness meditation. But, I could see that she either didn't agree or didn't understand him.

I interrupted and asked, "Can you please speak to her in Thai?"

"No. I tried to get an interpreter for her while she is here, but he is unavailable right now. She appears to know a little English."

"She doesn't seem to know what is happening," I said with concern to the teacher.

He turned his gentle attention back to her. "Semry, what is going on?"

"Big ugly things keep coming at me. I see them." She made clawing motions with her hands and waved her arms around her head, indicating her defense against big flying monsters. We just sat and listened to her with great compassion and intent. As her tears dropped to the floor, she tried to demonstrate her visions, again gesturing scratching motions with her hands toward her face and neck.

This was a terrifying state, especially if she lacked the capacity to continue to practice mindfully and watch them pass with sensate awareness. If one starts to believe the images that pass before the eyes, one can experience extreme psychological distress.

Her boyfriend twisted around in his posture, eyes widening, trying to gather how much she was struggling. He pleaded with her, "Semry, this will go away, and you will feel better."

She looked at him, tight-lipped, closed her eyes, and turned her face away, not appeased by his words or the mettā meditation instructions. I know what it is like to not feel heard. I sensed that this was her predicament, but I did not know what to do. She asserted, shaking her head, "Not go away. All last night and today."

I wanted to validate her fear, but I didn't know Thai. The teacher sat still, present with compassion. It seemed like her boyfriend wanted to stay and continue practicing. *Was she taking care of him?* From the conversation, it appeared that she understood a little more English than I had thought.

Unsure of my role or place there, I raised my hand to ask a question. They all turned to me. I turned toward Semry and asked, "Semry, do you want to continue to stay here one hundred percent, fifty percent, or only a little bit?"

She stared back at me.

They all stared at me.

I looked at them looking at me.

I tried again. "Semry, do you want to go home," I paused, then said, "A little bit?" showing the space between my thumb and forefinger. Pause. "Maybe fifty-fifty?" I shrugged one shoulder, then the other. Another pause. "Or one hundred percent for sure want to go home?" I put my hands together with a firm nod.

Without a second's hesitation, she asserted firmly, joining her hands together, "I want to go home one hundred percent now!"

We three laughed!

Semry's demeanor was still solemn and guarded.

We all took several breaths in silence. Then, she nodded at the teacher, and he nodded his assent.

I turned to her boyfriend. "You brought her here. Will you take her home?"

He nodded, looking a little disappointed for himself and yet concerned for her.

The clock chimed 6 p.m. We sat for a few more minutes while the teacher instructed her, "Please stay and rest overnight; it is good to rest first before traveling." We shared the moment together, knowing that she would go home.

After the nighttime meditation, she pulled me aside, slipped me her phone number, and thanked me earnestly with a heartfelt hug. She said they were going to leave before light. They wanted to get an early start because it would take two to three days to travel by ferry, train, and bus to her small town in northern Thailand. I patted the note with her phone number in my pocket, glad that I could check in with her later to see how she was recovering. I hoped that someday she would return to practice with the support of her native tongue.

When Semry left, I felt her absence. We had practiced together for two and a half weeks. She sat on my left at every meal. She'd always pull out the little stool from under the table for me to sit beside her. Now her stool was empty. Our considerate gestures for one another had affected my practice, making me feel safe and supported. Wishing her well, I returned to trusting the process, mine, hers, ours—the whole lot.

One of the nuns came upstairs and sat very still, maintaining a straight posture and barely perceptible breath for hours. During walking meditation, a smooth Grace flowed through the placement of each of her footsteps, seeping into my own steps without separation.

Another female Malaysian yogi kept coming in every so often. She worked as a hospital nurse with an odd schedule, coming to the center on her days off. She'd go straight to the teacher, recite the precepts in Pāli, find a spot, and meditate like a craftswoman, steady and true. As she was leaving one day, I asked her how it was that she came and went. Her face glowed as her chin lifted toward me, telling me about her love of the Dhamma. Her pure commitment radiated an unshakable faith.

During our revolving sitting and walking meditation sessions, which changed every hour, I crossed the a&p during a walking meditation. I began to look closer and closer into the arising of consciousness itself. For this, the teacher said I should just do standing meditation for a while to avoid feeling dizzy when walking.

I talked with my teacher about how suffering continues in a new way.

He replied, "Constance, you are very fortunate."

"I do not always feel so fortunate."

"But Constance, you are fortunate. You are in choiceless awareness now. You will adjust."

He was right; there was an assimilation going on for unrestricted awareness. During my practice, a thought often arose, *of course*, because I was seeing how conditions arose on their own. The evaluation of "unfortunate" was being fed by the perspective of the personal self, which was falling away. The "me" did not know what to think because this *knowing* is so intuitive and basic to humanity. However, I was also seeing that there was some relevant effort in tracing back into

Knowledge with less resistance and evaluating options for making choices.

I had been struck many times by the sweet admonishments from the teacher during the Sunday classes. He once said, "Yogis want to develop insight but they find undesirable distractions that can be likened to the rain, the sun, or the wind." I nodded, knowing how cold those winds can feel and how soothing the sun can be.

CHAPTER THIRTY

Being

ONE DAY, when Gho and I were washing our white clothes under the tap together, I softly commented, "I'm finding the peace I was looking for." I hoped she would share in my deep gratitude.

"What are you saying?" she asked.

"I'm discovering what I need to know."

"You think you are an arahant?!"

"Oh no!" Oh my, how could she think that? I shook my head and murmured, "Only stream-entry."

"Have you checked with the teacher on this?"

"Yes."

"Do you believe you are fully enlightened now? If you do, then, no one can help you."

I put my head down to resume scrubbing my clothes and whispered back, "No, no beliefs. So much to learn all the time."

She asked me if I knew certain terms in Pāli, which I didn't know. I wanted to connect from a place without concepts. I wanted the entire world to see that if there is a desire to look inward and face the three perceptions of existence, then perhaps more people would follow the meditation instructions and discover this profound Truth. When I patiently answered her questions, staying true to my intention, she smiled with me.

~~~

After several sessions of walking and sitting and walking and sitting, a new fruition, review, and a&p arose. Suddenly, I began hearing every word of Dr. Martin Luther King, Jr.'s "I've Been to the Mountaintop" speech, the final address he delivered before his assassination. It was as if I were standing beside him, brushing against his dark wool gabardine suit with my own hand, hearing and seeing the stirring among the crowd, and watching his chest rise as he drew breath, his melodious voice thundering with wisdom that echoed out over the mass of people. I could almost smell his aftershave.

His deep voice boomed in my heart all afternoon. It was more than him; there was a shift in our collective consciousness among his audience and in the entire world when he spoke these words.

When the teacher asked to see me, I was still immersed in the powerful sensations of this experience. He inquired about my practice, and as I spoke, the clarity of MLK's speech flowed through me with pure patient *knowing*, embodying the determination to face challenges ahead with unwavering resolve.

A large tear formed and slid down the side of my cheek as I continued to slowly recite Dr. King's words to my teacher. Tears welled up in his eyes too as we both shared a deep respect for the power of Dr. King's expression, which radiated beyond.

My teacher serenely ended the interview, "Continue, Constance."

All day I sat and walked with the heavy vibrations of a string bass thrumming through my ears and heart. In this rhythm, the earth seemed to quake within me, laying bare the bedrock of lunacy that underpins slavery and oppression in our world.

An acute knowing of the great harm being done to people of color and impoverished communities brought me down into prostrations. I saw how the formation of the United States had its roots in colonization, patriarchy, imperialism, white supremacy, and exploitation, and how it remains woven into many world systems. Awareness of this extensive spectrum of ignorance rattled my very bones.

Within the silent cacophony of sensations, I stayed with the rise and fall of the abdomen, with the rise and fall of my feet on the cool wood floor, with the movement or stillness expressing itself, extending its reach into each conscious moment.

As I returned to the teachings of the Buddha, an unfettered compassion ignited in my heart. Whiteness was what I was born into, and though I did not come from money by American standards, there was a reason I was born. One of those reasons was to be an ally to anyone suffering from the corrosive impacts of greed and power, without fear, and to join Dr. King in creating a better world for us all.

~~~

One rainy morning, the roof began to leak, and water dripped onto the beautiful floor. A nun and I found buckets to place around the room.

On my way downstairs later on, I saw Uncle Choo and suddenly blurted in an even tone, "I am a carpenter. The wood floor is being harmed. The hole in the roof needs to be fixed."

He said, "It is too high up there, and we had someone look at it before and they said it could not be fixed."

I shot back, "We could get a ladder and some tools and shingles and go fix it together."

He looked at me in shock. A roof is a roof; shingles can be woven in and lapped to prevent the leaks. This could be solved. We both paused, looking at the floor and then up again at the roof. I reflected to him, "This roof *is you-us.*"

He nodded and said he would bring it up to the committee of trustees and see what they thought. I hoped that the roof would be repaired in the near future, (although I had left before I could see this happen). We bowed to one another and returned to our respective practices.

Once the sun peeked out from the clouds and the downpour subsided, I took a walk outside to see an assertive old mottled dog sniffing around the back of the main building near the kutis. I stood there watching him. He appeared to be a smart scrapper, used to finding food on his walking trails. The kitchen was completely closed. What could I do?

Then, I tuned into his being; spoke to him in my mind, urging him to go on. It was like giving a gentle nudge with loving energy. I had done this a hundred times with my children to help them focus on their homework. He came to a stop, looked up and stared at me, then turned his head to the exit, then back at me, then finally scampered back around the corner out of the center's yard and toward the street. I wished him well. May he find nourishment in his life.

At the end of lunch that day, the cooks handed out chocolate-covered ice cream on a stick to the monks, the nuns, and the male yogis. They did not have any more for the female yogis. I sat and noted the painful sensations from my saliva glands working overtime as I smelled the chocolate and watched a male yogi in my peripheral vision slowly lick every single drip of melting creaminess from his fingers. The succulent vibrating sensations actually became a delight in that process alone, and the craving lessened.

I had been losing weight, which seemed fine to me, but I happened to overhear Uncle Choo say to the cooks, "Why she not eat more?" and then I forgot about it.

The food we yogis did not eat was given to the assistants in the meditation center. Maybe because I was taking less, he ended up receiving more food, and that made him curious about me. After the assistants had finished eating, any remaining food was distributed to other monks residing in the area and donated to the Salvation Army, where they fed families and children each day. Nothing went to waste. It was considered rude to take more than what one needed when so much could be shared. If I wasn't sure whether I would be able to eat something, I'd cut off a small piece and test it before taking a larger portion.

Uncle Choo came alongside me when I was in walking meditation in the garden. He said he was going to the store and wanted to take me with him. I happened to be thinking about offering dāna to the teacher, so I agreed to go with him. It was a rare treat to sit in a car and ride around. I was more interested in my shifting weight as the car turned corners than anything else.

During the drive, Uncle Choo asked me, "What do you eat for breakfast at home?"

"I like to have an egg with gluten-free toast."

"You have egg every day?! What do you mean you cannot eat gluten? What is that?"

"It is anything made with wheat flour."

Before I knew it, we were in a small grocery store, and I was simply noticing the sensations of standing. I asked him, "What does the teacher need?"

"He needs batteries for various things."

I picked out several packs of batteries and was ready to pay and leave when he stood right in front of me and asked again, "What do you like to eat for breakfast?"

I glanced around, nodded in the direction of a box of cornflakes, and said that would be okay. He quickly went and brought it back to me. Then, it occurred to me that he wanted me to eat more breakfast food. The way his feet were planted, I saw that we were not going to leave until I bought something I could eat.

"But," I said, "I cannot have this because I must do as the other yogis are doing, and it is not fair. I cannot buy for everyone."

"You can do this for you."

"But how? I cannot. I need to practice, and accept everything as it is. I cannot be a disturbance."

"You can keep this in the cupboard and get it at breakfast with your milk and serve yourself. You will not disturb anyone."

I quickly looked around and also chose seven little yogurts, since I had eaten very little dairy, and chocolate soy milk to pour on my cornflakes.

We each paid for our things, and I was back in the meditation hall within a short time.

The next morning, after sitting at the table for a moment, I remembered the cornflakes in the cupboard and stood up. The group of cooks stepped back in surprise, murmuring quickly to each other in Malay. They watched keenly as I stepped mindfully to the refrigerator and carefully took out the soy milk and yogurt Uncle Choo had made me mark with my name the day before. I walked to the other side of the kitchen, found a bowl and a spoon, sat down at the table, set aside my yogurt, and poured milk onto my cereal. It was like being on stage while touching each item, not as though it were me or mine—just pouring, just eating, and just sitting. The familiar food was a gift and supported my practice.

Later, after showering, I left my shoes on the step to my kuti as usual and tiptoed inside. As I was about to step on the little old white hand towel I used as an entryway rug, it suddenly slid about six inches away. Curious, I leaned down to return it to its place near the door when I saw what appeared to be a long worm sticking out from under it. I remembered all the worms on the sidewalk back home after a summer rain. My children and I enjoyed picking them up and putting them back in the dirt. I thought I'd do the same for this one, and carry it to the garden outside. I figured the rains had been so heavy that the viaduct had overflowed, bringing it up.

Without my glasses, I had to bend down very closely to see it. As I reached down, one end lifted straight up in the air with only a little bit of its brown tail on the floor. With a round head and two eyes, it turned its innocent face toward my nose. In the dim light of my room, I gasped. *Worms cannot do that. It's a snake!* It seemed to sniff for a moment, an inch from my nose, then made a hump in its foot-long rope of a body and slithered out under the door crack. The funny thing about it was the curious delight in the way this baby snake moved.

Afterward, I sat down on my cot and realized that it could have been dangerous. I was fortunate there was no problem.

The next day, a nun asked me why I had made a noise from my kuti the day before. I didn't know what to say; I barely remembered it. She asked, "You had a lizard in there?" I had to tell her it was a snake. She told all of the nuns to cover the entrances to their kutis with a towel to prevent the snakes from entering. It was gone, but still, precautions needed to be taken.

One day when I was making regular trips to the trash, Gho asked me how I was doing. I shared that I was having my period. She exclaimed in her usual whisper with little movement of her lips, "Oh, that is so good for practice!" I turned to face her and smiled, joyfully mystified by her cheerful remark. I'd never heard a woman say this.

There was some bloating and extra thirst, but due to the intensive meditation practice, I did not feel any pain or cramping for six days. I didn't even need any of the ibuprofen I had brought. In the past, my menstrual cycles did not often affect my emotional state and sense of inner strength like the usual stigma. The pinching nerves and the tension shooting down the legs vitalized my intensive practice. Wearing only white clothes raised mindfulness to not make a stain, and to spend extra time and attention in the bathroom collecting the crimson stream. The flow was heavier than usual, and because my teacher was a man, I did not want to discuss this with him.

Knowing this blood brought up awareness of birth and death. Seeing myself as a corpse, bloated and rotting, dissolved attachment for the body. This brought forth a tremendously rich gratitude for each moment—knowing the vulnerability of life with the wisdom of impermanence. It was a gift to see this reminder that we are not the body and that we are not to cling to it. Form changes within the Peace of all.

~~~

One midmorning, perfection permeated every cell in my body. I sat in a state of equanimity, relaxed and open. Then, I saw a heart pumping blood approximately sixteen inches in front of my chest. Above it, I saw a bright diamond about the size of a softball. My eyes were closed, but I experienced this vision quite clearly.

Being curious, I looked closer at the diamond and the heart, discerning each and toggling attention between them. I saw the luminosity of the diamond and the fresh pumping heart with its three layers, the outer layer, the middle layer of muscle, and the inner layer with the pumping blood, blood vessels, and heart valves, the sinew and thin purple skin. The valves were attached with strings that anchored the valves to the muscles of the heart.

I started to notice the process I was engaging in, and I thought it was kind of funny. I generally like hearts and diamonds. I sat and noticed "sitting, just sitting," but the images remained. I opened both eyes and could still see the sparkling diamond and the pumping heart.

What is happening here? How did this get going?

I looked into the heart for some time—the blood, the pumping mechanisms, the veins going everywhere. Eventually, I chose to concentrate on the diamond, which was level with my forehead. There were endless avenues within the diamond where colors lit up in a fascinating display like the aurora borealis. New paths unfurled, blissful and vast. Attention followed different colors, which opened different feelings in the body, intricate pathways curving and enfolding—there seemed to be no end to the opulent exploration.

Then I heard the bell for lunch. I was hungry and wanted to go, but the fascination was magnetic. I considered skipping lunch and just staying with the process, but I knew I would regret that. There would be no food until the next day.

Before I knew it, thirty minutes had passed. I looked around and saw that everyone had left. As I got up and started to walk, my calves felt heavier than my thighs, as if I were wading through water. Each foot placed itself on the ground in minute articulation. Heel to toe was as sublime as it could ever be. I shook my head, but was unable to stop what was happening in the body.

I arrived late to lunch because I simply couldn't move any faster. When I slowly slipped into my seat, I saw the teacher look at me out of the corner of his eye. I ate slower than my usual style, each bite as succulent as the last. When I finished before the monks, I watched the lizards run around catching flies and bugs along the walls with a subtle smile.

After lunch, I returned to my kuti and tried to rest. My body felt like gravity itself, pulling toward the earth, my mind helplessly remembering the diamond and heart. Something wasn't right. I got up an hour late for the sitting meditation, exhausted, as if I were recovering from jet lag. I hadn't slept, but was floating in a strange state. I slid into the building with heavy limbs. As I rounded the corner, trying to shake off this state, my teacher called my name and signaled me to follow him immediately.

I wondered if I should sit on the floor, but he motioned quickly to take the other chair and firmly said, "Just sit."

I was worried and sheepish about what he wanted.

"Constance," he hesitated and spoke firmly, "We do not do samatha here."

"Oh. Yeah. Right." I stared at him, relieved to have him name it. He knew what was happening. I wanted to know what I had done.

"This is very hard on you to do this."

"This diamond and heart appeared! I didn't know what to do."

"Constance, just do vipassanā, insight meditation, do not stay in samatha."

"Okay."

"You will cause too much fatigue. This is very hard on the mind. Broaden your attention."

I couldn't agree more. How touching that he was watching me, worried about me, even a little upset.

"Okay? We do not do samatha."

We both maintained eye contact while I absorbed this wisdom.

Then, with a firm nod, he said, "Constance, continue."

I nodded slowly, and with heavy limbs, I pushed up from my chair and bowed. It was gut-wrenching to learn I had been practicing in an unwholesome way. I felt a little ashamed and worried, which was silly because I didn't know what I didn't know.

As I later found out, samatha meditation can also be used to stop pain. Some people can even undergo surgery with this type of meditation. I was doing samatha in the beginning to calm the senses, (which is a common practice) but then, perhaps I unintentionally immersed myself in the process. I can be curious and I can be overly curious. It is not useful for moving through the stages of insight as the attention is too narrow. Vipassanā meditation is more open to being here in the body, being present and open to insight.

That night was the only night I did not go back to the meditation hall after my shower. I stayed in my room and lay in bed, totally wiped out and needing to review. On some level, perhaps I had not noticed a subtle form of clinging and slipped into clinging within the process of fascination. It was helpful to learn and feel how, in samatha, there can be stress in solidifying an apparent object.

In addition, I saw that there were other possibilities around this experience. I saw spirals within spirals where some paths expanded over vast periods of time, and some interacted with other levels of consciousness outside of time. I trusted that more would be revealed in the years to come.

The nighttime chanting echoing in the hall soothed my nervous system with soft bodily vibrations. The loving kindness in their voices radiated a heartfelt understanding that we are all learning in our own ways. I remembered the Heart and Diamond Sutras[43] and how they had affected me at the Zen center. Then, the unwavering wisdom of the Heart Sutra echoed through my mind as I turned over and drifted off to sleep: *Gate gate pāragate pārasaṃgate bodhi svāhā. (Gone, gone, gone to the other shore beyond. O what an awakening, all hail!)*

After that intense experience, I decided to do more grounding activities, like filling the water supply, taking care of the body, and cleaning my room. The mind had become more powerful, so I needed to be careful. It was as if I had been driving an old 1984 Chevrolet Chevette with a rusty muffler and a lousy clutch, and now I was driving a Maserati on the Autobahn. I didn't quite know how to handle the tight curves the mind was taking. The smooth and dynamic steering was constantly monitored by Awareness, with close attention in every detail. This new quiet engine was at one with its surroundings, no longer held back by as much fear and ignorance. What a wonder to be fully alive!

I was also humbled to learn how the nonsingular *me* would function in the world. How would I learn to integrate this Awareness? They don't give astronauts a rocket ship without a great deal of training first. Here we are with these incredible minds, yet many do not receive proper training in meditation. Meditation fosters resilience, lowers stress, and offers priceless insights.

Cooking for me means first reading the recipe, putting all the ingredients on the counter, and trusting it will all work out one step at a time. I had followed a recipe from the Satipaṭṭhāna and cooked "Constance" right out of the pot, but now what? I hadn't read a single thing about what to do next. My teacher simply said, "Continue." I had no choice but to deepen my faith in the process growing in my heart.

Most days, anyone passing by offered a bright smile with a polite bow—deep respect and mettā radiated in the center. The next Sunday, one of the community members gave me a small book of Ajahn Chah sayings, called *No Ajahn Chah: Reflections.* I opened it at random and read:

---

43 Edward Conze, *Buddhist Wisdom Books: The Diamond Sutra and The Heart Sutra*

In meditation practice, it is actually worse to be caught in calmness than to be stuck in agitation, because you will at least want to escape from agitation, whereas you are content to remain in calmness and not go any further. When blissful states arise from insight meditation practice, do not cling to them.[44]

We try to be aware of all states, treating them equally without prejudice, meeting the distinct sensations in the body—each one, like a wave, rising and eventually subsiding. Attuning to this with balanced Awareness is essential. I nodded with respect at this important boundary.

The little Ajahn Chah book was perfect because each passage was short. However, after a few days, I noticed a painful pressure behind the eyes when reading more than a few lines. Much like in a reversible figure-ground pattern, the eye organ kept ripping back and forth between the ground, white element of the spatial, indistinct back-ground and the black letters on the page, mopping up a greater breadth of optical awareness. The teacher said this was part of the process as the root of eye-consciousness removes its attachment to objects of perception.

Night held few differences from daytime practice. The dream world took on a whole new dimension, with choosing to see or not see what was before the mind. In a dream, when running down a flight of stairs, as though I were searching, I would suddenly stop, see that I was running, and ask why. If a nightmare arose and someone was at my throat, I would stop and ask, "Why is this happening?" And it would simply vanish—no more fear. Dreaming and knowing it was new to me.

After many more days of practice, when I arose one morning, I remembered a story I heard from a spiritual teacher, Gangaji, that resonated with me. She said a student had complained that he could not meditate because he lived on top of an auto shop, and the noise all day, every day, was too loud. The teacher looked at the student and said, "Move."

---

44 Venerable Ajahn Chah, "Meditation Practice," in *No Ajahn Chah: Reflections*, pp. 82.

Was it time for me to move from this wonderful place of practice? I still had about a month before my plane ticket to return home. I wasn't in any rush, but wasn't sure where to go. I started to think about how my kids were doing. While I sat there, I popped home, and saw them sitting next to each other on their respective computers, helping each other find things on the Internet. These thoughts started to pull at my heartstrings, making me think about leaving the center. But a new type of pull also started carving into my process deeper than before.

One night, when the rain was pounding down in torrents for hours, it seemed we were going to be in a flood—I resolved to go further. This meant that the level of understanding that had been coursing through my system would be cut under for new wisdom. This willingness would broaden the stream and allow deeper currents to arise.

I discussed this with Sayadaw Thuzana, and he agreed it was best to continue, but noted that it can also be good to rest and take it easy for a while. The ability to concentrate was so easy that I could see through my eyelids at times. The goal had been accomplished much faster than I ever expected. Using maps had initially helped me find faith to practice diligently, but now I needed to let them go and be sincerely with what *is*. Grounding activities such as grocery shopping, cooking for my family, organizing, and solving carpentry problems appealed to me. But the cost of an earlier one-way ticket home was too steep.

Before long, another amazingly beautiful sit, and a distinct message came.

All comes in its own time.

~~~

Monastic settings are not without the usual difficulties in life. There had been a conflict between two of the nuns. One of the yogis told me they had to resolve it themselves because if they brought it to the attention of the monks in charge, they would both be asked to leave. This was generally how they resolved disputes in that environment. There was nothing more important than the intensive practice. It was a good lesson for me to not idealize the monastic environment.

When I was in walking meditation one evening, I overheard a female yogi shouting at the teacher in his office. That was anathema to me. It seemed her nervous system was under great strain. I wondered how much more she could take. When there were a few treats at mealtime, she often took more than her share—we could all count. She dripped in sweat while she ate, her hands trembling as she walked. The practice is intense. I could relate to the pressure on the nervous system. But she was causing dissension by moving around, trying to get closer to a fan that was already being used by others. I simply stayed out of her way. Being greedy for the Dhamma is not the way to go.

In a short time, she was gone.

Others came and went, too. Each one, I hoped, was furthering their practice at least a little. How could one not in this kind atmosphere? But many cannot endure the constant practice with what the mind will do in silence. One needs to first cultivate an intuition for self-care and balance with the practice.

For forty days, I hadn't glanced in a mirror or considered my appearance, apart from maintaining cleanliness. I rotated the same two sets of white clothes day after day and walked barefoot. This was helpful for practice because identities disappeared. I simply forgot what I looked like. I had to smile inwardly about this because it was such exquisite freedom.

One evening, I sat in a chair and drank a cup of hot water as the sun set over the piles of rubble in the neighboring masonry plan. Equanimity arose to *be*; the feeling of perfection in Being was incredibly sublime while swallowing water. I didn't believe a single thing. Seeing the truth of no separation generated a fullness that also emptied on its own.

Sitting and soaking with an infinite enigma.

Being.

Looking inwardly and closely at the sensations of the thought, I saw that pain arises when any thought is held onto. It was simply a thought or belief, and I stayed with the process of investigation until it was absolutely clear that it was not true. Then the idea and tension in the body vanished. I gently watched and stayed with the process through and through.

The following day's stifling heat caused me to spontaneously fill two buckets of water near the hose for washing. I melted on a stool, rolled up my pants legs, and put my left foot in one bucket of cool water and the right in the other. Leaning over, I held the hose and let the water flow over my head—relieved from potentially fainting from heat stroke. I remembered playing with my kids when they were little and sitting with them under the sprinkler on a hot summer day.

The nuns shook their heads at me as they walked past. I was definitely bending the norms at the center. Another indication that it might be time to leave. It's important to do what is fitting with one's psyche. If I was concerned with basic needs while trying to practice, then I needed to slow down.

Later that day there was a knock on my door. It was my neighbor Achara asking me in pantomime to return to the upper hall to meditate. The upstairs hall, however, was extra muggy that week, with the afternoon sun beating down and the temperature hovering around 105°F. I shook my head and said it felt too hot for me to be upstairs that afternoon. I found drier comfort in my kuti, sitting in my underwear in front of my fan, drinking water for my health.

When I told Gho, via a little note, that I was thinking of leaving the center, she sent back a gracious reply inviting me to stay at her home in Kuala Lumpur on my way out of the country in a few weeks. Her invitation was a great honor, so I made a simple plan with her for our time together when she'd be home to pick me up at the airport.

After letting the teacher know I needed a break to contact my family one afternoon, I called Jamel, the kind taxi driver, who took me to an Internet café in order to email my family and a friend in Thailand. I reached out to Preston and asked him to review travel and hotel arrangements for me. I told him I'd be back in touch soon. It was nice to have someone handle those details for me. There was much to adjust to with all the intense energy blasting through my body. I needed to put on the brakes and allow space to accept this newfound insight in the body/mind.[45]

---

45 *A Path with Heart* by Jack Kornfield was supportive because he writes about many of the states and working through them with compassion and wisdom.

Preston double-checked that my return ticket was fixed. He booked a very low-cost deal for me to fly to the island of Langkawi on the west coast of Malaysia and stay at a remote resort on the edge of the jungle there. I was also invited to visit a yogi I had met in an online forum in Thailand. Plans started to take shape that I would visit Langkawi, then Thailand, then Kuala Lumpur on my way to Singapore for my flight back home. Exploring these remote islands on our beautiful planet was a once in a lifetime opportunity!

Our earth called me to touch in with Her by the sea to watch experiences come and go.

The earth does not argue,
Is not pathetic, has no arrangements,
Does not scream, haste, persuade, threaten, promise,
Makes no discriminations, has no conceivable failures,
Closes nothing, refuses nothing, shuts none out,
Of all the powers, objects, states, it notifies, shuts none out...
...Whoever you are! Motion and reflection are especially for you,
The divine ship sails the divine sea for you.[46]

46   Walt Whitman, "A Song of the Rolling Earth," in *Walt Whitman: Poetry and Prose*, ed. Justin Kaplan (New York, NY: Library of America, 1982), pp. 362-368.

CHAPTER THIRTY-ONE

Peace

A FEW DAYS BEFORE I left the center, the teacher's young novice monk approached me while I was in walking meditation in the late morning and told me to go see the teacher. I was working extremely closely through a tense state of mind, so I simply replied, "No," and walked on.

He raised his eyebrows, stepped closer to me, and abruptly repeated, "Come, see teacher."

In that moment, I'd been meditating on the importance of my practice with the teacher, so I stepped closer to him, thinking perhaps he couldn't understand what I said. He quickly stepped backward.

"Not now," I asserted softly and firmly.

His jaw dropped while he considered me. "Well, then, later," he said with some perplexity.

"Yes, later." I could feel the tense muscles in my forehead.

He left as I continued working with the anxious sensations of desire for deliverance or re-observation. I felt silly, because I hadn't meant to offend him. The process was my teacher. I *had* to pay attention to what was happening in the moment. Funny that I was contemplating my relationship with the teacher precisely when the monk approached. I noticed my subtle clinging to his presence, so saying "no" aligned with what I was facing at the time.

I had to laugh at myself for refusing. I had broken one of the center's rules. If the teacher wanted to see you, you were to see the teacher. It was understood. I had signed a form that said as much when I arrived.

There was a consequence to this. The teacher wanted to let me know he was going to be gone for a few days on retreat, so I wouldn't be able to say goodbye when it was convenient for us. When I learned this later on, I wrote him a note of apology, asking whether I could return for a visit in a few days before flying to Langkawi. Later in the day, he agreed via his assistant. How nice to have a closure meeting arranged after all!

I kept feeling a wonderful newfound peace, yet I started to wonder: *Was I clinging to peace?* Not having known this kind of peace, which is so sublime and exquisite, it seemed important to let it saturate every cell of my body, like I'd been dehydrated for ages and needed this thirst quenched. I trusted that subtler aspects of the process would be known in due time.

With deep gratitude, I made financial contributions, or dāna, as is the custom. I asked to make a special donation for *all* the female yogis to have yogurt or ice cream at one of the upcoming lunches. I took some pictures around the campus with Gho, got my bag all packed, and firmed up plans to visit her in Kuala Lumpur in a few weeks. Despite the added expense, it was an honor to be invited to her home.

One of the monks who was also leaving the center and had transferred into lay clothes offered to take me to see a local Theravāda Buddhist publisher to select books, and to drive me to my hotel. His generosity touched me. I was given a book by my teacher's teacher, Sayadaw U Paṇḍita, called *Beautifying the Mind*, along with some smaller books to share with others.

The hotel presented several cozy amenities, like air conditioning, a spacious shower, room service, a pool, and a quiet environment. The cool air in my room calmed my hot flashes as I continued to feel like an elusive vapor evaporating into everything.

I went down to the pool for a swim, but when it started raining, I took shelter underneath a cabana. Three young men were drinking beers and chatting nearby.

One of them posed the question, "Why get married?"

Another said, "Don't your parents expect it for you?"

He replied, "Sure they do, but look at what happens: first you get married, then you need to buy a house, then you need children, then the children need education. It never ends. No, I will not get married. It is a sure way to suffer."

They all laughed.

"I see your point, but my parents expect me to marry a girl this year, and I barely know her."

"You'll know her eventually. My mother said she knew my father after twenty-five years, but not before then."

They all laughed again.

I had to laugh too!

He understood the causes of stress and how we were perpetually wanting. The desires were endless. How could we see desires as just arising and passing? How could we move past desire to make wise choices rather than foolish ones?

Every other day I would find myself gazing inward and hearing, "Home."

Then, the moment would disappear and...

I am home.

I am.

I am not.

I am neither.

Oh, how open!

I could have just stayed at that hotel for a month to wait for my return flight, but plans were already made for an interesting trip to Langkawi. Jamel came to the hotel to help me find a place to change money. I asked if I could stop to purchase a small knife on the way. This upset Jamel.

He turned around at a stoplight and examined me, "What on earth do you need a knife for?"

"I want to buy some of the red fruit, but I need a knife to peel and cut it."

He sighed with relief. Then, he started to drive toward a market where I picked up a small knife. There were fruit vendors offering the red fruit, which I learned was papaya, all around the area. Papaya, so wonderful! I also described my favorite brunch that had been served at the center a few times. He told me it was called Nasi Lemak.

Later in the afternoon, I walked to a nearby museum. However, my interest gravitated far more toward sitting in the cool air-conditioning of the space and watching for any clinging to the idea of self than studying the antique furniture and art.

The eye organ meets with an object and it passes through.

On past travels, my habit was to bring along a best-selling novel or science-fiction adventure for some escapist reading, so I stopped into a bookstore. But then I noticed that I had absolutely no interest in escaping! I checked the science section, curious whether any scientists knew how penetrating this insight could be. Perhaps Einstein did. But with the few Dhamma books I had picked up at the publisher's office, I already had what I needed.

How little I needed or wanted was confirmed again and again. I walked around the bookstore, and the only thing I wanted to buy was a map of the area, which proved useful. Less reading was also easier on the eyes at the time, as they became channels for a new way of seeing. The "outer eye" could easily process information, but the "inner eye" could no longer attach to an object. Wisdom and faith arose, allowing me to adjust and trust the process.

The body needed to rest when it needed to rest, eat when it needed to eat, wash when it needed to wash, and move or walk for circulation, each a meditation in the *here and now*. Both pleasant and unpleasant sensations were perceived intensely. Joy, happiness, equanimity, raptures, delight, and wonder were all enhanced and more readily available. Learning not to attach to these byproducts of enlightenment, however, would be a new level of maturity. Ultimately, there was a shift in the relationship between deluded ideas and desires, which had ruled in the past. They no longer held as much sway over the true desire to live in congruence with Reality.

Spirit processed a wise power and love. It did not let me veer far from its nourishing flow. There was an endless illuminating quality that continually refilled the mind and body. Stillness is like a vibrant openness with loving kindness for all beings, happening instantaneously without manipulation. There was a sort of purifying process happening in cycles, and now arose a desire to be more skillful in living with direct Knowledge. I had an established preference for honesty, and I continued to look at any denial, illusion of control, dualistic thinking, or external referencing, but now my attention rested on a subtler sensate level.

Just as we each have our own unique circulatory, digestive, and hormonal systems, so do our bodies have genetic karma. With a heavier menstrual flow, I was undergoing hormonal changes, which brought on sporadic hot flashes.[47] Due to more frequent loose stools, it appeared my gluten allergies required closer observation of key triggers in my digestion. These areas need attention just as much as anything else. These were good reasons to consider resting more, practicing on my own schedule, and shifting my attention for a while. My physical health was paramount given that I was halfway around the world from home.

~~~

Transitioning my attention while traveling required extra mindfulness in different ways with many things: passport, tickets, luggage-weight restrictions, hotel reservations, finding food, finding bathrooms, packing and unpacking, etc. In retrospect, this was a burden I would not recommend.

Much of the time, I preferred to return home after a retreat to observe any clinging within the safe confines of familiarity. I could be more relaxed to accept the new input assimilating within the body.

The mind was still focused on every sensation, looking into any holding pattern in that vibrating tension. Handling luggage and making sure I had all my things together required effort in a different way.

How to bring up carefulness? I posed the question to myself as I paused for some time on the curb before crossing the street outside my hotel. Then a group of motorcyclists zoomed by me, and one boy grabbed the strap on my backpack. As in tai chi, I spontaneously

---

47   I learned later this was perimenopause.

rotated toward and then away, spiraling around, and his grip on my bag released in a flash as they sped off. If he'd had a tighter hold, I would have had to replace my backpack, passport, wallet, and camera!

I walked quickly around the corner, checking behind me to see if they were going to make a second try. Without looking where I was going, I ran smack dab into a monk, who then gave me clear directions to a restaurant.

I could only consider how fortunate I'd been. I was in a new environment, and I had to be mindful of everything and make quick decisions—what a challenge! Thereafter, I kept my passport and wallet in a waist pack inside my pants.

A primordial peacefulness was underlying all events, insights, and sensate awareness. I had been so used to suffering that this rooted peace was like being enveloped in a larger, interconnected body, one that required less, preferred less than before. Ajahn Cha wrote about this:

> There are two kinds of peace — the coarse and the refined. The
> peace which comes from samādhi is the coarse type. When
> the mind is peaceful there is happiness. The mind then takes
> this happiness to be peace. But happiness and unhappiness are
> becoming and birth...so happiness is not peace, peace is not
> happiness. The other type of peace is that which comes from
> wisdom... the mind which contemplates and knows happiness
> and unhappiness as peace. The peace which arises from
> wisdom is not happiness, but is that which sees the truth of
> both happiness and unhappiness. Clinging to those states does
> not arise, the mind rises above them. This is the true goal of all
> Buddhist practice.[48]

To turn inward with Awareness felt so simple and divine no matter what was happening. There is no place to go except to focus inwardly, and this is available at any time. *An all-pervading Peace is already present.* I still find this amazing as I write this today. The goal had been

---

48   Venerable Ajahn Chah, "The Path in Harmony," in *A Taste of Freedom*

achieved, but there was more brightness to uncover with practice and discriminating evaluation. With equanimity in samādhi, release into the deeper stage of sakadāgāmi was possible.

A process of receiving: seeing, hearing, smelling, touching, tasting, and knowing grew in a fresh new way without clinging. This wasn't happening all the time, but more often each day, influencing contracted states like fear, misery, disgust, desire for deliverance, and re-observation.

The knowledge and friction from going through these changes tugged at me:

Further.
What is always here?
Rise above.

~~~

The day came for my last meeting with my teacher. As my feet carried me up the steps and into the center, my heart swelled.

When I approached him, I saw that he was standing with a volunteer going over some details. He looked up and offered his wonderful, inviting, soft smile, motioning for me to sit. Then, he joined me on the floor.

After our respective bows, he inquired, "Constance, why did you choose to leave when you did?"

"Primarily, it was the heat during the daytime, and concern for my physical health."

He nodded. We sat, just being together.

Then, I shared, in a contemplative tone, "I didn't realize I held the idea that I was an abandoned daughter. My father left when I was young, then died when I was twelve, and my mother had nothing to give me. Now, I understand that it was a belief, and I feel so free. Awareness is showing me these energetic adhesions now."

He nodded and understood with empathy, "No, you are not an abandoned daughter."

We both paused, breathing in and out and looking into each other's eyes. There was something about him that resonated in my heart. It was such a profound gift to be with someone who was truly present. His gentle manner and humble attitude provided the ocean of support I needed during intensive practice. I often felt the entire world could fall into his wide, radiant smile.

"I did not want to lean on you, that is why I did not see you before. I saw how busy you were with your teacher and all of the things you had to do."

He smiled and nodded, glad to be seen as well.

I knew that I could not predict when I would ever see him again. As much as I considered him one of my root teachers, I was grateful for release from attachment to him.

We are not separate, the connection is real, as it is with all things.

"How is your practice?" I asked.

"Oh, Constance, it is just here, wherever I sit."

This truth struck a chord with me. He had done what had to be done.

We both paused again.

"I plan to continue intensive practice. I hope to be at Spirit Rock in March, and if I do not make steady progress through the next stages, then I will be back. Have you been to Spirit Rock?"

He nodded. "It is very nice there."

We both smiled.

I expressed my deepest gratitude for his attention, all of the practitioners, the volunteers, and the entire place. He said he didn't answer letters or emails, so I'd only have ongoing contact if I joined him at the center. The joy and faith we both shared in the Dhamma softened the tinge of sadness in my heart for our parting. Monastic centers like this, where you can go when the call arises, are a priceless gift to all of humanity.

"Constance, you are very present in each moment. You are in Choiceless Awareness now. Follow the Eightfold Path. You have much wisdom Constance, continue."

I put my hand on my heart. His sincerity graced me.

Choiceless Awareness.

A part of me questioned the term, *choiceless. What part was that?* Like a koan, reflection continued.

His volunteer offered to take a picture of us, and he kindly obliged. As we stood up, she urged us to move in front of the Buddha statue, and a deep unified knowing arose:

We are not separate.

The Venerable Abbot Sayadaw U Thuzana & Constance Casey, 2008

CHAPTER THIRTY-TWO

Harmony

A FTER I SETTLED into my cottage on Langkawi, I arranged a call
with Daniel Ingram, with whom I'd spoken before I left home. I
wanted to talk about how to navigate more intense and rapid sensory
perceptions, and connect. He does warn yogis in advance on his website
that he is "into very hard-hitting Dharma, and sometimes lets it out
with both barrels." I liked that he was not into projections onto me, or
mine onto him.

He got right on task. "How do you know you have stream-entry?"

"Because I *know*. I verified it. I am cycling differently. Awareness
is here. Everything is inside of everything, which is inside of everything else; it is endless."

"What did the teacher say?"

"He said, 'You are in choiceless awareness now.'"

"Oh, that sounds good."

"How to practice now?" I asked.

As he responded in his usual rapid speed, I pulled out my pen
and took some notes to keep track of the fast-paced interaction.[49]
I quickly accepted his style because I needed some feedback. His
cogent yang approach counterbalanced some aspects of my yin
personality.

---

49 Post Retreat Notes can be found at https://www.constancecasey.com/
2008retreatnotes/

He suggested a focus on the vibrations, which was validating, because they were unavoidable at that point. The various intensities of tension, and where they activated in the body demanded skillful attention. As these sensations danced through the body, I used breath energies intuitively to nourish and balance the mind/body through difficult states into equanimity. The new raptures were whirling through and within. It also helped to establish a routine and some structure in my day as these chaotic swirling energies arose and passed away.

I began writing in my journal about integration and dialed into the material conditions of my life: our low income, unfinished house, parenting teenage boys, the deleterious political landscape in my town, the fact that almost no one I knew in my local community was going to understand what I had been through, and the loneliness that would result from time to time were upcoming challenges.

However, these very factors served as nourishment for my ongoing practice of awakening with compassion. For me, that included enjoying simplicity, moving slowly in my own methodical way, harboring less ambition, loving more, and reducing the hindrances with Awareness.

In taking in all of these views, a lightening-up was happening more on its own. I sat enchanted on the balcony as the sky took on blending and twirling hues of red and purple, with being, non-being, and neither blessing every breath with Presence and unity.

Happily, I picked up my colored pencils and drew a small sketch of shapes that came to me as the sunlight sparkled across the moving water on the edge of the jungle. A dozen long-tailed macaques sat serenely below along the shore, sharing the view.

Underneath my bedside table, I found a fifty percent off coupon for a single massage. I called to find out that with the coupon, I could enjoy a nurturing treat within my budget. After the massage, stretching out my limbs in the pool made my body vibrate with rapture.

Sitting, swimming, and slowly moving extended into loving kindness meditation. Being alone in my little cabin, and walking back and forth along the shore, I reflected with kindness toward whatever was arising, which filled me with a wellspring of Grace, softly showering me when more tension arose through sporadic spirals of insight.

View of the Andaman Sea

Continuing to become friends with the mind is at the core of my practice, often nurturing wise boundaries for self-care and deeper inquiry. I say a word or phrase and let it accompany the in-breath, just letting it subtly touch into the mind and body and do its own dance to affirm the beauty of being.

In Buddhism, there are four sublime states to be cultivated: Loving kindness (mettā), compassion (karuna), sympathetic joy (mudita), and equanimity (upekkhā).

These four attitudes are so similar to the beatitudes and the underlying tenets in the great religious traditions for peace, love, and kindness among all humans. Returning to these states made me feel at home with my practice wherever I was. I reminded myself of the importance of this friendliness as I went about my daily activities and met people in the areas I was traveling.

It took some continued effort to release patterns of worry. In practicing compassionate, loving, kind attention toward finding brunch, eating, resting, breathing, and washing—stress lessened, giving way to a broad open field of Awareness. The cloud of delusion kept lifting, with less "me." Even in the midst of the most difficult times, I found a contentedness and calm delight in the breath. *What is happiness? Notice clinging to unhappiness.* By tuning into the bare sensations in the body with kindness, a sense of delight arose on its own. And, at other times, the power of concentration kept the hindrances at bay, providing the calm of equanimity for release.

When sitting in my cottage after a relaxing sit, I thought that surely after stream-entry I would be more decisive about my future. The insight had clarified my human birth, and the need to know the Dhamma directly had been met, but for clarity around my marriage—*I really didn't know.*

As I sat with the not knowing, I realized it was okay. I hadn't known what to do for a long time, but not knowing was becoming more of a way to be, rather than grinding life down into some known quantity. It seemed illogical to make any big life changes because I had been reborn and was learning how to live straight from Mystery.

How could I know, when each moment was brand new? If I could meet each moment as each moment was meeting me, in fresh open awareness, then anything was possible.

~~~

After resting alone for several days, I learned that I could rent a motorcycle, for only $15 for the day, to explore the island with its lush biodiversity. Why not?! I went far to the north and down through the center of the island. I learned that Langkawi is home to several types of monkeys: the gliding monkeys, with small wing-like arms, that travel across tree tops; the dusky leaf monkeys, who were very shy; and the gray/brown macaques—having learned that tourists equal food, they could be a nuisance. The slow loris monkey moved like a sloth, and the flying lemur leapt among the trees. This was all totally new to me.

Near an area that appeared like a nature reserve park, I slowed down and stopped because more than a dozen long-tailed macaques were combing through dumpsters and some had lumbered out across the narrow road in front of me. Being cautious, I kept my distance as they sat and stared back at me. There were several large males in the group, about three feet tall, with big strong teeth. I looked behind me; there was no one around for miles. The new resorts had encroached upon their feeding territory. They were just doing what they needed to do, forage for food. But now there was waste in their midst, strewn across the road and up the hillside.

I lightly pressed the accelerator, my knee almost touching them as I crept slowly through their troop. As I passed the corner, I heard a whooshing sound and saw dozens of smaller monkeys leaping long distances through the jungle trees. They were the flying monkeys, smaller and well-camouflaged. I thought about how limber and strong they were, and how they could have jumped onto my motorbike as I went by. I didn't want to frighten them, and prayed that we could live in harmony. I wished for them to find nourishment that was more congruent with their needs, rather than the rubbish they were combing through.

A street-side restaurant caught my eye and I placed an order for Pad Thai, one of my favorites. I sat there, wondering how we might live more in harmony with our earth. If more people could awaken, we might see how interdependent we are with each other and realize the need to respect and care for all of the planetary species and resources. We would all benefit.

When I returned to my motorcycle, I didn't remember how to start it. The guy I'd rented it from already had it running when I left. I asked some people to help me, but I didn't speak the language.

One woman kindly came and stood by me, pointing tentatively at different things as we investigated. It was getting dark. I had many miles to navigate to get back. I tried the key several times and thought perhaps I had flooded the engine. "Shit!" I mumbled under my breath.

She looked at me quizzically, and softly asked, "Hmm, what is 'shit'?"

I laughed, feeling so grateful for her innocent approach. I just started touching each thing and watched with her while the mind worked it through. When I allowed the attention to drift and the hands and feet to peruse carefully, it occurred to me to push a little button, which appeared to prime the carburetor. It was a remote memory from starting an old lawn mower, but it started the bike, and we both smiled widely. I bowed and thanked her profusely as I drove off.

I spotted a wide inlet driveway with a view of the ocean, which seemed like a good place to pull over to check my directions. As I studied the map, out of the corner of my eye, I saw four men in white uniforms carrying rifles stride toward me. They shouted and pointed fervently at the road, ordering me to leave the area. I acknowledged them immediately while stuffing the map in my pants pocket, watched for an opening in the oncoming traffic, and sped off. Glancing over my shoulder, I surmised that it was a military base.

Farther down the road, I pulled onto an old unpaved driveway overgrown with weeds near an old house. A little girl, about four or five years old, emerged from behind a hut. As I checked the map, she approached me and observed my bike. Her bright eyes and undeterred curiosity compelled me to offer her the cash in my pocket. As soon as I handed her the bill, three boys ran to her from behind a shack and tried to pry it from her hands. She immediately kicked them in the shins, holding tight to the cash. They sorely retreated, and she threw up her hand, smiling and waving as I rode onward to the resort.

When I returned the bike, I asked about the base. I was told I was lucky not to be arrested by the military for approaching the entrance. They could have taken me into custody and searched me for a suicide bomb. Again, my laissez-faire American attitude was shaken by this kind of potential violence. I had never considered that happening in my home town. So much suffering goes unnoticed and unrecognized in society. If I'd had darker skin, I sensed they'd have pointed their rifles at me instead of pointing their fingers at the road.

~~~

On my last night in the cottage, I had time to sit and contemplate life back home. Stewart had been suffering in his own way. Out of love and curiosity, I decided to call him to try to connect, and see how things were going. Just after I got him on the line, macaques jerked the handle to my room, shaking the entire wall structure.

I quickly glanced out my curtains on the balcony side and saw two monkeys climb up the pillars supporting the neighboring cottage in the water. Would they climb up here too? Perhaps this was why I got such a reduced rate for this particular cottage? A monkey bite was the last thing I had anticipated on this trip.

While I tried to establish a connection with Stewart, the monkeys' scratching and screeching intensified. I stood there trying to find words as the monkeys pounded and rattled my only exit.

His voice crackled through the receiver, "Maybe I should go?"

"What!? Monkeys are trying to get in!" I said anxiously.

It was about 9 a.m. where he was. He always had trouble with interruptions, and talking with me all of a sudden made it hard for him, especially with the clamor in the background.

I waited for the monkeys, wondering if the doorknob lock would hold or if they would give up. I was fortunate they didn't come to my balcony; I had no food to distract them, and would it even help? It was such a strange sensation to toggle between trepidation and simple curiosity.

Many thoughts whirled through my mind. *What was Stewart feeling? What did I want from him? What could he do anyway? What do I want him to be doing? Why would I want him to be different than who he is?* I have been practicing total acceptance of what *is.* I did not want anyone to be with me who did not want to be with me. What is *is. Only now!* As my mind moved quickly into the sensations of these thoughts, time disappeared.

"Are you there?" I asked.

"Yeah. I just finished extending wires into the family room."

The monkeys decreased their pitch.

"Huh!?" I shook that off. "I don't know what to do. There's no bolt lock on this skimpy thin door." I realized he was waiting for a direct request. I put across to him, "I'd like you to stay until they are gone."

"Okay. I will stay," he echoed.

We sat together in silence, and as much as I wondered how the monkeys had come to my door, I wondered what I was doing in this relationship. *How had I come to this cottage?* Something happened where the mind stripped nude to unveil that it was all dependent on a series of conditions so complex that the unfathomableness of them could only go on humbling me.

My body wanted to let go—to free up tension for peace and harmony. A divine logic unmasked that holding onto anything was futile. I could feel Life. Intimacy is simply truth between two people. He is doing what he is doing. I could accept that as my breathing slowed down. The scratching and screaming stopped. *Quiet.*

I asked him about the boys and the house. He said things were fine.

Feeling completely drained, I said goodbye. I could only be grateful to have a place to rest for the evening. I closed my eyes for a moment, sending them all my love, and breathed in peace.

There is a choice for being.

When I called the office to ask about the monkeys, I was told that the island is their home and they were here first. If the monkeys entered, I was warned to keep my distance; they usually ran toward the refrigerator and would leave if they couldn't find any food. Good to know.

Home is here. We are here to share.

The next morning, I left my cottage to take some pictures when a big old male monkey jumped onto a railing right next to my shoulder. His left arm grabbed at my camera. I jumped back and screeched, hoping this would frighten him away. Instead, he just sat there observing me, not in the least bit startled. He brought his hand to his face and began tracing his finger along his chin.

What? Suddenly, he became my teacher. He couldn't help but be himself, open and free, wanting and curious.

Then a passerby threw him a peanut, and he quickly turned to break it open and chew it. Even though the person helped distract the monkey so I could move on, the occasional toss of a peanut created the cause for his arrival to begin with, and so it goes, around and around.

The incongruities between my husband's personality and my own were like a few perfect peanuts life had thrown to each of us. If I'd had a husband who was more in sync with my needs and desires, perhaps I would not have been driven to investigate my suffering so deeply. I could only feel grateful for him and his support. Without him doing every single thing he had or had not done, I would not have come to be where I was at that moment. I'd come to trust the process even more. Living with him again would be the real test.

~~~

My next destination was Thailand, where my new yogi acquaintance, Jenn, picked me up at the Bangkok Airport. It was clear on an overhead TV that Obama had won the election, and my ballot had been counted for that to happen. She drove me to a nice and quiet, inexpensive resort west of Bangkok where I could hang out in peace, visiting me every other day for an outing together.

After settling in, I called Semry to see how she was feeling. It was wonderful to hear her voice and connect with her. I asked if she was all right after leaving the center, and she exclaimed, "Oh yes, so glad to be home!" We could only speak briefly due to the language barrier, but she thanked me for my concern, and I thanked her for her kindness because we were like Dhamma sisters.

The busy city engaged every sense for exploration. Jenn and I zipped around Bangkok in a tuk-tuk, a three-wheeled taxi, tilting back and forth as we rode through the busy, winding roads. She also stopped me from ordering Pad Thai and said she'd order so that I'd experience more variety in the Thai cuisine.

Off the corner of a market, I bought a little ornament from a skinny little boy with no shoes. He had taken a long reed and ingeniously transformed it into a cricket. She took me to visit Bangkok's Grand Palace. Every square inch was covered by a colorful mosaic display of fine craftsmanship! The eye organ reached out and invited colors and designs to pass through. Her generosity in showing me around and translating helped me enormously throughout my stay.

The humidity caused me to look around for shade, and I often suggested to Jenn that we step back into some coolness to take in the scenery. I continued to feel alarmed by sudden flashes of heat arising in my body. I'd start sweating from pores that I never knew could sweat, soaking my clothes; I carried a dry shirt in my backpack to change into. After a hot flash, my body swung into a freezing cold flash, and then it would eventually return to a balanced body temperature.

Numerous scraggly dogs roamed the streets. My heart sank seeing some of them curled up on a warm road for comfort while others, some with open gashes and wounds, howled or whimpered in pain. These were things I'd never seen before due to the cold climate and animal care laws back home. We pay taxes to have dogs picked up, and if they are not adopted, they are euthanized. However, in Thailand, I saw dogs living out their karma and not being murdered.

~~~

The beauty of the lush vegetation and surrounding water lilies outside my window helped me settle into some mettā meditation practice with rest and reflection. I regularly explored the sensations of pleasant, unpleasant, or neutral, using breath energies creatively for support. Breath awareness brought attention to any leaning in or pulling away from a sensation, alleviating the painful pull of the mind to figure things out and allowing for openness. Some state shifts felt like a twenty-pound weight over my entire body had been lifted.

Through quietude, I found more clarity and strength to confront some emotional patterns of despair and unworthiness I'd learned in our culture and from my family of origin. Some of my deep work around despair and fear revealed ways of relating to a subtle form of nihilism. At times, the sensate force of these new lessons was so intense, they simply moved through the body and I didn't know what they were because I was focused only on the sensations. It was going to be a lifelong process of learning to get used to these subtle energetics in this mind/body.

Sometimes, I noticed formations, senses of self that had been so conditioned to feel hurt, arising in my aura before they came into the body. This was a new way of noticing, of peeling back the layers. Sometimes I saw other beings and ghosts hanging around the body and learned to send them along their own path firmly and compassionately.

Other times, waves of friction from those around me quickly penetrated my heart. I breathed through this process, and then watched it pass into a greater field of Awareness from which I was not separate. This made it difficult to see what was *me* and what was *not me*. The boundaries between conventional reality and ultimate Reality blurred, again and again.

While my long-term practice was a ripener for awakening, it was also wise to find some reflective support for the "me," "Constance," who had not felt seen, heard, or understood much over the years. I finally saw how my perceptions had contributed to not feeling seen because I hadn't understood what I was in Spirit. As I've heard many spiritual teachers say over the years, we are spiritual beings having a human experience. Spirit is free. I needed to know Spirit directly and regularly. And Spirit needed to experience Spirit through this form "me" in order to really feel whole. And *that* was what I'd been seeking all of my life.

Woven into this seeking was a fundamental need to investigate Stillness, leading me to become quieter and more withdrawn. Two different processes intertwined: one included journaling, or talking with an empathic friend or teacher to learn new ways to digest unresolved hurts and grief; the other unfolded naturally in each and every breath, grounding me with the acceptance needed for healing old wounds and loosening up old patterns of belief with Love.

In daily life, we must function through many rational beliefs, like that a bee will sting, or a bus will arrive. However, seldom are we aware of how we hold them. Many believe "this" is who they are, for instance, constricting one's reality into an unchangeable, solidified resin. In spiritual practice, we hold provisional beliefs in the form of faith and trust in the process. To wake up, I needed to know my involvement in beliefs directly so the mind/body would find release. Just like the smell of lavender, words cannot describe it to full satisfaction. With *knowing*, there was no need for me to believe.

Basically, old habits were stored in my energetic field and needed to be worked through with Awareness. This took time, practice, and support. For instance, I participated in being invisible in my biological family to feel safe, which had the side effect of denying many of my gifts and talents. But this tendency could not go unseen anymore. Awakening brought more loving awareness of these unresolved issues with my family of origin, as Higher Power now called for an even deeper release.

As my flight home approached, these thoughts of my life surfaced and shook me up into realizing my adherence to them as ideas of "me." What am I? This "me" felt like an eddying vortex, pulling any ideas into a void that varied in intensity depending upon my concentration.

The deep love I felt for my life and my family had, in large part, caused me to seek and find the Truth, for which I am forever grateful. My husband's behavior and his habitual thinking patterns were hard for me. Would more affection and intimacy be possible? I could only focus on my own behavior and respond to his behavior with new skills. That old illusion of control was staring me in the face, inviting me to let go and trust the tenderness and love that flowed from my heart.

Connecting with others and seeking support was crucial for the well-being of my family, especially due to our low income and demanding life circumstances. Looking back, it's as if Life herself demanded that I exude a higher level of energy and openness. Each day was a delicate balancing act as I juggled responsibilities as a parent. My children relied on me for guidance, emotional support, and stability. While their presence brought immense joy and purpose to my life, it also necessitated frequent interaction with the world outside my comfort zone.

Had circumstances been different, without the responsibilities of parenthood and with financial abundance, my humility in reaching out might have taken a backseat. I imagine I'd have been far more reclusive, choosing more solitude and introspection.

People with a strong sense of self, especially extroverts, often want to come out to tell everyone about their insights and express themselves. Being a little more of an introvert, I just wanted to be intimate with this Divine process. Still, I wanted to connect with people. I desired conversations that would allow me to openly discuss my practice in a straightforward, relaxed, and intimate way. However, I really didn't know anyone who would be able to understand this, so I had a tendency to diminish incredibly intense blissful moments and withhold "my" radiance.

To share openly and authentically includes being seen and heard clearly and safely. I did not have much experience with that throughout my life due to familial estrangements and the marriage I chose. Knowing that I am not even a particle lightened *me* up to see that I could heal from unhealthy patterns and move with more authenticity. As these insights arose, there was a call to move deeper into Stillness and a sweet healing process called me home.

Some of the Thai people I encountered carried a gentle and kind manner about them. They inspired me to embody the harmony between the sweet softness of the heart and the crisp clarity of the mind. I was reminded of the statue of Mañjuśrī I had back at home. Depicted as a bodhisattva, which could appear as male or female, it held a lotus flower in the left hand, representing love and compassion, while also wielding a flaming sword held lightly in the right hand, representing the realization of transcendent wisdom so as to swiftly cut through ignorance and duality.

I love to swim. While on the island of Langkawi, I swam every day, either in the ocean or the pool. In Thailand, floating in my long bathtub helped me cool down and relax when returning from an outing. The buoyancy of being in water helped me relax, accept, and work with the energies.

Relaxing tensions as they arise is an important part of the practice that includes getting out of the way. I continued to surrender to the best of my ability. *Relax into that too.* The universe is in a state of perpetual harmony, so making adjustments with the breath along the way reduced the clinging to ideas of "me" or "mine" that created inner discord.

The arising and passing of all phenomena is true, but that is not the whole Truth; rather, it is a doorway to the Truth.

Resting in Stillness.

I sought out my old story and reflected on how unnecessary it was to hold onto it. It was a passing configuration of vibrations and colors that engaged ideas, and my habit was to unconsciously cling to those ideas. Harmony became a new conscious priority.

Many edges, or points of connection, melted into a fabric of non-separation that existed in all things. Everything was full of movement and had its own unique character. It was like coming to a place with no vista, just open and unknown, an unraveling mystery. I could worry, or I could wonder. Wonder was the obvious choice, while worry was the habitual choice to unlearn.

~~~

My yogi friend Gho and her husband greeted me at the airport in Kuala Lumpur. We drove to their home for my short stay before I left SE Asia. She was incredibly gracious to show me around the city and treat me to the best Malaysian cuisine.

The attitude toward marriage was quite different there and rarely about romantic love. Although she appeared content with her marriage, practice was far more important to her. We both agreed that life was about knowing Truth and living in it each moment. She stated that they aspire to accept and understand one another, even if it takes many decades—that's a good start. They do not even expect it to happen in one lifetime!

That required a great deal of patience. I had more to learn to integrate this raw connection with Life into my marriage. Gho shared vehemently, "Constance, marriage to Truth is the best of all possible marriages!" I loved that! I had much to learn from her.

With patience, and less "me," harmony seemed more likely between Stewart and me. We could meet in the middle, even if we were quite different. To a large extent, even with my bewilderment around Stewart's behavior, we shared a vitally important mutual respect for one another.

Going forward, seeing ideas as just ideas brought a crisp spark to each moment!

Our existence is like clouds over the lake
on a blustery autumn afternoon
The birth and death of Mother Earth's many creatures,
a lilting dance.
Lifetimes pass like a shooting star
in the vast open sky,
streaming as briskly as dawn turns to day and
dusk to night.

~ Poem from my 2008 journal entry ~

CHAPTER THIRTY-THREE

Home

JOURNEYING BACK HOME, after my brief stay in Kuala Lumpur, I found myself in Singapore, ready to embark on the next leg of my adventure. Picking up some t-shirts for my boys, I carefully packed my bag at an airport hotel, preparing for an early morning flight.

Settling into the first long flight back from Singapore to Tokyo brought an unexpected twist—the flight attendant's call bell kept ringing and ringing. Much like everyone else, I was annoyed at first and didn't understand why it kept echoing throughout the cabin.

The flight attendant passed by and informed us that they were unable to turn it off. Since no announcements could be made due to the glitch in the intercom system, the captain's copilot walked through the aisles to soothe the many anxious passengers, asking that they please be patient as they coordinate with ground control.

I chose to use the event to relax and take the sound of the bell as an object. Each time it rang, I stayed with the felt vibrations of the sound and let thoughts of it be "only hearing." As people panicked in a frenzy around me, I continued meditating until the boundaries of the body and sound fused into Stillness. I experienced a very deep and relaxing samādhi that went beyond space and time while the sound of the bell receded further and further away, like I was *being meditated*.

Time slipped away unnoticed as the plane drew closer to the tarmac. As I soaked in sensations, moment by moment, feeling the changing cabin pressure while staying with the breath, a flight attendant crawled through an upper chamber just above my seat. He disconnected a wire, and the dinging stopped. Opening my eyes, I turned to look out the window and was delightfully greeted by the sight of my familiar Minneapolis neighborhood dusted with snow.

At baggage claim, I was bowled over by the two tall, handsome young men with big smiles and open arms. Per Malaysian custom, I bowed to Forrest and Preston. We exchanged long, warm hugs. They looked a little skinny to my discriminating eye.

Home is where the heart knows.

Stewart was rocking side to side, squeezing and unclenching his car keys, waiting in shy anticipation for me to greet him. I signaled him to come over. As he attempted to give me a side hug and a polite kiss on my cheek, he tripped over the luggage. After a hurried scuffle to gather it up, he marched us toward the freezing airport garage. I had been moving in slow motion, attuned to peaceful rhythms.

Accept.

On the ride home, I shivered without a coat and turned up the heat. The kids asked, teasingly, "When are you going to cook supper for us?" I had to laugh. They wanted to taste my home cooking.

For months, I had enjoyed delicious, inexpensive meals without having to cook. It would take some time to transition back home. However, cooking is one of the ways I show love. In preparing some of our favorite recipes together, I had an opportunity to reconnect with mettā.

With mettā and mindfulness, activities can happen with ease.

This whole retreat had given me freedom from the role I played as "mother," not only to our children, but often with Stewart. I needed to transform my relationships with them into more harmonious ways of living and being together.

The next day, while replacing the eighth dead lightbulb, I chuckled: How many household members does it take to replace a lightbulb? Then, I remembered the trash container needed to be out on the curb and emptied the next morning. I walked by the boys on their computers and asked if it was taken care of.

"Yes, Mom, we already did it," said Preston.

I looked outside, and sure enough, the can was out there, ready to be picked up!

"It took a few weeks to get into the habit, but we got it, Mom."

"How did things go with your dad while I was away?"

"We mostly took care of ourselves. I was really busy with school," Forrest said, and Preston simply nodded.

While I returned to the mother role, I knew it was just a role—not me, not mine, not all that I am. What a relief! And, since they each had had many health problems over the years, which required intensive care, it was a relief that Stewart and the kids were all right.

Glancing out the window, I saw that Stewart had ordered too much rock for the retaining wall project in the back yard. Some progress had been made while I was away, but the extra-large pile of gravel sitting in the driveway made it impossible to put the car in the garage. With my usual determination to be thorough, I would not have considered the wall finished until the area around it was also cleaned up. I sighed, breathing into the dissatisfaction with the huge pile of rocks: I would have to figure out how we'd use them. A sensation of tightness in my head dissolved into spacious Presence. *Once I've rested, there will be a way* to take care of the rocks.

When I brought this up to Stewart, he fell silent as usual, probably searching for clues about what to say. A temptation to enter into some resentments mingled with acceptance of our differences. I'd grown weary of supplying verbal prompts for him on communication and sensing that my feelings were not heard. I pondered how to move our relationship in a more positive direction.

In the past, I might have felt like a sponge wrung out trying to communicate. I might also have felt stuck, alone, and separate. But now an inner water sprinkler nourished resilience. Wisdom provided a gauge valve on this never-ending flow, inviting me to accept each of us as we were, and recast my will into God's will for our individual and common welfare as a family. My responses came from a new place, a place of depth and compassion. I could not argue with *what is. We are not separate. Love was present.* I could only humbly listen to the incredible flow of energy in the body despite our divergent paths.

"Thanks for building the wall and being here. I couldn't have practiced so well without your support."

He nodded with a big smile.

"There is so much to learn about how you and I do things," I said, gently smiling back. "Maybe we can come to understand each other more now."

He stood there, awkwardly shifting from side to side. I couldn't tell to what degree he agreed.

Let thinking happen, I thought, and sighed, while my gaze focused on the blue sky out the window.

Then, I looked at him as if for the first time.

He spoke hesitantly, looking down, "When you were gone, I could see how much I rely on you for a sense of order, and your attention with the kids."

"Hmm," I murmured, taking a brief pause before sharing, "It will be interesting to see what we each learn now."

We stood parallel, gazing out the window, an accustomed stance for us, as his eyes often darted around. He promptly pointed to our birch tree, enthusiastically recounting in detail his sighting of a finch and the particular aspects of its distinct chirp, unstreaked brown-blackish wings, and feeding habits.

I felt sad that he did not turn toward me. I understood his interest in the bird was his familiar way of coping with interactions, but this way of his often left me feeling somewhat invisible to him. My need to reunite with affection or tenderness was not recognized.

Nevertheless, Stewart's admission was a rare moment of connection and urged forgiveness to arise in my heart. Maybe he'd enjoy understanding his own perceptual patterns more? And, with Awareness, I could meet him right where he is. There were certain things about him that I appreciated, like his sincere willingness to assist when asked. There was much to consider going forward. *Go with the flow.*

I wondered, *Does time apart make the heart grow fonder?* Not all wounds can be healed with time. It takes daily practice, commitment, and skills for the heart and mind to grow in compassion. I'd appreciated the break from his particular habits. The solitude had been healing and helpful for getting to know myself. However, I needed to face our mismatched differences and honor my own needs more. I loved him, and yet love alone does not fully sustain a functioning partnership.

I could finally see that for many years he had been coping with sensory overload by limiting his social interactions. He appeared to be compensating for a great deal of social confusion on a daily basis. No wonder he had been drawn to highly specialized programming projects.

~~~

Stewart and I first met in 1985 at a block party, where we happened to dance together. We connected over having emigrated from families that didn't nourish our unique ways of being. I found his eccentricities sweet, and we enjoyed many biking trips together.

His living situation and finances were a mess, and he was going through a divorce at the time. I helped him sort his possessions and move out of the condominium that he shared with his wife and into a rented room. When I was in a fix, he showed up to help me with a few projects, and he was on his best behavior as we moved through the many platonic dates that we shared.

When I looked around, this pattern of helping men wasn't unusual for most of the women I knew at the time. Stewart didn't drink alcohol, didn't smoke, and didn't date any other women. He seemed to want to be with me. Given his divorce, I assumed that he would learn new skills for a healthy relationship. And, in the first year after we got married at the courthouse, before we had children, he showed an interest in communication and connection with me, and I felt closer to him. We attended several intensives with Anne Wilson Schaef, and he expressed his appreciation for all of the new information about recovery. His work life began to improve with positive feedback from his colleagues.

After the marriage grew more complex due to the challenges of parenting a seriously ill child, he began working late into the day and taking on assignments that required him to travel farther from home. When our family left the house, I knew that windows had to be closed, the shades lowered, water bottles filled, snacks prepared, and the doors locked. He would often ask, "What do you want me to do?" and if anything was forgotten, he'd say, "You didn't tell me." It was true; I could hardly remember everything. We were both responsible, yet his recurring need for specific instructions and lengthy time away from home led me to shoulder more than my share.

During our outings, I worried more about losing Stewart than the children. Despite trying to lay out a plan and make things clear in case we were separated, there remained great confusion from him time and time again. To solve this problem, I made four tie-dyed shirts in the same color, aiding each of us in finding one another at state park outings and crowded events.

After discovering that he preferred to go off alone and read *Dune* for the umpteenth time, I asked him about it. He said he resonated with an incantation from *Dune* called "Litany Against Fear" that stated, "Fear is the mind-killer." While I respected the courage of his inquiry into fear's influence, I thought the negative framing around fear could be limiting, much like how too much shame, born from anger or fear, can stop us from learning and growing. I considered how this confrontation of suffering with stoicism might circulate feelings of paralysis. When I turned toward fear with compassion, it transformed or slowly faded away.

We discussed our feelings, and he shared his struggle to take in the idea of softening toward fear; that it was not an enemy. The book appeared to offer comfort in holding a warrior stance toward fear. My process was becoming more porous and open, while he seemed to reinforce his guard with each revisiting of the book's ideologies. Without my ongoing facilitation, the openness to communication that I needed for mutual intimacy often clashed with the armor of his warrior stance.

With our small income, we needed to focus on making enough money to cover basic needs, which kept us both busy and too tired to fully reconcile our differences. I had been very accommodating with Stewart while dismissing many of my natural needs to be seen and heard. Yet, I could no longer ignore the impact his behavior had on me. I felt a natural leaning in to understand him more and learn how I played a part in feeling conflicted around him.

Out of concern for us all, I asked him if he'd participate in an online assessment for a mild form of autism called Asperger syndrome. He appeared quite curious and nodded vigorously. He took the test right away, and reported back that his score was notably high on the spectrum. We sighed in relief, knowing there was a name for his process. I also took the test but was not considered to be on the autistic spectrum.

I knew I needed to find some additional support, so I invited all four of us as a family to visit a local clinic that specialized in autism. Despite this being a difficult subject to acknowledge, I knew it was time. If Stewart could gain a better understanding of his neurological processes by developing more specialized relational skills, it would help us communicate better. It had been much easier to believe that there was something wrong with me and that I needed further help, which I did reach out for, but he was also a participant and interacted in a different way than most of my friends and I did.

Stewart quickly made arrangements in his schedule to set up an appointment right then and there. After he completed the official assessment at the clinic, it was confirmed that Stewart displayed strong traits within the Asperger's spectrum. The counselor educated us, offering literature, workshops, and practices for living with an autistic family member. Forrest and Preston also sat in on some of the sessions where the therapist explained Stewart's needs for more explicit communication and validated the challenges we faced together. Stewart met with a group of folks also on the spectrum and shared that he finally felt recognized and supported for his way of being. The clinic also offered a support group for families of adults with autism that Preston, Forrest, and I participated in. It was a huge relief for us all to have this named with compassion.

We were each actively learning and unlearning. Stewart was learning to openly accept his autism by paying closer attention to his thinking processes, style of relating, and how we might react when he withdrew from the family to cope. He also appeared to have noticed a shift in my behavior. I felt hugely relieved for being more integrated with Life. He seemed sensitively aware of that by softening his tone more often when he approached me.

One day when we sat on the window seat together peering out into the back yard, he shared, "I see that it can really happen. Sometimes, it really scares me, knowing it's possible for me too. I'm not sure I'm ready for this." Moments where he would be open like this touched my heart.

"That's true," I said. "Fear definitely comes up. And, the 'little me' gets nothing out of this process."

He nodded with a chuckle at that. There appeared to be some consideration regarding his own aspirations for practice.

Awakening blended into everyday life with a calm directness, producing less reactivity to his behaviors. Even amidst the societal stigmas surrounding autism and awakening, we as a family and individually risked more constructive discussion to talk about our differences so that we could understand each other in a more functional way.

Stewart truly respected the work I was doing, and appreciated my discovering Adya, which led to several helpful conversations recalling our respective family histories around religion. However, he shared that it was too difficult for him to focus his mind on the breath in sitting meditation. He preferred listening to binaural beats with a certain tempo as a form of walking meditation, or tuning into Adya satsangs while doing simple chores. Given that the Buddha taught many different forms of meditation, I encouraged him to find his own form of connection with the Divine.

Whatever we are, however we are—Life expresses itself through each of us. During my interactions with him, I could see that whatever he did was not personal, nor was anything I did. Stewart showed love by completing household tasks and fixing certain things for us. And in my love for him, I respected his different forms of expression and gave him space to explore what fit for him.

We were each doing the best we could. To transform my relationship with him meant learning new ways to communicate and, even more crucially, letting go of expectations for how he was handling his relationship with me.

~~~

After arriving home from Malaysia in November 2008, I felt hesitant to step into parent-school relationships so soon. Even though Stewart hadn't come with me to a teacher conference in over ten years, I asked him to join me. However, he said he had to go to a job interview downtown.

Forrest had been getting good grades in all his classes except one, advanced honors American history. He'd hoped there would be more discussion and small-group sharing, but instead it had the same familiar hierarchal focus on the teacher, who practiced a rote teaching style. Forrest was getting an average grade, and didn't want to do the work. His teacher looked at Forrest and me with scorn over his missing assignments.

After hearing about the coursework, along with his five other classes, I suggested he end it. He was completely flabbergasted. I said, "Why struggle with it? If you do not want it, let it go, take a different class. Perhaps that is best anyway. Give yourself three days to consider." I encouraged him to be completely honest with himself about what he wanted and what he would commit to. I also knew that after three days, a problem would usually resolve itself.

Forrest decided to withdraw from the course. He shared his dismay at the lack of philosophical and cultural discussion. It didn't help that the course's focus on traditional white history contrasted with other lessons I'd given my children about the United States. I could see why he wanted to do something else.

Forrest told me of his teacher's stern response, "You don't want to do that," adding that he also refused to sign the necessary form to exit the course.

I stepped in to help negotiate the situation. The school counselor also pushed back at Forrest, saying it was a big hassle, and that he'd lose credit and have a "W" for withdrawal on his record this late in the semester. The counselor appeared annoyed that I didn't see that as a problem, and told us to sit in the hall for a bit because we were interrupting his already busy day. After some time, I went to his door to let him know we were still there. He appeared seriously flustered. After working assertively with the school counselor, we found an independent study course in architecture to fill the credit.

The counselor had looked a bit askance at me, so before we left the school I went to the bathroom and noticed that my shirt was buttoned on the wrong buttons, my hair was a mess, and my shoulders were still coated with sawdust from cutting plywood before we left home. I peered into the mirror again, this time seeing with the "inner eye" a form not limited to ideas of beauty or ugliness; it was simply expressing a fullness of the world. I stood back and stared in awe at this transcendent and immanent Mystery and how the mind creates a seemingly separate sense of self. And yet, I couldn't dispose of the little "me" that others perceive from this face or how my mind interprets it. Those imaginations just arise in the dance of Life.

Afterwards, Forrest was taken aback when I drove straight to his favorite fast-food restaurant and invited him to order whatever he wanted. He quickly apologized for being lazy. I didn't see it that way. I admired him. I knew how bright he was, so I reminded him that he hadn't had any trouble doing any of the work in classes where he felt a meaningful connection, and so it was perfectly reasonable to make a different choice. This teacher expected learning through memorizing and regurgitating information without questioning and discussion, and that style doesn't suit everybody.

As we shared the French fries, I asked him to consider the wisdom of withdrawing energy when it feels futile to continue. I invited him to think that he was not a failure; he could feel content for being honest.

He had interpreted my practice as some idealization of struggling on in the face of hardship and thought he had to do the same. I had demonstrated perseverance, but I wanted him to know that my practice was more about surrender, peacefully sitting and watching the clouds in my mind clear. I took another spoonful of ice cream, glad that he too had been listening from within. Before the next semester, he also decided to change high schools and attend the arts high school his brother had attended.

~~~

At first, I figured I was just adjusting to the time changes of travel, and the late November weather in Minnesota was a freezing contrast to the tropical Southeast Asian humidity. But my abdomen hurt, so I visited with my eastern medicine doctor who diagnosed that I had a parasite that had to be cleansed out of my system.

My poor health interfered with a fun train trip we had booked for our Thanksgiving tradition of visiting the families of my paternal cousins and my stepmother. I wanted this adventure as much for the kids as I did for myself and worried that we would not get our money back if we canceled our tickets. My sponsor helped me realize I had to decline the trip, take care of my health, and stay home. The kids were disappointed but accepted that I needed to rest, and fortunately, we got a full refund.

There are always many causes that go into making decisions. In retrospect, my extended family rarely inquired into our well-being. In my prior work with Anne Wilson Schaef, I grieved the loss of family and, through that process, learned to let go. I came to understand that we each have our own way of being, and living far away with little correspondence makes for a strained relationship. Even though I still care for all of them, the lack of reciprocity after my attempts to reach out led me to put more emphasis on creating a family within my local community that would also accept Preston's emerging queer identity.

I needed to heal and rest. For about three days, I sweated out my fever in solitude with penetrating insight as the parasite left, and my health eventually improved.

Stewart was still actively looking for employment. I needed to share those responsibilities. My website clients had hung in there, having worked with Preston for their basic updates while I was away. However, I had a pile of new work requests. Most of our bills were covered since we had them on auto-pay, but my credit charges from my trip needed a calculated payment plan immediately.

As much as I modeled organization and foresight, it was distinctly not on the kids' radar to put things away or use the grocery list to plan meals ahead of time. However, they demonstrated care for their own hygiene, homework, and washing dishes. The only near-casualties were two thirsty, shamrock houseplants clinging to life. There were no terrible storms, the roof was intact, and the house was secure. They both received excellent grades in college and high school with negligible supervision. Our dear Ruby seemed a little overfed but was okay. Our funny little furry friend stuck to me like glue, helping me with every step. Overall, I kept feeling amazed at how fortunate I was to practice.

One evening, while I awoke from a nap on the couch, I overheard Forrest and Preston engaged in conversation in the kitchen.

"Mom sure seems happier now." Forrest remarked.

"Yeah," Preston said. "She isn't perturbed like she was before."

"She keeps bringing home documentaries from the library."

"I think it's her creative way of showing us places and learning things without having to go there. She wants us to learn more about the world."

"And what's with her and Dad?"

"She said her happiness is not dependent on him, so he's free and she's free. She didn't mean it in a mean way, just like it's a fact."

"Do you think she'll get a divorce?" Forrest asked.

"She might. She is a little unpredictable, but whatever she does, she is so careful. I'm not worried."

"Things feel funny around her now. I mean, like more fun."

"Yeah." Preston said.

"She's different."

"Yeah, she's proven it's possible. It's pretty amazing. There is something really different about her. I don't think I'm ready to face into fear like she has. I sat with her a few times before she left, and she went through some tough stuff."

"I'm not sure I understand it."

"She says no one can until they practice well."

"Wow!"

"Yeah." Preston said, sighing deeply.

~~~

Prior to stream-entry, I saw paradoxes within my life story. Now I was seeing *no* solid story—more of a vibrant Presence in every cell of my body. *Only here and now.* Today, I look at the moon and know, "Hello, sister!"

Not consistently feeling a solid sense of self brought up a new kind of wonder for living. I didn't know how I would express myself from such a big vibrating orientation. But I knew I could trust this beautiful Being shining through and dissolving the sense of a separately existing self. Ideas about who I thought I was were dropped on the road and washed away, presenting more openness. I remembered my teacher telling me to follow the Eightfold Path; trust that, with honesty, it will carry me across the stream. Walking around with equanimity illuminated the path with more ease while I inquired, *Show me the way.*

I had no one I felt comfortable speaking with who understood about deep awakening. Adyashanti satsangs provided helpful support, but he only did one-on-one interviews online, with little chance to get through to him. I wanted to talk about the factors of enlightenment and adjusting to this new way of seeing in my daily life. Finding a local, preferably female, enlightened teacher who had personal experience with parenting more than one child, was aware of neurodivergent thinking, and understood economic challenges would have been extremely supportive for integrating and orienting the newfound energies coursing through my system. But, I knew it was not likely that I'd find one. I've found that many teachers who don't share similar experiences aren't very adept at responding to struggles that arose for me or helpful in navigating this terrain.

One or two friends were understanding of some of the ways I had changed. For those who weren't, our relationships were meant to change. Some friends had replaced me in their circle and weren't sure how to fit me back in when I returned.

It appeared that many of my old friends often saw themselves through a lens of limitation, not abundance. I often heard them say the phrase, "I can't." I was no longer interested in acquiescing to cynical discourse. What felt strangely different was that I didn't have to try so hard anymore. I was accepting people more and feeling more patient. I saw a basic goodness in us all.

While there is obviously greed, hatred, and delusion all over the earth, I was called to look closely into my own participation. The courage to change the things I "can" became more natural to Being. Some friends had also been holding ideas of blame, victimization, and helplessness for a long time.

We simply don't know what we don't know.

Several people were drawn to me, but quickly reckoned I was crazy based on their misconceptions of awakening. Some friends were more curious than caring. We all do what we do until we are done doing it.

On occasion, this perceptual difference made me feel lonely. The words from Sayadaw U Paṇḍita, "Be careful who you keep company with," echoed within me when choosing to call someone or arrange a meeting. I noticed some sensations of loneliness and watched them pass as I accepted that I needed to continue to be a friend to myself.

The nourishing qualities of enlightenment cascaded through again and again. Reciprocity arose as a desire, but I didn't want to nurture a sense of lack, so the process continued to be my primary teacher. Compassionate friends with whom one can openly discuss one's spiritual practice are a rare gift.[50] However different we each were, I couldn't help but love them all.

~~~

With Awareness, I finally understood the Twelfth Step: "Having had a spiritual awakening, we tried to carry this message to others and practice these principles in all our affairs." Spiritual awakening is made up of infinite awakenings all along, including abiding awakening. The priceless gift of serenity invites more and more openness and compassion, nourishing a gradual awakening process. Every moment we are mindfully Aware is an awakening.

How this would translate into changes in my marriage, home life, or vocation was not a problem because living with uncertainty about those things *is* reality. I was more interested in finding solutions than dwelling on problems. It's much better to trust; let the gentle path of learning and unlearning be a discovery with the present unfolding Beauty.

The Twelve Step program asks us to lovingly detach, and that felt easier as I became aware of my habitual clinging. As Ram Dass said, "Once you have tasted something as sweet as spiritual awakening, you

---

50 This is a reference to the teaching on admirable friendships. For more, see Saṁyutta Nikāya, 45:2, "*Upaḍḍha Sutta: Half of the Holy Life*," translated from the Pāli by Ṭhānissaro Bhikkhu.

want to share it with people you love," but "You cannot force the human heart."[51] The desire for all to awaken to this Spirit within all of us is a desire that should be carefully embedded with boundaries. While I wanted to carry this message to others, I did not want to evangelize. I knew I had to do so in a way that was congruent with meeting people where they were, in their current level of truth and form of practice.

Learning to detach with love in this way is an ongoing effort. I'd become somewhat enmeshed with my husband's idiosyncrasies over the years, so I needed to learn more skillful boundaries. Amends are a shift in behavior as well as attitude. I continually invited more patience and a softer tone from Stewart and my children.

How to gracefully stand in my own truth and invite more openness and understanding from others in my life? Awakening was like pulling back the curtain on old patterns of fear that fed into some of the people-pleasing I had learned in our culture. I now knew that my own happiness was foundational to being alive and living. And this happiness was dependent on my practice and could not be diminished; it could only grow brighter.

Each day I try to model healthy ways of living in authenticity with my family. We are each different, but let us feel the *fun* in functional! I wanted to learn how to be more powerful at fostering a cooperative culture in my home. Options for growth are possible among all of us, but they require an interdependent effort and mindfulness. There are more parts to an apology, for instance, than just saying you are sorry. There is a repair process involved where each person sees themselves as a participant. There is making the past into a lost era of forlorn desire, or there is a choice for healing, knowing what you know now that you didn't know before. There is no erasure of past deeds, but there are possibilities for reconciliation through peaceful communication and right effort.

Waking up to Reality freed me from beliefs that had encumbered me my entire life. I had been released from believing that I was a wife,

---

51   Ram Dass, "Sharing Our Awakening," in Ram Dass Love Serve Remember Foundation Website

an abandoned daughter, a martyr, a victim, a mom, a cook, a maid, a friend, a homeowner, a rescuer, a counselor, an artist, a manager, or any other role I took on. Those are roles I play, but they are not me.

When I sat with Sayadaw U Paṇḍita in Malaysia, he said, "Waking up is so bright, that is why we wake up in stages." This fresh, compassionate openness was so clear and blinding at times. And in this waking process, I'm embedded in a core processing as no-thing and everything, and neither no-thing nor everything, and not that either, with a spontaneous sense of responsibility given to any situation.

I wanted to cook and play and skip down the street!

This human birth had a reason—to know the Heart of all Hearts and to open to the Brightness of Being in every cell and breath.

I continued to surrender in receiving this knowing:

Truth is available, right here, right now.

Chapter Thirty-Four

Remembering

A S CLEAR AS THE DAY IT HAPPENED, a powerful memory came
to me when I was recovering in bed after returning home from
my journey in Malaysia and Thailand. I was nine years old. It was
after Christmas when we were off school in a house we had recently
moved into. Had it been a Saturday, I would have had to finish all of the
vacuuming, dishes, and laundry before venturing outside.

Winter always meant slipping old plastic bread bags over my
double thick wool socks, then putting on my shoes and rubber over-
boots to go sliding in the freshly fallen snow with my brother. To save
money, my mother bought me bigger shoes to grow into, so they weren't
too tight with the extra socks.

My little brother, Trevor, and I trudged out to the big sliding hill
just a few blocks away. I had my warm peacoat over my heavy blue wool
sweater, with snow pants, a scarf, hat, and mittens. My mittens were
extra nice because they hugged the cuff of my jacket. I had to use my
teeth to pull them up and over.

My mini toboggan was yellow, his was red. The sun was bright
and the snow banks were piled high as we trudged up the sidewalk
to the hill. Only one busy four-lane street to cross and a little ways
more until we spotted the big banks of snow at the end of the church
parking lot across the street from the hill. A big plow had lifted the
snow and piled it really high. The piles must have been over nine
feet tall.

We dragged our sleds over to the mountain, and we could hardly believe how tall it was. We climbed up and started walking around. It was so high! Trevor decided he was a king, and I was a queen. We made big chairs to sit in, carving out the snow and patting it down.

Then we started digging. We found some small sticks, a flattened beer can, and a piece of cardboard in the parking lot to help dig down and scoop out snow. I wanted to make a hole. Then Trevor made a hole about six feet away from my hole. The sunshine made me sweat from all that digging, even though it was very cold.

After a while, we each dug down to where we could stand up inside our own holes and not see out. So, *hey,* we thought, *let's make a tunnel!* I started digging, and he scooped it out behind with the cardboard. We had no sense of time, just scraping, pulling, pushing, and lifting out big chunks of compacted snow.

We'd stop once in a while. Trevor had some old candy in his pocket and we chewed it greedily through sighs of smoky exhales. It tasted so sweet. Then, we ate snow cookies to fill us up the rest of the way and tucked into our respective tunnels. When our holes met in the middle, we made it just big enough for one of us to crawl through. We started to slide down one end, crawl through, and climb up out the other end. Swish, swish, swish, the sound of us crawling along the snow on top and back down again, head first like squirrels. I came out and Trevor went in, around and around, in and out.

All at once, after I came out, the top caved in on his side. Trevor was down there. I shouted, "Trevor! Trevor!" For a second I waited, thinking he was going to come out of the hole on the other end, but he didn't. Unsure of which end he would be closer to, I just started digging where I thought his face would be. We had packed the snow down and with the melting from the sun, it was turning to ice, so I threw off my mittens and used my hands to burrow down with my fingers, then chopped with my stick, and pulled out some more big pieces.

Silence.

I looked around for help, but no one was around. Not a single car in the parking lot. The street seemed too far away. My heart pounded in my ears.

Quiet.

Just keep digging. Finally, I could see the corner of his jacket and pulled at it. Was he knocked out? He was quiet. I dug some more and freed up his neck and head, then he lifted his bright red and purple face, covered in snow, and he pleaded, "Help me out of here!" His legs were still stuck and it took me a few more minutes of frantically scratching and kicking chunks of snow with my boots to loosen up enough for him to climb out. As he scrambled up, gasping for air, I realized we had gotten down pretty far into the snow bank. Then we wiggled and clawed our way back to the top of the mountain into the sun, blowing onto our freezing red hands.

I just sat there with him, breathing hard. He started bawling big sobs of fear and pain.

I stared at him in shock and relief.

All of a sudden, he stood up, and kicked me hard in the side; announced angrily, "I'm going home. I'm gonna tell Mom what you did."

I couldn't speak. He could have died. Right then I faced death. I had been in a state of misery and despair as I dug him out, and now fear and relief gripped me in a strange combination. I looked around. We were alone.

I watched helplessly as he grabbed his sled and climbed down the snow bank and tromped away.

At this point, it had been hours since we had left home. And even though I was hungry, the hopelessness clung to my ribs. I knew it wasn't going to be good to go home with him blaming me for what happened. I was just over a year older than him; I was supposed to know better. My mother would give me hell. I would stand there and just take the blame.

Nope. No way was I going home. I sat for a while and slunk back down into the hole where no one could see me and felt waves shudder along my back and into my gut.

My ribs heaved as I gasped with sobs.

Mom might take me to see the priest for this. But that didn't matter because I liked saying Hail Marys and Our Fathers. I decided to do my penance right there, just in case, so I wouldn't go to hell. *Isn't God in the prayer somehow?* I said ten Hail Marys and ten Our Fathers, and I jabbed at the wall of my cave hole with the tin can for each prayer.

My shadow sulked like a walking lump with a big long tail and carried me across the street. I wondered, *Am I over there? Or am I here?* My breath reached out into the sunny sky and dissipated into free-flowing wisps.

I started toward another hill: step-crunch, step-crunch. The twist of the rubber sole made a small squeak, then when lifting the foot: all quiet, breathe out, watch air become smoke, step down, pull sled, feel mitten wet, press thigh into the hill, press, step-crunch, cold wind touch face, watch shadow. Stop. Shadow stop. Move. Shadow move. Feel lifting leg, swishing snow pants, moving rhythmically, stepping, lifting, breath, stepping, breath, step breath, crunch, crunch. Then, at the top.

Deep breaths take in the vista, the wonderful openness. With the shadows getting longer, it was harder to see scary low spots, so I put my sled down and sat for a while. Then I decided to go down head first. Why not? The hill starts slow and picks up fast with a rush of freezing cold air, piercing the eyeballs and making them weep, faster and faster, then slow, slow, slow, stop, rest.

Roll over. Lie on back. See sky. Rest. Then, back up: step-crunch, breath, step-crunch, breath. Climb up hill, step, step, step...Put down sled. Lie down. Release. No time. No need, just each moment felt through wet mittens.

Slide down, roll off sled onto my back, struggle to get up, and back up the hill again. Step, step, breath, step, breath. I overheard a dad say to his little girl, "Time to go home now and go to bed."

The stars came out, the sky a deep blue over the white hills. The water tower reminded me of thirst, so I ate more snow. Nobody was around after I got to the top, so I scooped out a little hole in the midst of the pine trees to pee in. It was hard to pull everything down and make it work. Paying close attention, I made it work; steam rising from the little pit. That made for more relaxing steps and faster, riskier parts of the hill than before.

With nothing to lose, I headed for the bigger sections of the hill. Second by second turned into minutes and hours. Alone and not alone, being with the snow, being cold, then warm, watching the shadows change with the setting sun. Wondering, *What knows this?*

Glittering whiteness, so beautiful. The snow started to squeak and crunch in a stiffer way as the day wore on; the sun saying goodbye made the snow freeze faster. The deep slushy spots on the hill froze into hard ridges that hurt my knees on the way down.

I could feel my toes now, cold, but still all right. The rest of the body felt warm. Staring up at the sky I asked, *Why can't the heat from the center move down to the toes?* Then, it did.

It started snowing lightly. The beauty of it, how wonderful. I felt happy. I took my sled and started the walk home. I took the hard way along the top of the hill where the snow was deep past the water tower and quickly crossed over the busy street. By the time I got to our block, two inches of snow coated the sidewalks. My boots made swooping brush strokes in the snow. I turned to look at them. *How was I just there, and now I am here? Whose footfalls are those?* Cold toes, not me.

Tired and relaxed, I tossed my sled down on the sidewalk and lay down on my back. As I grabbed the twine with my sloppy mitten and pulled it over my shoulder, snowflakes touched my cheeks and eyelashes, and I gazed at them on my dark blue mitten. Each one so big and pretty. I opened my mouth to catch them on my tongue and noticed they didn't always land there.

I pushed with one leg, then the other—push and slide, push and slide. I closed my eyes and breathed in, belly rising, when all of a sudden, the sky opened up. They weren't only snowflakes any more. They were stars falling, big huge stars all around. I opened my eyes, amazed. The wonder of it all! *I was a snowflake. I was the snow falling, I was the "earth crunching beneath my feet. I was the car that passed by on the street, I was the slush landing near me from the car passing, I was more than one snowflake, I was all of them combined and also each one. I was the whole universe! I was seeing and being as One and this was Home. There was only being with each sensation, each noticing, nothing left untouched; all the senses came alive in wild wonder with joyful knowing, deep knowing.*

Occasionally the universal foot would push along, slide, push along, slide, stop, see all wonder of all wonders, push along, slide. Stop. Wonder.

For a long while, I lay on the sidewalk in front of our house.

Someone passed me at one point, their pant leg brushing my shoulder like caressing another galaxy. I was falling without fear, falling through the universe. Flying without end.

The house was dark when I entered that night, everyone had gone to bed. I lay down in my bed and stared out the window all night, curling up with countless galaxies in my heart.

No one ever mentioned Trevor's near-death experience.

~~~

I had completely forgotten this experience until I returned home from Malaysia. This memory from childhood, of our unified connection with all, pulled me along and deepened my resolve to keep going. The graceful gift of Mystery opened up a myriad of other memories and answers that I had always been searching for. Being home, in my familiar habitat, helped me relax and know what it is to be human.

Sādhu. Sādhu. Sādhu.

I could see my teacher's face and hear his voice gently reminding me:

"Constance, continue."

Afterword

WHEN PERSONAL STORIES ARE SHARED, it fosters hope and understanding. I'm carrying this message forward to show a way out of the addictive system that trapped me in a cycle of stress. The Buddha Dhamma provided me with more direction in understanding a progressive path for liberation. It is my wish that my sons and whoever else might benefit from these words will be drawn toward this freedom. Real, abiding, transformative change can be done here, right now in this very life!

My relationship with the world has changed. I can no longer solely identify with my personal story, so I don't attend recovery meetings quite as regularly. Having genuinely experienced the promises of the program, I embrace a more flexible approach to anonymity, as advocated by Lois W., which empowers us to carry the message, offer support, and provide guidance to those in need. Therefore, I choose to offer my full name and hold my anonymity lightly.

My moral training in Christianity, Twelve Step recovery, Quakerism, and Unitarian Universalism was like the Buddha's first training in "*sīla*," or ethical conduct; a grounded path to start practice that pulled me along. Meditation is learning to live in touch with the Dhamma in all aspects of life. I was no longer meditating but *being meditated*. Deeper stages of understanding and insights have emerged since the events of this memoir, so it was sometimes challenging to maintain the perspective of a stream-enterer when giving this testimony.

The question is commonly posed whether it is best to go full-fledged into insight practice or to work on psychological issues first. The answer comes down to psychic readiness. They are different forms of insight. If there is a constant effort to deliberate about concepts related to your inner dilemmas, then it is probably not helpful to do concentrated insight practices. Inner conflict can be distracting, so it helps to be gentle with oneself, have a somewhat stable lifestyle, and be interested in practice. Eventually, psychological issues are revealed and melt away as wisdom arises.

For most of my life, I felt like one of my handmade wooden scrap cutting boards—workable, but dry, with tautly warped fibers arching into distorted forms. With the freshly saturated, watchful wisdom of meditation practice, my inner grain relaxed into a more pliable, natural readiness. As I approached each task in front of me, I considered the life, shape and purpose of the raw material more than its rudimentary form. It curves, bends, breathes, designs, supports, and faces death. It is a mutable amalgam, changing through time, requiring care and attention, much like we do.

After more than a decade, many of our household projects came to a conclusion with patience. We can all enjoy cooking in our finished kitchen now. There are several other projects and some trim work to complete. We continue to take it one step at a time, saving what little we can to apply to the cost of fresh wood, but more often our savings go into essential daily needs.

Preston and Forrest have certainly grown into admirable young men, each pursuing their own directions after college and working to reduce their college debt load. They continue to be valuable contributors to the community and actively participate in household projects. Just like the majority of us, they're learning about the complexities of this human life. They're currently in search of their individual paths, gradually discovering their place and purpose as they move forward.

Spirit Rock offered me a space with a partial scholarship for the March 2009 retreat, and I continued to go on retreats at centers around the country when I could afford to do so. From 2010 to 2012, I completed the Community Dharma Leaders Training Program with

Spirit Rock and have been teaching online. You can learn more at www.constancecasey.com.

Insight can rush far ahead of the ability to articulate or harmonize with the intellect when what is being seen has no name. The language sectors of the brain and body needed time to catch up with the process. Being at Naropa University in Boulder, CO, and completing a Masters in Divinity in 2016 helped sharpen aspects of my intellect with Heart wisdom. My master's thesis, which I'll be publishing in the coming year, focused on unique ways one can find meaning using alternative metaphors in the midst of a terminal or difficult diagnosis.

In 2019, I practiced with my root teacher, Sayadaw U Thuzana, for a month at Tathagata Meditation Center in San Jose, CA. It was during this time that he gave me my Pāli name, Aggañāni, which means "supreme wisdom," and encouraged me to share the Dhamma.

I continue to study the texts and learn because I love wisdom teachings. We will all experience old age, disease, and death. A deep compassion grew in me for those going through cancer, difficult diagnoses with ill health, chronic pain, or in hospice care. My concern fed a desire to work with many diverse patients in various hospital settings. I've devoted thousands of hours providing interfaith spiritual support and guidance in many areas of hospital care.

In my compassion for those with different abilities, I want you to know that the Malaysian Buddhist Meditation Center is not an accessible building. There are many steps, and no elevator or ramp.

Before I left, the administrator mentioned that they were pleased to see that I was practicing in line with the Dhamma and doing well there. MBMC welcomed me, but they do not have the resources to support foreign yogis if they fall ill, or experience other difficulties. Going away can be nice, and I will always cherish the experience, but it is wise to find support right where you are now; many retreats are online, allowing people to practice from the comfort of their own home. In my case, I needed to go away to reduce all distractions; to sustain inner concentration as continuously as possible.

I'd appreciate hearing how my awakening story has impacted your journey. For further connection or inquiries, feel free to reach out at constance@constancecasey.com. I'm organizing some weekend retreats in the Midwest area so that we can practice in nature with one another. It's also possible to set up a nice and safe home retreat and check in with me or another teacher for support.

It's best to find authors and teachers with whom you resonate. You never know what makes you feel drawn in certain ways to different lineages and unique forms of prayer or meditation. I deeply value you finding your own authentic path and what can best support you.

The call renews in each moment for the personal will to bake like an apple pie in an oven of Love. And amidst this deep love with Spirit, sensations and vibrations are met in each moment with peace, harmony, and playfulness.

The beauty of Universal Love, God, Spirit—whatever you call this profound underlying expression is difficult to express in words, but continues nevertheless within us, in all things and at all times, no matter what.

May you practice well.

May all beings be well.

With kindness,
Constance

Sources

Print

Alcoholics Anonymous World Services, Inc. *Alcoholics Anonymous: The Story of How Many Thousands of Men and Women Have Recovered from Alcoholism*, 3rd edition. New York, NY: Alcoholics Anonymous World Services, Inc., 1976.

Al-Anon Family Groups. *One Day at a Time in Al-Anon*. United States: Al-Anon Family Group Headquarters, Inc., 1989.

Al-Anon Family Groups. *How Al-Anon Works for Families & Friends of Alcoholics*. Al-Anon Family Group Headquarters, Inc., 1995.

Chadwick, David. *Moments with Shunryu Suzuki: Stories of a Zen Master Told by His Students*. Portland, OR: Broadway Books, 2001.

Chah, Venerable Ajahn, *No Ajahn Chah: Reflections*. Penang, Malaysia: The Penang Buddhist Association, 1997.

Chah, Venerable Ajahn, *A Taste of Freedom*, DharmaNet Edition. Berkeley, CA: DharmaNet International, 1995.

Conze, Edward. *Buddhist Wisdom Books: The Diamond Sutra and The Heart Sutra*. New York, NY: First Harper Torchbooks, 1972.

Dhammadharo, Ajahn Lee, *Keeping the Breath in Mind*. Valley Center, CA: Metta Forest Monastery, 2010.

Gibran, Kahlil, "On Children." Poem in *The Prophet*. New York, NY: Knopf Doubleday Publishing Group, 1923.

Gunaratana, Henepola. *The Jhanas in Theravada Buddhist Meditation*. Kandy, Sri Lanka: Buddhist Publication Society, 1988.

Gwen Westerman and Bruce M. White, *Mni Sota Makoce: The Land of the Dakota*. St. Paul: Minnesota Historical Society Press, 2012.

Hua, Hsuan, *The Vajra Prajna Paramita Sutra.* Buddhist Text Translation Society, 2003.

Holy Bible. New International Version, Zondervan Publishing House, 1984.

Kornfield, Jack, *A Path with Heart: A Guide Through the Perils and Promises of Spiritual Life.* United Kingdom: Random House Publishing Group, 1993.

Ramakrishna, Sri. "Dive Deep, O Mind." Poem. In *The Gospel of Sri Ramakrishna,* translated by Swami Nikhilananda. New York, NY: Ramakrishna Vedenta Centre, 1942.

Rūmī Jalāl ad-Dīn, "A Great Wagon." Poem in *The Essential Rumi: New Expanded Edition,* translated by Coleman Barks. New York, NY: Harper Collins Publishers, 2004.

Sayādaw, Venerable Mahāsi, *The Progress of Insight: A Treatise on Satipaṭṭhāna Meditation.* Kandy, Sri Lanka; Buddhist Publication Society, 1994.

Schaef, Anne Wilson, *Beyond Therapy, Beyond Science: A New Model For Healing The Whole Person.* New York, NY: Harper Collins Publishers, 1992.

Sona, Ajahn, *Life Is a Near Death Experience: Skills for Illness, Aging, Dying, and Loss.* British Columbia: Birken Publications, 2021.

Suzuki, Daisetz Teitaro, *Manual of Zen Buddhism.* United States: Grove Press, 1960.

Ṭhānissaro Bhikkhu, *The Buddha's Teachings: An Introduction.* Valley Center, CA: Metta Forest Monastery, 2016.

Ṭhānissaro Bhikkhu, *Into the Stream: A Study Guide on the First Stage of Awakening.* Valley Center, CA: Metta Forest Monastery, 2011.

Ṭhānissaro Bhikkhu, *The Karma of Questions.* Valley Center, CA: Metta Forest Monastery, 2016.

Ṭhānissaro Bhikkhu, *Selves & Not-self: The Buddhist Teaching on Anatta.* Valley Center, CA: Metta Forest Monastery, 2011.

Ṭhānissaro Bhikkhu, *With Each and Every Breath*. Valley Center, CA: Metta Forest Monastery, 2012.

W., Lois. *Lois Remembers: Memoirs of the cofounder of Al-Anon and wife of the cofounder of Alcoholics Anonymous*. Virginia Beach, VA: Al Anon Family Group Headquarters, 1979.

Whitman, Walt. "A Song of the Rolling Earth." In *Leaves of Grass*. Brooklyn, NY: Fowler & Wells, 1855.

Wilber, Ken, *The Integral Vision*. United Kingdom: Shambhala, 2007.

Suttas

Numbered Discourses: A Sensible Translation of the Aṅguttara Nikāya, translated from the Pāli by Bhikku Sujato. Eastwood, Australia: SuttaCentral c/o Alwis & Alwis Pty Ltd, 2018.

Sayings of the Dhamma: A Meaningful Translation of the Dhammapada, translated from the Pāli by Bhikku Sujato. Eastwood, Australia: SuttaCentral, 2021.

Middle Discourses: A Lucid Translation of the Majjhima Nikāya, translated from the Pāli by Bhikku Sujato. Eastwood, Australia: SuttaCentral, 2021.

The Foundations of Mindfulness: Satipaṭṭhāna Sutta, translated from the Pāli by Nyanasatta Thera. Kandy, Sri Lanka: Buddhist Publication Society, 2012.

Saṁyutta Nikāya: The Connected Discourses of the Buddha, translated from the Pāli by Bhikkhu Bodhi. Ukraine: Wisdom Publications, 2000.

Handful of Leaves, Volume III: an Anthology from the Saṁyutta Nikāya, translated from the Pāli by Ṭhānissaro Bhikkhu. Valley Center, CA: Metta Forest Monastery, 2017.

Handful of Leaves, Volume IV: an Anthology from the Aṅguttara Nikāya, translated from the Pāli by Ṭhānissaro Bhikkhu. Valley Center, CA: Metta Forest Monastery, 1999.

336   Constance Casey

Web

Ingram, Daniel, "General Advice on Retreats." Integrated Daniel, 2008. https://www.integrateddaniel.info/retreats.

Ram Dass. "Sharing Our Awakening." Ram Dass Love Serve Remember Foundation. Be Here Now Network, July 16, 2020. https://www.ramdass.org/sharing-our-awakening/.

Venerable Mahāsi Sayādaw, "Practical Vipassana Exercises," BuddhaNet Ebook Library (Buddha Dharma Education Association Inc.), November 28, 2006. https://www.buddhanet.net/pdf_file/mahasit1.pdf.

Film

Harrison, John Kent. *When Love Is Not Enough: The Lois Wilson Story*. DVD. United States: Hallmark Hall of Fame, 2010.

Appendix A

Glossary

aggañāni (Pāli) — agga means supreme, and ñāni means wisdom

arahant (Pāli) — a person whose mind is free of defilements, who has abandoned all ten of the fetters that bind the mind to the cycle of rebirth, whose heart is free of mental effluents, and who is thus not destined for further rebirth

bhikkhu (Pāli) — fully ordained male monk, (or bhikkhuni, nun, fully ordained female)

clinging — creating a sense of I, me, or mine and believing it

dāna (Pāli) — generosity, giving

Diamond Sutra — refers to the Vajracchedikā Prajñāpāramitā Sūtra, which can be translated as "The Perfection of Wisdom Text that Cuts Like a Thunderbolt" and dates to the 5th century CE. This sanskrit text contains the discourse of the Buddha to a senior monk that expresses the teachings on not-self, the emptiness of all phenomena, the liberation of all beings, and the importance of sharing the teachings with others.

Dhamma (Pāli) / *Dharma* (Sanskrit) — the teachings of the Buddha and also "the way things truly are." There are also "dhammas" or "phenomena," referred to in many different ways: interrelated elements that make up the empirical world, constituents of experience, the practice of virtue, meditation and wisdom, the liberating path.

deva (Pāli) — refers to a class of celestial beings or a path of the six paths of the incarnation cycle, often characterized by their long life, joyous surroundings and blissful states of mind

337

dukkha (Pāli) — stress, unsatisfactoriness, suffering

Goenka retreats — A retreat that follows the vipassanā teachings of S.N. Goenka

Heart Sutra — refers to the Prajñāpāramitāhṛdaya, which translates as "The Heart of the Perfection of Wisdom" and dates to the 7th century CE. This brief sanskrit text summarizes many of the fundamental Buddhist teachings and is commonly recited in Mahayana schools of Buddhism.

jhāna (Pāli) — refers to concentrated states of absorption

kamma (Pāli) / *karma* (Sanskrit) — action, deed, doing

karuna (Pāli) — compassion

kinhin (Japanese) — walking meditation

mettā (Pāli) — loving kindness or friendliness

mudita (Pāli) — sympathetic joy or happiness for the well-being of others

mudra (Sanskrit) — refers to the use of hand postures during meditation that express or nurture various energetic flows within and around the body

nibbāna (Pāli) — enlightenment, the end of suffering or stress

ōryōki (Japanese) — meditative form of eating in Zen practice that emphasizes mindfulness awareness by abiding to a strict order of precise movements

Pāli — the language of the Pāli Canon, the original written texts of the Buddha

pasāda (Pāli) — combination of confidence, perseverance, and ardency

sādhu (Pāli) — repeated three times, it is interpreted as referring to three elements: a disciplined body, words, and mind. It is a profound expression of gratitude for the teachings and often chanted at the end of a Dhamma talk.

samādhi (Pāli) — concentration, unified attention

samatha (Pāli) — generally considered a focused form of meditation for calming the mind

sāmaṇeras (Pāli) — assistants to monks or nuns

saṃsāra (Pāli) — worldly existence, the indefinitely repeating cycles of birth, dukkha, and death

saṃvega (Pāli) — feeling of futility with the cycle of saṃsāra, urgency for spiritual clarity

satsang (Sanskrit) — a gathering with a spiritual teacher for teaching and discourse with the teacher

sīla (Pāli) — ethical conduct, moral discipline

sotāpanna (Pāli) — a stream-enterer, referred to in Theravāda Buddhism

Sōtō Zen (Japanese) — a branch of Zen Buddhism

Suttas (Pāli) — the second division of the Pāli Canon, consisting of discourses given by the Buddha or his closest disciples

Theravāda (Pāli) — the oldest branch of Buddhism referred to as the Elders Branch

upāsikā (feminine)/ *upāsaka* (masculine) (Pāli) — a dedicated Buddhist practitioner following the eight precepts

upekkhā (Pāli) — equanimity

vipassanā (Pāli) — insight, a profound truth

yogi — Buddhist meditation practitioner

Appendix B

Reflection Questions

What areas of the book touched you?

What areas of the book had an effect on you to deepen your practice?

How do you relate to Constance's story?

How do you take time for contemplation?

What are some options for you to nurture peaceful acceptance into your life?

Have you known others who might be in a state of saṃvega? In what ways are they able to cultivate more supportive pasāda?

What was your response to the arising and passing away (a&p) experiences referred to in this book?

What is an unforgettable spiritual experience that you can share?

What are your favorite spiritual words for the numinous? Like God, Stillness, or something else?

How can you relate to Constance's story from your particular faith tradition?

How were your perceptions about your particular faith practices challenged by this story?

In what ways are you loosening your grip on roles that you play or nurturing new roles in your life?

How has this story changed your understanding of Buddhism or meditation?

What were some aspects of gradual awakening as part of Constance's awakening process?

How does this story of a woman's journey affect the body of spiritual literature today?

How is this story different from other spiritual memoirs that you have read?

What did you notice about the impact of patriarchy in the book?

What other lingering questions or reflections arise for you?

———————————•———————————

Invite Constance Casey to speak at your book club,
meditation group, or venue.

Contact her at www.constancecasey.com/contact.

Gratitude

The process of writing and publishing this book held greater significance than the book. Discussing this story and the tenets of Buddhism with my family brought up a variety of insights and reflections that were healing for each one of us. Editing with my sons gave me an opportunity to transmit to them the basics of spiritual practice so that they can turn to this for their respective practices—however that unfolds for them. Primarily through their efforts and ongoing support, this book is here for you to read.

A deep bow to Stewart, not only for his support throughout my writing process, but also for his effort in providing for our family's basic needs and looking after our home and sons during my retreats.

Preston Casey Palmer helped me in the early stages of editing and gave me some helpful feedback. Preston also provided graphic design skills in creation of the cover photo, converted my drawings for each chapter, and participated in formatting the book for print.

Forrest Casey provided extraordinary detailed grammar and line editing, along with design formatting throughout the entire book.

All of my teachers: Anne Wilson Schaef, Sayadaw U Thuzana, Jack Kornfield, Trudy Goodman, Gil Fronsdal, Adyashanti, and Mukti have all been sources of support and empowerment.

I thank my early teachers in Zen, Norm Randolph, and Steve Hagen and all the folks at Dharma Field.

I appreciate the wise friendship from Daniel Ingram, Wes Vaught, Kamala Masters, Steve Armstrong, and Vincent Fakhoury Horn.

Special heartfelt thanks to Nancy Manahan for her encouragement and editorial feedback. With her help, I learned to breathe more life into my storytelling by showing more and telling less, and by dropping details that detract from the narrative's essence.

Many thanks to Esther Porter, Sun Yung Shin, and Angie Jabine for their editing expertise.

Cathey Flickinger provided invaluable guidance, expertise, and service perfecting both the book design and cover.

I appreciate those who provided comments on the first draft: Devin Berry, Roger Wiard-Bauer, Chris Hafner, Jim Vilendrer, Pat Samples, Kathy Houser, and an anonymous reader.

Thank you to Sara-Jane Wilson, Ollie Stocker, Kathy Connelly, and Pamela Ayo Yetunde for their helpful feedback and questions.

I'm very grateful for my wonderful Twelve Step Recovery friends and their support for ongoing learning, integration, and kindness.

I also thank the Universe. Many words and phrases came to me in dreams, through everyday practice, or while simply drinking a cup of tea. Walks with our pup, visits to the rose garden, or holding my heavy tape measure to fix something at home encouraged reflection for the writing process. To create something of this depth and magnitude was a monumental task for a first-time book project, offering insightful and sometimes challenging learnings, so much so that I could write another book about the process of writing and editing. With all her myriad displays, Spirit moved through my writing journey in all the inseparable happenings along the way.

Permissions

Every effort was made to contact copyright holders to obtain permission to use the quotes in the book. If any work has been used without permission, I extend my apologies. Please contact me so that credit can be given in future updates of this book.

Thanks to the following for their gracious permission:

Special thanks to Coleman Barks and Maypop Books for the express permission to reprint the excerpt of the poem "A Great Wagon" by Rūmī Jalāl ad-Dīn, from *The Essential Rumi: New Expanded Edition*, translated by Coleman Barks and © 2004 Coleman Barks.

The excerpt of the poem "Dive Deep, O Mind" by Sri Ramakrishna, as found in *The Gospel of Sri Ramakrishna*, translated into English by Swami Nikhilananda is reprinted with permission from the Ramakrishna-Vivekananda Center of New York.

The quote from "Āsīvisopamasutta: The Simile of the Vipers," is © 2003 Wisdom Publications, *The Connected Discourses of the Buddha* and is reprinted by arrangement with Wisdom Publications, Inc., wisdomexperience.org.

The following quotations are considered to fall within the realm of fair use or are in the public domain:

The excerpts from *Alcoholics Anonymous: The Story of How Many Thousands of Men and Women Have Recovered from Alcoholism*, 3rd edition., published by Alcoholics Anonymous World Services, Inc. (A.A.W.S.) (New York, NY: 1976) are considered fair use. The use of these excerpts does not mean that A.A.W.S. has reviewed or approved the contents of this publication, or that A.A.W.S. necessarily agrees with the views expressed herein. A.A. is a program of recovery from alcoholism only. Use of the Twelve Steps in connection with programs and activities, which are patterned after A.A. but which address other problems, or in other non-A.A. contexts, does not imply otherwise.

The excerpts from *How Al-Anon Works for Families & Friends of Alcoholics*. (Virginia Beach, VA: 1995), *One Day at a Time in Al-Anon* (Virginia Beach, VA: 1989), and *Lois Remembers: Memoirs of the cofounder of Al-Anon and*

About the Author

CONSTANCE CASEY, MDIV. was invited to teach meditation by her teacher, Sayadaw U Thuzana, of the Theravāda lineage in 2008. She is a graduate of the 2012 Spirit Rock Community Dharma Leader Training Program and was empowered to teach by Jack Kornfield and Trudy Goodman. Constance obtained a Masters of Divinity from Naropa University in 2016, where she is also endorsed to teach Mindfulness Meditation Instruction.

Constance's practice is primarily informed by the suttas in Theravāda Buddhism. Her long-term engagement in Twelve Step Recovery, Christian contemplative, and Sōtō Zen practices have also affected her open way of teaching.

Constance volunteered compassionate care for hundreds of people, including dying patients and their families as an interfaith hospital chaplain. Grief and loss, as well as joy and peacefulness, are natural expressions of being human and authentically free. Through her experience with addiction counseling, she respects and values your unique spiritual practice and journey while supporting you to find balance and significance in the face of adversity. Constance will encourage you to attune toward being more mindful and aware for release and serenity.

Speaking engagements, group teaching, and individual sessions are all part of Constance's mentoring practice. Constance lives with her family, including their pup, in the home they continue to renovate together.

With meditation practice and study, there are ways to learn more about being human through deep inquiry and embracing your own experience with dignity and integrity. If Constance Casey's journey and teachings have touched your heart, there are several meaningful ways you can show your support. You can purchase her books and artwork, or invite her to your book club, meditation group, or event as a speaker.

Great sacrifices were made in the process of bringing this book to fruition. Please consider making a donation as part of the traditional practice of generosity in Buddhism called dāna. Your contributions play a vital role in helping her continue to teach, write, and share her wisdom with a wider audience, including those in need. Together, we can create a ripple effect of positive impact in the world.

Learn more about her offerings at *constancecasey.com*.
There you can also find suggested resources
that are updated regularly.